APHRAHAT AND JUDAISM

SOUTH FLORIDA STUDIES IN THE HISTORY OF JUDAISM

Edited by
Jacob Neusner
Alan J. Avery-Peck, Bruce D. Chilton, Darrell J. Fasching,
William Scott Green, Sara Mandell, James F. Strange

Number 205

APHRAHAT AND JUDAISM
The Christian-Jewish Argument
in Fourth-Century Iran

by
Jacob Neusner

APHRAHAT AND JUDAISM
The Christian-Jewish Argument
in Fourth-Century Iran

by

Jacob Neusner

Scholars Press
Atlanta, Georgia

APHRAHAT AND JUDAISM
The Christian-Jewish Argument
in Fourth-Century Iran

by
Jacob Neusner

Copyright ©1999 by the University of South Florida

Originally published by E. J. Brill, 1971

Publication of this book was made possible by a grant from the Tisch Family Foundation, New York City. The University of South Florida acknowledges with thanks this important support for its scholarly projects.

Library of Congress Cataloging in Publication Data
Neusner, Jacob, 1932–
    Aphrahat and Judaism : the Christian-Jewish argument in fourth-century Iran / by Jacob Neusner.
       p.   cm. — (South Florida studies in the history of Judaism ; no. 205)
    Originally published: Leiden : Brill, 1971. With new introd.
    Includes bibliographical references and index.
    ISBN 0-7885-0577-7 (cl. : alk. paper)
    1. Aphrahat, the Persian Sage, fl. 337–345. 2. Judaism
Controversial literature. 3. Judaism—Controversial literature—
History and criticism. I. Title. II. Series: South Florida
studies in the history of Judaism ; 205.
BR65.A386N48 1999
261.2'6'09015—dc21   99-35108
                         CIP

04 03 02 01 00 99   5 4 3 2 1

Printed in the United States of America
on acid-free paper

TABLE OF CONTENTS

Publisher's Note: This volume is reprinted with permission from the E. J. Brill edition of 1971. The Preface to the Second Printing is set apart from the original text in a pagination format of "*iii," etc. This format maintains the integrity of the pagination in the original text and assures the continuing usefulness of the original index.

PREFACE TO THE SECOND PRINTING

Nearly three decades after its original publication I reprint my *Aphrahat and Judaism* because I believe Aphrahat represents the exemplary figure in the religious dialogue between Judaism and Christianity, an enduring voice of civility and rationality amid the cacophony of mutual disesteem. In the American language Aphrahat should have a hearing in yet another generation, the original edition having sold out, because of what he represents, because of the human achievement embodied in the words of his that endure, even across the ages and in a very different world.

What makes Aphrahat remarkable and exemplary? It is his embodied faith in the power of the reasoning intellect to sustain religious conviction even amid conflict. His counterparts in antiquity and their continuators in medieval and modern Christianity, until nearly our own day, in no way approach his confidence in the power of a reasonable reading of the universally acknowledged facts of a shared Scripture to compel assent. He is a model for the Judaic participants because, though representing the minority living in a hostile majority, unlike more than a few of them, he does not dissimulate. He is a model for the Christian participants because, unlike most of them, he shows that Christianity can find a voice that is not shrill and a message that is not demeaning to Judaism, — that Christianity can speak confidently, therefore in humility, to its Judaic competition. What accounts for his remarkable achievement? It is the uncertain context in which Aphrahat's Christianity found itself that made necessary the invention of a Christian voice of reasoned argument for the purposes of disputation with a confident Judaism, as I shall explain, but it is the unique achievement of the man himself that makes the difference: an intellectual of faith and self-evident dignity speaks across the ages, representing a kind of Christian that Judaism seldom has known, speaking to a kind of Judaism that Christianity has rarely acknowledged — a unique moment in the unfolding of the Christian-Jewish argument of twenty centuries.

The small Christian community represented by Aphrahat, who flourished in the first half of the fourth century in Babylonia, then a province of the Iranian Empire under the Sasanian dynasty, lived side by side with an ancient and sizable community of Judaism, rooted in the region from 600 B.C.E., for nearly a thousand years. His writings make clear that he encountered a living Judaism, competing on equal terms — whether political or intellectual — with an equally vital

iii

Christianity. His encounter with Judaism, his shaping of the Christian response to Israel's challenge, his modes of demonstrating his case, and his appeal to a common Scripture to make the Christian point — these represent a unique moment in the two millennia of Judaeo-Christian argument. Here, in the Zoroastrian empire, Christianity not only enjoyed no political advantage but found itself under serious scrutiny as agents of a foreign power. In perpetual tension and occasional war with Iran, the Roman government under Constantine and his heirs made itself the protector of the Christian minority of Iran. But as a hostile power Rome only succeeded in marking Christianity as a danger to Iran's empire. Under Shapur II, in Aphrahat's time, the Iranian government adopted a variety of laws meant to humiliate Christians and separate them from their faith. The Jews of the time, so Aphrahat tells us, adduced in that fact evidence that God did not favor Christianity, but preferred Judaism, the Jews living in security and practicing their faith, in most of the fourth century, without interference. So here a persecuted Christianity addresses a Judaism generally at peace with its political setting. Christianity but not Judaism then had to explain why it was persecuted. The Christian theologian, not the Israelite sage, had to spell out how persecution represented evidence not of divine rejection but of a divine plan of an altogether other order.

So far as I know, Aphrahat's situation bears no counterpart in the entire history of Christianity in its encounter with Judaism, and the Twenty-First Demonstration, so far as Judaism is the particular debating-partner, has no parallel of which I have heard. Here is the voice of a Christianity that Judaism rarely encountered, not triumphant, not privileged by power, not sustained by state support. It is a Christianity that, no other power being accessible, appeals to common reason, to argument meant to compel, based on evidence shared by all parties to the debate and historical evidence and philosophical rationality accepted by each. Aphrahat embodies the voice that Judaism would shape for itself in Christian countries when required by Christian governments in alliance with the Christian Church to dispute the truth of the faith, on pain of death, win or lose. So Aphrahat stands for the Christian as the eternal Jew. And what he embodies is the power of Christianity to confront a powerful and hostile world and a Judaism that on the whole manages more comfortably in that world than does the other heir of Israelite Scripture.

What I contribute is a translation of the Demonstrations on Judaism and a set of studies of them. In these systematic studies, first I present an account of the critique of Judaism, second, I compare the exegesis of Aphrahat with that of the rabbis on verses of Scripture important to Aphrahat, third, I situate Aphrahat in the larger framework of the Patristic critique of Judaism. In this way I show that Aphrahat is fundamentally original, an important instance of the potentiality of a Christian critique of Judaism. What I find admirable in Aphrahat is his mode of argument, his forthright address to the view of the other party, his appeal to shared facts, his reliance on a common rationality — traits that characterize the

Judaic participants in the medieval disputations, and, if truth be told, the Jewish, but less commonly the Christian, participants in contemporary Judaeo-Christian *Auseinandersetzungen*. Today, as for a thousand years past, the facticity of Christianity, its givenness as "of course" the truth, frame the agenda of Judaeo-Christian dialogue. That Judaism is a religion too, that Judaism sets forth its system on its own grounds, constituting not merely the Old Testament without Christ as its climax — that consciousness rarely shapes the perception of the Christian party to the dialogue.

Here, then, we meet a different framing of the Christian component. Aphrahat forms his rational apologetic in a way that is in part autonomous of the Judaic critique and in other parts responsive to it. Specifically, he met the Judaic critique of Christianity on the common ground of the Scriptures that both parties to the debate shared, the Hebrew Scriptures of ancient Israel. On the basis of those Scriptures he built his arguments in favor of Christianity in its Syriac statement and against the competing Judaism. I do not think any Christian participant to the Judaeo-Christian argument of antiquity approached with greater respect for the requirements of reason and rational exchange the tasks of theological apologetics and polemics. No Rabbinic document of the same period — let the full truth be told — begins to compete in the articulate address to points of difference. Not for a thousand years did Judaism produce a figure of equivalent weight, able to confront Christianity in its own terms and context and to compose a Judaic apologetics and polemics worthy of the name. And for our own time, Aphrahat embodies the model by which all parties to the theological encounter are to be measured. That is because Aphrahat combines reason with learning and the dignity of honest interchange. Rehearsal of standard canards, recapitulation of conventional abuse, repetition of one's own position in place of an honest confrontation with the other's — these common traits of the medieval and modern continuation of antiquity's argument find a contrary model in Aphrahat.

This book enjoys a special place in my heart, partly because of my admiration for its subject, Aphrahat, and partly because it marked the conclusion of my first major scholarly project beyond the dissertation, which was my *Life of Yohanan ben Zakkai* (Leiden, 1962: E. J. Brill). This beginning of my independent labor, as a fully autonomous scholar, came to fruition as my *History of the Jews in Babylonia* (Leiden, 1965-1970: E. J. Brill) I-V. I turned in that work to Aphrahat, because represents the only substantial literary evidence on Judaism in Sasanian Babylonia. In that context, *Aphrahat and Judaism* served as an appendix to the *History*, though standing on its own as well. As I explain in the shank of the book, some of the Demonstrations on Judaism had been translated, others not. While some work on Aphrahat and the Jews opened many doors — cited at length in this book — little systematic study of Aphrahat and Judaism, apart from Marcel Simon's occasional references in his magisterial *Verus Israel,* touched on the subject. As part of the larger project, therefore, I determined to rework the existing translations of Demonstrations and to undertake the first translations from Syriac into English of the others. To do so, I commuted weekly from Providence to New Haven and studied Syriac at Yale University in the Syriac-seminar of Professor Franz Rosenthal in 1968-1969. This took place in my first year as Professor of Religious Studies at Brown University. In the same year I attended Professor Judah Goldin's seminar at Yale in Midrash. In those days Yale was a magnet for Semitics, and many of the leading figures of our generation flocked there as students. At that time I met such distinguished figures of the generation coming to maturity after my own as Professor Stephen A. Kaufman, Hebrew Union College-Jewish Institute of Religion, who was the superstar of the Syriac seminar, and Professor Anthony J. Saldarini, Boston College, a major player in the Midrash seminar.

In that decade, from 1960 to 1970, I engaged in a fair amount of post-doctoral study of languages and texts. In that same context, in the earlier 1960s, for a summer and a year I had studied classical Armenian and ancient Armenian history, to consult the Armenian sources on the Jews in Mesopotamia and Babylonia, and for three years Middle Iranian (Pahlavi, Pazend) to examine the Zoroastrian ones. While never pretending to be a master of Syriac, Armenian, or Pahlavi, I was able to locate and provide accurate accounts of the evidence pertinent to the Jews in Babylonia. I also spent some years in sustained, if informal, study of the art of the synagogue of antiquity and of Hellenistic Judaism with Professor Erwin R. Goodenough, who spent his post-Yale retirement career at Brandeis University, where from 1962 to 1964 I held a post-doctoral fellowship. After 1970, while I continued my interests in Syriac, Armenian, and Pahlavi (Zoroastrian) studies, I turned in a different direction altogether. The work of that period, 1960-1970 — the *History* and *Aphrahat* — has not been superseded, and, in English, has no competition at all even now.[1]

From my decade in the Orientalist world I proceeded in a different direction, first toward history, quickly thereafter into history of religion. In Oriental studies as the approach to the Rabbinic literature that formed the focus of my life's work I found little to value and still less to respect. I find negligible what was at stake in the historicism, the low-brow positivism, the fact-mongering and the vacuity of Orientalism's self-validating scholarship. I did not conceive that what was important in the Judaic sources of antiquity registered in the desiccated academicism that dominated, and still dominates, that alien world. A bit more than a decade later, my decision to turn away from the Oriental Society proved prescient. Evidence of its hopeless incapacity to engage in scholarly argument spread itself out in the pages of the *Journal of the American Oriental Society,*

---

[1] Y. Gafni's work in Hebrew on the Jews in Babylonia in Talmudic times has never been translated into English.

which in 1984 simply refused to permit me to reply to Saul Lieberman's posthumous — and trivial — diatribe against a few pages of a volume of my *Talmud of the Land of Israel: A Preliminary Translation.* Others tell me, that, as a matter of policy, the *Journal of the American Oriental Society* — unlike *the Journal of Biblical Literature* and *the Journal of the American Academy of Religion* and their principal European counterparts — simply will not permit academic *Auseinandersetzungen* in its pages. I cannot say I blame them for forbidding what their discipline does not sustain, which is mature exchange of critical views, such as Aphrahat represents.

That fact presents no surprise. From the end of the 1960s forward, I found no reason to think that Oriental studies offered even a critical program of scholarship, its historical work in my area being puerile and gullible. Orientalism succeeded in teaching the ancient languages but not in much else. So for history I went models in a different direction in search of, beginning with *my Formation of a Legend: Studies on the Traditions concerning Yohanan ben Zakkai* (Leiden, 1971: E. J. Brill), and then the *Rabbinic Traditions about the Pharisees before 70* (Leiden, 1973) I-III. After fifteen years in Oriental Studies and in history, in the 1970s I started afresh, with the history of religion and its disciplines as these would illuminate the sources of nascent Rabbinic Judaism. A straight line commenced at *A History of the Mishnaic Law of Purities* (Leiden, 1974-1980: E. J. Brill) I-XXII. There I have walked, on that straight path, for more than a quarter of a century, and there I plan to progress.

Jacob Neusner
UNIVERSITY OF SOUTH FLORIDA AND BARD COLLEGE

For
Noam Mordecai Menahem

TABLE OF CONTENTS

I

TRANSLATIONS

II

STUDIES

Map: Northern Mesopotamia

Source: F. M. Fiey, O. P., *Assyrie Chrétienne. Contribution à
l'étude de l'histoire et de la géographie ecclésiastiques et
monastiques du nord de l'Iraq* (Beirut, 1965), vol. I.

PREFACE

Outside of the Babylonian Talmud, Aphrahat (fl. ca. 300-350 A.D.), a Christian monk in Mesopotamia, provides the only substantial literary evidence on the state of Mesopotamian-Babylonian Judaism in Sasanian times. His Demonstrations furthermore were given final form by the end of the fourth century, if not earlier, and hence antedate the Babylonian Talmud by a hundred years or more. They moreover testify about Judaism and Jews who probably were little affected by rabbinical influence, as we shall see, and thus constitute especially rare and valuable data. In connection with my *History of the Jews in Babylonia*, it therefore seemed useful to prepare an English translation of Aphrahat's Demonstrations relevant to Judaism, together with studies of some pertinent issues. The result was to serve as an appendix to vol. V, comparable to vol. III, pp. 339-353, Armenian traditions on Babylonian and Mesopotamian Jewry; vol. III, pp. 354-358, Adiabenian Christianity; and vol. IV, pp. 403-424, Zoroastrian traditions on Judaism. Since Aphrahat's Demonstrations and related studies proved too long for an appendix to the foregoing volume, I decided to allow them to stand separately.

It is hardly necessary to point out that only a small aspect of the life and thought of Aphrahat is under consideration here. Although he was the first Father in the Iranian Church known to us, Aphrahat is practically ignored in histories of patristic Christianity. Not all of his demonstrations are available in English, only a few in other Western languages, except for Parisot's Latin and Bert's German. Mine are the first English translations of Demonstrations XI, XII, XIII, XV, XVI, XVIII, XIX, and parts of XXIII.

My effort is to make use of Aphrahat as a source for the study of Judaism east of the Euphrates. To do so, I have had to discuss his place in the context of both rabbinic Judaism and early Christianity. My argument—for the study is intended as an argument—is that Aphrahat was not a "docile pupil of the Jews" but a Christian, standing in important ways within the conventional structure of the argument of the Church on the matter of Judaism, completely original, however, in his development and application of that conventional argument. He was truly a "docile pupil" of no one, but a powerful, independent mind.

The Christianity of Aphrahat requires further study. The shape of his piety and spirituality needs to be appreciated, placed into relationship with the religious life of the Christian tradition in all its immense variety and richness. For such a study, Demonstrations XIV and XXIII are primary, those treated here far less important. Demonstrations I through X, in which he presents something like a systematic account of the faith, need to be read in the light of the piety of XIV and XXIII.

Aphrahat provides a glimpse into the perception of reality shaping the mind of a particular kind of Christian, living in a world alien to much of Christianity West of the Euphrates, but in important ways similar to Palestine in the early centuries A.D. (This was F. C. Burkitt's view, here seconded.) It may not be too much to allege that, if not Jesus, then certainly the writer of the Fourth Gospel and of Revelation would have understood Aphrahat on Judaism more readily than he would have comprehended the Alexandrian, Cappadocian, Antiochian or North African fathers on the same matter. Yet if this is true, then we must reconsider our conception of the distances and discontinuities separating the Christianity of those centers from the Semitic Middle East, for in one very central aspect, namely the Christian theology of Judaism, Aphrahat reveals the persistence of widely-followed conventions.

For an outsider, the most moving, indeed spiritually affecting writings of Aphrahat are, as I said, Demonstrations I through X, XIV, and XXIII. Here the believing man stands forth, the defense of the faith and critique of the opposition are muted. For the study of the history of religions, the ways in which various sorts of Christians took up the cross and imitated Christ, the morphology of the Christ-centered human experience, the perception of the world shaped by the New Testament and its reading of the Hebrew Scriptures — these are · important, illuminating issues. Aphrahat seems to me a richer source of insight for the consideration of such questions than do those systematic theologians, writing in Latin and Greek, who receive substantially more attention. But it is for historians of Christianity to raise these issues in the study of Aphrahat himself.

My translation depends upon the texts of Wright and Parisot (below, p. 7), and especially on R. Payne Smith, *A Compendious Syriac Dictionary*, edited by J. Payne Smith (Mrs. Margoliouth) (Oxford, repr. 1957 of 1903 ed.). My knowledge of Syriac, as of Armenian, Pahlavi and Pazend, is elementary and by no means sufficient to the task. While what follows hopefully is an accurate and careful translation, I do not claim to contribute in *any* detail to the study of Syriac literature, philology, or text-criticism. I am grateful to my teacher Professor Franz Rosenthal,

Yale University, for instruction in Syriac, but he in no way bears the onus for either my limitations or errors.

My student, Rabbi David Goodblatt, assisted in proof reading.

In addition, my thanks are due to Professors Joel Kraemer and Wayne A. Meeks, Yale University, and Henry A. Fischel, Indiana University, for providing materials otherwise unavailable to me; and to Brown University, for bearing the considerable costs of transcribing the translations and typing the final manuscript, preparing the indices, and other research expenses. A fellowship from the American Council of Learned Societies greatly assisted my research. My teacher Morton Smith contributed learning and criticism. To him, as always, I am deeply indebted.

JACOB NEUSNER

Providence, Rhode Island
Purim, 5730
March 22, 1970

LIST OF ABBREVIATIONS

'Arakh.	=	'Arakhin	Mal.	=	Malachi
A.Z.	=	'Avodah Zarah	Matt.	=	Matthew
b.	=	Babylonian Talmud	Meg.	=	Megillah
Ber.	=	Berakhot	Mekh.	=	*Mekhilta deR. Ish-*
Bekh.	=	Bekhorot			*mael*, ed. Lauterbach
Bez.	=	Bezah	Men.	=	Menahot
Bik.	=	Bikkurim	M.Q.	=	Mo'ed Qatan
Chron.	=	Chronicles	M.T.	=	Massoretic Text
Col.	=	Colossians	Naz.	=	Nazir
Cor.	=	Corinthians	Ned.	=	Nedarim
Dan.	=	Daniel	Neh.	=	Nehemiah
Deut.	=	Deuteronomy	Num.	=	Numbers
Eph.	=	Ephesians	Par.	=	Parah
'Eruv.	=	'Eruvin	Pes.	=	Pesahim
Ex.	=	Exodus	Pet.	=	Peter
Ez.	=	Ezekiel	Phil.	=	Philippians
Gal.	=	Galatians	Prov.	=	Proverbs
Gen.	=	Genesis	Ps.	=	Psalms
Ginzberg,	=	Louis Ginzberg,	Qid.	=	Qiddushin
Legends		*Legends of the Jews*	Qoh.	=	Qohelet
Git.	=	Gittin	Rev.	=	Revelation
Hab.	=	Habakkuk	R.H.	=	Rosh Hashanah
Hag.	=	Haggai	Rom.	=	Romans
Hag.	=	Hagigah	Sam.	=	Samuel
Heb.	=	Hebrews	Sanh.	=	Sanhedrin
Hor.	=	Horayot	Shab.	=	Shabbat
Hos.	=	Hosea	Sheq.	=	Sheqalim
Hul.	=	Hullin	Song	=	Song of Songs
Is.	=	Isaiah	Sot.	=	Sotah
JBL	=	*Journal of Bibli-*	Suk.	=	Sukkah
		cal Literature	Ta.	=	Ta'anit
Jer.	=	Jeremiah	Thes.	=	Thessalonians
JE	=	*Jewish Encyclopedia*	Tim.	=	Timothy
Josh.	=	Joshua	y.	=	Palestinian Talmud
Jud.	=	Judges	Yev.	=	Yevamot
Ket.	=	Ketuvot	Zech.	=	Zechariah
Lev.	=	Leviticus	Zeph.	=	Zephaniah
Mak.	=	Makkot	Zev.	=	Zevahim

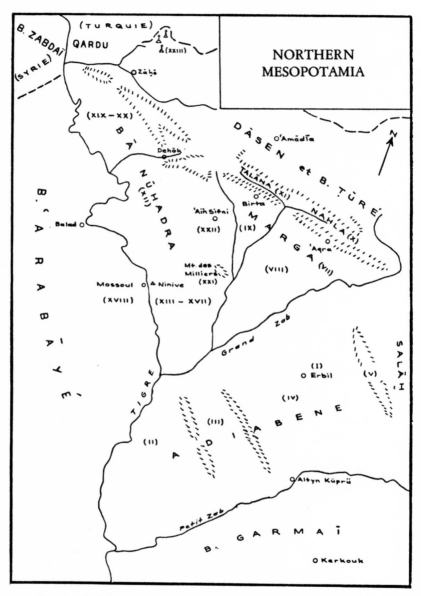

Source: F. M. Fiey, O. P., *Assyrie Chrétienne. Contribution à l'étude de l'histoire et de la géographie ecclésiastiques et monastiques du nord de l'Iraq* (Beirut, 1965), vol. I.

CHAPTER ONE

INTRODUCTION

I. EASTERN CHRISTIANITY

Christianity in the Iranian empire cannot be called *Iranian*, for it was largely the creation of Semites, chiefly Jews along with other Aramaic-speaking peoples in northern Mesopotamia in general.[1] While various kinds of individual Iranians converted to Christianity, the eastern church consistently used Syriac as its primary language and in large measure was composed of non-Iranian peoples. Indeed, the boundary between Iran and Rome did little to distinguish among differing sorts of Semitic Christians, though Nestorians tended to predominate in the east, Jacobites in the west. Aphrahat could as well have written his demonstrations in Edessa, on the Byzantine side of the border, as in Mar Mattai on the Iranian side. Just as the Jews lived an autonomous life and knew and cared little about the religion and culture of the Iranian peoples, so Syriac-speaking Christians formed their own autonomous community in the polyglot satrapies of the Iranian west. The Tigris-Euphrates valley, like the Balkans and Eastern Europe, was peopled by a multitude of ethnic groups. Christians were, moreover, acutely conscious that they constituted a new such ethnic group, "the people which is of the peoples," and Aphrahat repeatedly explained the new social entity formed by the disciples of the Messiah. Since a peculiar religion was part of the self-definition of each ethnic group, it was important to underline the fact that the Christians likewise constituted not merely a cult, but a true "people."

It is hopeless to seek the origins of so complex a phenomenon as Christianity across the Euphrates, for the stories of where and how churches were first established in fact were composed long after these churches had become well-developed, permanent institutions. What we have is two traditions, pertinent to two of the older churches of the east,

---

[1] On Christianity in the Sasanian Empire and its relationships to Judaism, see the summaries of talmudic and related evidence in my *A History of the Jews in Babylonia I. The Parthian Period*, pp. 180-183; *II. The Early Sasanian Period*, pp. 19-26, 72-91; *III. From Shapur I to Shapur II*, pp. 9-16, 24-29, 354-358; *IV. The Age of Shapur II*, pp. 20-26, 56-61; and *V. Later Sasanian Times*, pp. 6-8, 19-29, 43-45, 92-95, and 119-122.

Edessa and Adiabene, but these scarcely account for the rest, and cannot be thought to testify definitively even about themselves. The movement of Christianity to the Iranian empire generally is parallel to that of rabbinical Judaism. In both instances, religious groups, formed within the heart of Palestinian Judaism, competed in the first place in winning over the Jews of the oriental diaspora. Christianity took root in the Jewries in Edessa and Adiabene, rabbinical Judaism in those of Nisibis and central Babylonia, probably by the accident of history. Where rabbis established themselves, they postponed the introduction of Christianity for roughly a century and a half; where Christians made headway in local Jewries, rabbinical Judaism scarcely took hold. Thus churches flourished in Edessa and Adiabene by ca. 150, while it was only ca. 300 that we find Christian communities of any size in Nisibis and central Babylonia. Papa, the first catholicos of Seleucia-Ctesiphon, the winter capital of Iran, which was surrounded by Jewish settlements under rabbinical leadership, came to office in ca. 314-5 and died in 344-5.

The numbers of native-born Aramaean Christians were, furthermore, greatly augmented by Shapur I, who deported large numbers of Christian captives from Syria and Asia Minor to the western satrapies. But these Greek-speaking Christians did not succeed in imparting a Hellenistic character to the Semitic church, and readily assimilated into the life of the pre-existing Christian community, so far as we can tell. Similarly, Shapur II moved Armenian Christians to Khuzistan with no perceptible impact on the shape of the Christianity of Iran.

My guess is that the Babylonian church-community also was augmented by Jews alienated by rabbinical leadership in the Babylonian Jewries. The rabbis, imposing their oral Torah in addition to the written Torah all Jews knew and revered, certainly must have found a mixed reception among the old communities. They claimed that their Torah would ensure the salvation of Israel. After nearly a century, central Babylonian Jewry found itself no better off than before, and at least a few must have come not only to resent rabbinical innovations but to doubt the theological foundations upon which they were made. Furthermore, the rabbis tended to identify themselves with the exilarch and proprietary classes, favoring the latter in decisions on land-tenure and in other matters. For example, while they gladly made use of the community's charity-funds for the redemption of captives, often traders in international caravans, they never did so to pay the cost of the oppressive head-tax, and so numbers of Jews had to sell themselves into slavery in order to obtain the necessary tax-money. The commercial classes, not the landless poor, thus enjoyed the use of communal resources. While we do not have evidence that on this account Jews converted to Christianity, we do have reason to conclude Jews who converted to Christianity posed a problem to late third-century Babylonian rabbis.

The eastern Christians drew on the heritage of the Essenes and Qumran, the rabbinical Jews on the legacy of first-century Pharisaism. Vööbus emphasizes the continuities between the fourth and fifth-century Iranian celibates and ascetics, on the one hand, and the covenanted community of Qumran on the other. The earlier parts of my *History* have shown the immense influence of Palestinian Pharisaism on Babylonian rabbinic Judaism—so profound an influence, indeed, that we can hardly distinguish, except in trifling details, between the law and theology of the two countries' rabbis. Vööbus persuasively characterizes Aramaic-speaking Christianity as fundamentally ascetic and highly millenarian. The backbone of the church was the ascetic monk, living mostly in community with other monks, and exerting overwhelming influence on the values of ordinary Christians. Similarly, the rabbis came to shape the life of Babylonian Jewry to conform to the legal and theological legacy of Pharisaism.

Of the shape of the Christianity that preceded Aphrahat we know very little. He is the first articulate spokesman known to us, and yet, by 336, Eastern Christianity was well developed in doctrine and liturgy. Aphrahat stands as a testimony at the end of two centuries of Christian life in Adiabene. This life began with the conversion of Jews, themselves a mere two or three generations away from conversion to Judaism and still surrounded by Jews loyal to the new religion of their fathers.[2] The character of early Syrian Christianity is best described by Vööbus (pp. 12-13):

---

[2] For the early history of Christianity in the Iranian (Parthian, then Sasanian) empire, see first of all Arthur Vööbus, *History of Asceticism in the Syrian Orient. A Contribution to the History of Culture in the Near East. I. The Origen of Asceticism. Early Monasticism in Persia* (Louvain, 1958), pp. 3-31, 138-172; J. Labourt, *Le christianisme dans l'empire perse sous la dynastie sassanide (224-632)*, (Paris, 1904), pp. 1-18; Frank Gavin, *Aphraates and the Jews* (Toronto, 1923; also *Journal of the Society of Oriental Research* 7, pp. 95-166), pp. 11-17; Martin J. Higgins, "Chronology of the Fourth-Century Metropolitans of Seleucia-Ctesiphon," *Traditio* 9, 1953, pp. 45-99 (for the dates of Papa); and, for a brief and lucid summary, Edward J. Duncan, *Baptism in the Demonstrations of Aphraates the Persian Sage* (Washington, 1945: Catholic University of America Studies in Christian Antiquity, ed. Johannes Quasten, No. 8) pp. 16-21. Other pertinent items are listed in the bibliographies of the several volumes of my *History*.

We are first impressed with the covenant-consciousness in the primitive Syrian Christianity. The Christian faith is perceived as a new covenant, and this is the decisive factor determining all others in the understanding of the new religion, even to the shaping of its implications. The covenant . . . assumes the structural position of moulding all its theology, ethics, and organization. This *qeiāmā*, which also means 'oath,' 'a solemn promise,' characterizes the believers even insofar as their name is concerned. These Christians are *benai qeiāmā* and *benat qeiāmā* translated 'the sons of the covenant' and 'daughters of the covenant,' actually in the Semitic simply 'covenanters.' Further, men and women in this new relationship . . . are called to struggle not only against evil but also against the physical-natural conditions of the world. Thus the covenant-consciousness expresses its content with a negative estimate of this world, and practically, by correlation, it results in asceticism. Possessions, marriage as well as any link with this world, are sacrificed for the sake of this new *qeiāmā* which God has established with His elect.

Vööbus stresses that on the basis of the new covenant a new community was formed, the True Israel distinct from the rest of the Jews. He notes a "common fund of thought" behind both Qumranian asceticism and Syrian Christianity.

II. APHRAHAT

Among the first great fathers (along with Ephrem) of the Iranian church, Aphrahat, a monk of the rank of bishop at Mar Mattai, north of Nineveh, near the present-day Iraqi town of Mosul (see map), wrote, in elegant, classic Syriac, twenty-three Demonstrations. The first ten, composed in 337, present a systematic account of Christianity, addressed to his fellow-monks. The next thirteen, written in 344, deal with various pressing issues facing the Iranian church, which was severely persecuted because of its resistance to the taxes Shapur II levied to pay for his war with Christian Rome. Among these Demonstrations, XI, XII, XIII, XV, XVI, XVII, XVIII, XIX, and XXI, as well as parts of XXIII, deal with the Jewish critique of Christianity. Since the Iranian church included large numbers of converted Jews—in the first instance having been established in some measure by Jews—the Jewish-Christian argument constituted a primary concern for Aphrahat. He himself was a convert, born probably of Iranian parents, but he obviously had mastered both Scripture and Christian doctrine. The Jewish critique was re-enforced by the peace and prosperity enjoyed by Jewry in a time of Christian suffering.[3] The everyday relationship between the two communities was vigorous, intimate, and competitive.

---

[3] Vol. IV, pp. 20-27, 35-56.

What is striking is the utter absence of anti-Semitism from Aphrahat's thought. While much provoked, he exhibits scarcely a trace of the pervasive hatred of "the Jews" characteristic of the Greek-speaking churches of the Roman orient, indeed of his near-contemporary John Chrysostom. On the contrary, Aphrahat conducts the debate through penetrating criticism, never vilification. Though hard-pressed, he throughout maintains an attitude of respect. He must be regarded as the example of the shape Christianity might have taken had it been formed in the Semitic-Iranian Orient, a region quite free of the legacy of pagan Greco-Roman anti-Semitism. In the Iranian empire, the Jewish-Christian argument was carried on heatedly, but entirely within reasonable limits, along exegetical-historical lines, through generally rational and pointed discussion.

Aphrahat's mode of argument is of special interest. He presents a case based almost wholly on historical facts derived from sources universally acknowledged as accurate by all parties to the argument. He does not wholly rely on interpretation based upon convictions held by Christians but not by Jews, although he does share Christian affirmations. He copiously cites the Hebrew Scriptures, rarely the New Testament, and then chiefly when addressing himself to his Christian readers. His exegeses of Scriptures are reasonable and rational, for the most part not based on a tradition held by the church and not by the synagogue, but rather on the plain sense of Scripture as he thinks everyone must understand it. More often than not, he quotes without exegesis at all, thinking that the meaning is obvious, the implication clear. It is frequently alleged that his arguments are exegetical, but this seems to me far from the case. The arguments are fundamentally historical. Exegesis of Scriptures actually plays a small part. What dominates is *citation* of Scriptures as one would cite a historical document, for facts available to anyone, not for interpretations acceptable only to the initiated. The Jewish-Christian dialogue in Aphrahat's formulation thus is an argument about events, the facts of history, not about theological doctrines. The assumption is that the Christian side wins because it is right about what has happened. Doctrine, faith, revelation play no considerable role in such an argument.[4]

---

[4] To be sure, Aphrahat remains well within the conventional Christian reading of Is. 53, Ps. 22, Zech. 13, and other Hebrew Scriptures understood by the Church to refer to Jesus, his life, passion, and resurrection. See below, pp. 199-214, for a survey of what Aphrahat learned from New Testament uses of Hebrew Scriptural testimonies to the Christ. While these testimonies are important to Aphrahat, they do not occupy a central part in his

How shall we account for both Aphrahat's stress on history and his effort to prove his case through the plain sense of Scripture? The answer is found in his hermeneutical principle, that Scripture seldom is to be interpreted in other than an ordinary, everyday sense; hence also in the context of the critique of Judaism one cannot greatly depart from that plain meaning.

Unlike practically all of the Church Fathers who wrote on Judaism in Greek and Latin, Aphrahat rarely allegorizes Scriptures. West of the Euphrates, particularly among the Alexandrians, it was commonplace to interpret Scriptures in terms other than those immediately present. Thus the earlier Fathers generally argued against Judaism's "carnal" interpretation of the commandments. Jews really believed God did not want them to eat pork. The trans-Euphrates fathers generally argued that he wanted them to avoid the vices of swine, to live in a restrained and dignified manner. Jews err when they understand Scripture to be speaking of real pigs, a real Sabbath, real circumcision, and a real, fleshly people descended from Abraham, Isaac, and Jacob. For Aphrahat, to be sure, one who obeys God is a true child of Abraham, but in this regard rabbinical theology did not differ. Both Aphrahat and the Jews with whom he argued firmly believed the commandments represented real, this-worldly observances, not merely symbols of some higher truth which, once realized, obviated the need for actual practice. True, Aphrahat occasionally made use of allegory. But if one compares his writing with that of his predecessors, who find the sign of the cross in Moses' gesture against the Amalekites, the apostles on the bells of the high priest's robe, a heavenly rest in the commandment to keep the Sabbath, a spiritual circumcision in place of a physical one (in this matter, Aphrahat does not greatly differ, since the New Testament had already introduced the theme of circumcision through baptism and faith), and a moral message in the dietary laws, Aphrahat stands practically alone. His arguments focus upon Scriptures and history, events believed by both parties to be normative and consequential, because an allegorical, non-historical reading of Scriptures was not a significant part of his hermeneutic. I cannot say why that should have been the case. Like the rabbis, Aphrahat was able to execute various forms of midrashic exegesis, but, like the rabbinical hermeneutic, these forms generally focused upon the interpretation of Scriptures according to the on-the-whole plain and clear meaning, a meaning located, to be

---

argument, except in Demonstration XVII, Part iii, in which he proves that Jesus was the messiah foretold by Hebrew prophecy. There he has little choice.

sure, by reference to antecedent convictions, e.g. on the rabbis' part, concerning Torah, and on Aphrahat's part, concerning Christ. From the Apostolic Fathers to Nicea, Aphrahat remains very much by himself in his concentration on Scriptures as fundamentally historical documents. In this respect, we find in him a version of the Christian theology of Judaism phrased mainly in historical, rather than theological terms. The theologians of the Greek and Latin-speaking West used allegory and hence found little need for history, while Aphrahat did the opposite.

III. EARLIER STUDIES

Texts and Translations

W. Wright, *The Homilies of Aphraates, the Persian Sage. Edited from Syriac manuscripts of the Vth and VIth centuries in the British Museum, with an English translation. Vol. I: The Syriac Text* (London, 1869; no further volumes) was the first edition of the text. I followed *Aphraatis Sapientis Persae, Demonstrationes,* ed. and trans. Ioannes Parisot, in *Patrologia Syriaca* I, i (Paris 1894) and I, ii (Paris, 1907), and afterward compared my translation with the text of Wright, generally following Wright where the two texts differed. Important variations are noted in the translations. Among translations I consulted Parisot, Georg Bert, *Aphrahat's des persischen Weisen Homilien, aus dem syrischen übersetzt und erläutert* (Leipzig 1888), and, for Demonstrations I, V, VI, VIII, X, XVII, XXI, and XXII, John Gwynn, *Selections . . . from the Demonstrations of Aphrahat the Persian Sage*, in Philip Schaff and Henry Wace, eds., *A Select Library of Nicene and Post-Nicene Fathers*, second series, XIII, Part ii, *Gregory the Great, Ephraim Syrus, Aphrahat* (repr., Grand Rapids, 1956), pp. 345-412. My translations of XVII and XXI do not significantly differ from Gwynn's. Existing translations seem to me accurate, though Bert often paraphrases.

Introductions, Bibliographies and Studies

I consulted Otto Bardenhewer, *Patrologie* (Freiburg in Breisgau, 1901), pp. 338-340; B. Altaner, *Patrology* (London, 1960), p. 400; William Wright, *A Short History of Syriac Literature* (repr., Amsterdam, 1966), pp. 32-3; and Anton Baumstark, *Geschichte der syrischen Literatur* (Bonn, 1922), pp. 30-1.

Wright's introduction (pp. 1-18) summarizes the earliest references to

Aphrahat in Syriac literature. The name Aphrahat was common in Iran, he says (p. 7). Our Aphrahat was not a victim of Shapur's persecutions. A monk of the rank of bishop, he drew up the encyclical letter of the council of 344, held at Seleucia, which comes down to us as Demonstration XIV. He knows Marcion, Valentinus, and Manichaeism, but nothing of Arius. Wright further describes the fifth and sixth century MSS. Wright comments that Aphrahat "seems to me to quote the Peshitta merely from memory." He is not always able to locate passages cited.

Bibliography will be found in Bardenhewer, and, to 1922, in Frank Gavin, *Aphraates and the Jews* (Toronto, 1923; and *Journal of the Society of Oriental Research*, VII, pp. 95-165; page references are to the former), pp. xi-xiv; to 1945, in Edward J. Duncan, *Baptism in the Demonstrations of Aphraates the Persian Sage* (Washington, 1945: Catholic University of America Studies in Christian Antiquity, ed. J. Quasten, No. 8), pp. xiii-xiv.

The best, also the most up-to-date, brief account is Arthur Vööbus, "Aphrahat," *Nachträge zum Reallexikon für Antike and Christentum* in *Jahrbuch für Antike und Christentum* III, 1960, pp. 152-155; with an excellent, selective bibliography, p. 155. Vööbus devotes considerable attention to Aphrahat in several of his important studies, including "Celibacy, a Requirement for Admission to Baptism in the Early Syrian Church," *Papers of the Estonian Theological Society in Exile*, I (Stockholm, 1951), pp. 35-58; especially in "Methodologisches zum Studium der Anweissungen Aphrahats," *Oriens Christianus* 46, 1962, 4th series Vol. 10, pp. 25-32; and in his monumental *History of Asceticism in the Syrian Orient. A Contribution to the History of Culture in the Near East. I. The Origin of Asceticism. Early Monasticism in Persia* (Louvain, 1958: *Corpus Scriptorum Christianorum Orientalium* Vol. 184), throughout, especially pp. 173ff. Bert's introduction (pp. vii-xxxvi) is excellent.

Among numerous studies listed in Gavin, Duncan, and Vööbus, I read the following: Edmund Beck, "Symbolum-Mysterium bei Aphraat und Ephräm," *Oriens Christianus* 42, 1958, 4th series Vol. 6, pp. 19-40; F. C. Burkitt, *Early Christianity outside the Roman Empire* (Cambridge, 1899); the same author's *Early Eastern Christianity. St. Margaret's Lectures, 1904* (London, 1904), pp. 81 ff., 121 ff.; Frank Gavin, "The Sleep of the Soul in the Early Syriac Church," *JAOS* 40, 1920, pp. 103-120; M. J. Higgins, "Aphraates' Dates for Persian Persecution," *Byzantinische Zeitschrift* 44, 1951, pp. 265-271; Ignatius Ortiz de

Urbina, *Die Gottheit Christi bei Afrahat* (Rome, 1933); J. Labourt, *Le christianisme dans l'empire perse sous la dynastie sassanide (224-632)* (Paris, 1904) pp. 31-42; and H. L. Pass. "The Creed of Aphraates." *Journal of Theological Studies* 9, 1908, pp. 267-284, a response to Dom R. H. Connolly, "The Early Syriac Creed," *Zeitschrift für die neutestamentliche Wissenschaft und die Kunde des Urchristenthums* 1906, pp. 202ff; and R. H. Connolly, "On Aphraates *Hom.* I, 19," *Journal of Theological Studies* 9, 1908, pp. 572-6, a reply to Pass. The passage under discussion is translated below in part. Pass holds that "by the change of a single word, possibly by the addition of a single letter in the Syriac text, we could convert this document into a Jewish creed." Pass here refers to the letter sent by Aphrahat's friend, to which he makes response in Demonstrations I-X. The friend, Pass says, was citing an originally Jewish creed. The ten elements of the creed included faith in God as creator of heaven, who made man in his image, and accepted Abel, Enoch, Noah, Abraham, Moses, the prophets, and "he further sent (Pass: will send) his Messiah (Pass: Christ) into the world." Connolly replies (p.573) that Pass "does not appear to have drawn the conclusion that Hom. I, 19 is directly based upon the Letter: he traces the resemblance rather to the independent use of a common source, —which on other grounds he conjectures to have been a Jewish Creed." Connolly refers favorably to Paul Schwen, *Afrahat, seine Person und sein Verständnis des Christentums* (Berlin, 1907) in *Neue Studien zur Geschichte der Theologie und der Kirche* II. Schwen provides the most thorough available summary of Aphrahat's life and works, biblical citations, and his theology: belief in one God, convenant and people of God, the sacraments, Christians in the world, and history. He quickly treats "Jewish traditions" (pp. 63-5), where he refers to Funk (below) and briefly comments on his findings.

Aphrahat-studies have been part of the larger Roman Catholic-Protestant theological debate about Christian origins, particularly the sacraments, Mariology, and Christology. F. C. Burkitt states explicitly, "Let me remind you in passing that this is not a merely literary question of *Quellenkritik.* On the contrary, it is the keystone of Protestantism. The one thing which historically justifies us in breaking with the Catholic tradition is this breach of continuity at the earliest period. We are entitled to criticize the Greek Gospels freely, to suggest on due evidence that phrases or figures have been wrongly or imperfectly apprehended, in a word we have a right privately to revise the judgments of the Church, mainly because the Church of the second century was so far removed in spirit and in knowledge from the life of Judaea in our Lord's day . . ." (*Early Christianity outside the Roman Empire*, pp. 6-7). Scholarship has therefore tended to concentrate on Aphrahat's views of the sacraments, especially baptism and celibacy, theology, and so forth. This is especially unfortunate, not only because important aspects of Aphrahat's thought have been ignored, but also because even the most obvious lower-criticism of the text has been neglected. As a result, sentences are sometimes repeated, misplaced, and confused, but neither the translators nor the editors have paid much attention to improving the text in even simple, obvious ways.

Fourth-Century Jewry

For Palestine Leopold Lucas, *Zur Geschichte der Juden im vierten Jahrhundert* (Berlin, 1910) provides an admirable account of the Jews and the fourth-century church fathers in the Roman Orient, and other aspects of the Jewish-Christian argument of that period. For general history the best work is Michael Avi-Yonah, *Bimei Roma uVizanṭion* (Tel Aviv, Jerusalem, 1952). For Babylonia this writer's *History of the Jews in Babylonia, III. From Shapur I to Shapur II* (Leiden, 1968), and *IV. The Age of Shapur II* (Leiden, 1969) are available. On the involvement of Jews in persecution of fourth-century Christians in Seleucia-Ctesiphon, I consulted the brilliant study of Gernot Wiessner, *Zur Martyrerüberlieferung aus der Christenverfolgung Schapurs II* (Göttingen, 1967: *Abhandlungen der Akademie der Wissenschaften in Göttingen. Philologisch-historische Klasse,* third series No. 67). Wiessner's data on Judaism derive mainly from Graetz, but his analysis of the pertinent martyrologies is sophisticated and persuasive.

Aphrahat and Judaism

The earliest work was S. Funk, *Die haggadischen Elemente in den Homilien des Aphraates des persischen Weisen* (Vienna, 1891), who gives fifteen instances in Genesis, eight in Exodus, two in Leviticus, three in Numbers, five in Deuteronomy, and six others, of Aphraates' affinity to rabbinic materials. Parisot adds others (in his introduction, p. xlix-xl). Louis Ginzberg, "Die Haggada bei den Kirchenvätern und in der apokryphischen Literatur," *Monatsschrift für Geschichte und Wissenschaft des Judenthums* 42, 1899, and his *Die Haggada bei den Kirchenvätern* (Amsterdam, 1899) contain some references to Aphrahat.

Ginzberg's "Aphraates, the Persian Sage," *JE*, I, pp. 663-5 competently summarizes some points in common between Aphrahat and the rabbinical literature of various periods. His judgment (p. 665) is noteworthy: "Aphraates showed not the slightest traces of personal ill-feeling toward the Jews; and his calm, dispassionate tone proves that it was only his firm conviction of Christianity that caused him to assail Judaism."

Frank Gavin's dissertation, referred to above, is the single most comprehensive study of the subject. Gavin comes to the topic of "the homilies of Aphraates in relation to Jewish thought" after offering observations on the general character of the homilies, the origin of the Iranian church, the Jews under the Sasanians, and so forth. He treats as a common element "the same envisagement of religion," then cites concrete instances of "Aphraates' dependence upon, or affiliation with, Jewish thought" (pp. 37-72), namely his doctrines of creation, man, the soul, the fall, sin and the evil impulse, original sin, eschatology and chiliasm. He further discusses Aphrahat and the *Didaché*, and Aphrahat's use of Scriptures. The method is much the same as Ginzberg's and Funk's. Gavin briefly describes Aphrahat's viewpoint on a subject, then cites parallel sentiments drawn from various rabbinic sayings. The whole is arranged by theological topics rather than according to the order of Scriptures as in the cases of Funk and Ginzberg. Otherwise the works are identical in conception and method (below, pp. 150-158).

I. Ortiz de Urbina, "La controversia de Afraate coi Giudei," *Studia Missionalia* 3, 1947, pp. 85-106, summarizes, in précis-form, Demonstrations XI, XII, XIII, XV, XVI, XVII, XVIII, XIX, XXI, and XXIII. He notes that the chief concern is to protect the faith of simple Christians. His summaries are comprehensive, but merely repeat what is in Aphrahat.

Further references to Aphrahat and the Jews and Judaism are found (among other places) in Labourt, *Le Christianisme dans l'empire perse* (Paris, 1904), pp. 39-41; Vööbus in *Jahrbuch für Antike und Christentum* 6, 1960, pp. 153-4; Jean Juster, *Les Juifs dans l'empire romain* (Paris, 1914), I, pp. 59-61; Stanley Kazan, "Isaac of Antioch's Homily against the Jews, Part Two," *Oriens Christianus* 46, 1962, 4th series No. 10, pp. 89-95; A. Lukyn Williams, *Adversus Judaeos. A Bird's-eye View of Christian Apologiae until the Renaissance* (Cambridge, 1935), pp. 95-102, a rapid summary of the chief references to Jews and Judaism; James Parkes, *The Conflict of the Church and the*

Synagogue. A Study in the Origins of Antisemitism (N.Y., 1961), pp. 117, 154, 276ff., who remarks that Aphraates' tone "is amazingly reasonable"; George F. Moore, "Christian writers on Judaism," *Harvard Theological Review* 14, 1921, pp. 197-254; Isaac Broyde, "Polemics and Polemical Literature," *JE* 10, 102-9; and elsewhere. None of these works (except Vööbus) does more than summarize or merely refer to a few salient points.

P. Aug. Spijkerman, O.F.M., "Aphrahat der persische Weise und der Antisionismus," *Studii Biblici Franciscani Liber Annus* V, 1954-5, pp. 191-212, reviews Demonstration XIX, on the hope to be gathered together in the land of Israel in messianic times. He describes the contents but adds little to the critical analysis of either the text or the substance of the demonstration. Professor Willard G. Oxtoby kindly supplied this reference.

Apart from Gavin and Funk, the only important studies of Aphrahat's relation to Judaism and the Jewish-Christian argument are Gustav Richter, "Über die älteste Auseinandersetzung der syrischen Christen mit den Juden," *Zeitschrift für die neutestamentliche Wissenschaft und die Kunde der älteren Kirche* 35, 1936, pp. 101-114, and Marcel Simon, *Verus Israel. Étude sur les relations entre chrétiens et juifs dans l'empire romain (135-425)* (Paris, 1948), in particular pp. 198-206, 369-379. Simon refers to Aphrahat throughout. Of greatest interest, he places Aphrahat into the context of contemporary Christian-Jewish polemics, showing the relationship of his arguments to those of contemporaries. Simon's is the only really original, thorough, and searching account of Aphrahat's place in Christian thinking on Judaism. Richter reviews some of the passages, concentrating on the meaning of *QYM'* in relationship to *BRYT*.

After a century of study, Aphrahat remains a figure of unusual interest. Much has been done, but much work remains. Comparisons between his exegesis of Scriptures and those of Talmudic rabbis have not been fully explicated, for the parallels which Funk, Ginzberg, and Gavin noted do not exhaust the illuminating studies to be made. Of still greater importance, the meaning and implications of the parallels suggested by Funk, Ginzberg, and Gavin require more careful definition. Scholarly conceptions have greatly changed since the days that people assumed a parallel could be readily specified and forthwith bore significant and obvious consequences. The conceptual advances of more recent times need to be brought to bear upon Aphrahat-studies. My purpose is set by the context of my *History*: What can be learned from Aphrahat about

Jews and Judaism in the Iranian empire? This limited purpose guides me throughout. Aphrahat's usefulness in dealing with this question by no means exhausts the larger issues of his relationships with rabbinic Judaism and with antecedent patristic thought on Judaism, both of which are discussed as well.

iv. Early References to Judaism (337 A.D.)

Demonstration I: On Faith

[16] 6. I now come to my first statement. I said that the Messiah is called by the prophets a stone. Of old, David said concerning him, "The stone which the builders rejected has become the head of the building" (Ps. 118:22). And how did the builders reject this stone, which is the Messiah? But they thus rejected him, saying in the presence of Pilate, "This one will not be king over us" (John 19:15). And again [they rejected him] in that parable which our Lord spoke concerning a certain man, the son of a noble family. He went to receive the kingdom, then to return and rule over them. They sent after him messengers saying, "This one will not be king over us" (Luke 19:13, 14). By these things they rejected the stone who is the Messiah. And how did it [the stone] become the head of the building? How else, than that it was set over the building of the peoples,[5] and on it is raised up their entire building. And who are the builders [who rejected the stone]? Who, but the priests and Pharisees who did not build a true building, but were destroying what he was building, as it is written in Ezekiel the prophet, "He was building a wall of partition, but they were shaking it, so that it might fall" (Ez. 13:10-11)? [Aphrahat further cites Ez. 22:30, Is. 28:16, and then proceeds.] For the people of the house of Israel fell on him, and he became their destruction forever . . . but the peoples believed on him and do not fear.

> *Comment:* Aphrahat here refers to the rejection of Jesus as the Messiah, saying that doing so led to the destruction of Israel. This point will frequently recur in later polemics; here it is simply part of his exposition of faith.

[28][Aphrahat cites Hos. 10:12, "Light you a lamp and seek the Lord." He further cites Is. 55:6, 7, "Seek the Lord, and when you shall have found him, call upon him . . ."] For that lamp shone, but they did not by it seek the Lord their God, so "its light shone in the darkness, but the darkness did not know it" (John 1:5). Then the lamp was set on a stand,

---

[5] Aphrahat uses 'MM' consistently to refer to the gentiles.

but those who were in the house did not see its light. What does this mean, that the lamp was set on a stand? But this, namely, [it refers to] his being raised up on the cross. By this means the entire house was darkened for them on his account. When they crucified him, the light became dark for them, but shone among the peoples . . .

(Parisot I, 28)

> *Comment:* The interest of this passage is in Aphrahat's careful specification of *when* Israel was rejected and the nations given Israel's blessing, namely, when they did not see the light of the lamp raised upon the menorah (lampstand): at Calvary.

[44, line 13] 19. For this is Faith: When a man believes in God, Lord of all, who made heaven and earth, the seas and all which is in them. He made man in his image and gave revelation [6] to Moses. He sent of his spirit in the prophets. He furthermore sent his messiah to the world. A man should believe in the resurrection of the dead. Moreover, he should believe also in the mystery of baptism. This is the faith of the church of God. A man should separate himself from observing hours, Sabbaths, New Moons, and festivals; from divinations, sorceries, Chaldaeanism, and magic; from fornication, from songs, and from empty doctrines, the vessels of the Evil One; and from the blandishment of sweet words, from blasphemy, and from adultery. A man should not bear false witness nor speak with two tongues. These are the works of faith set upon the true rock who is the Messiah, upon whom is raised the entire building.

(Parisot I, 44-45)

> *Comment*: Aphrahat's reference to *not* observing the Sabbath, New Moons, and festival seasons is excellent testimony to the presence in the Church of Sabbath-observers. Keeping the Jewish festivals and holy seasons is made equivalent to fornication, sorcery, false witness, and other evils. Among the works of faith is *desisting* from them all.
>
> Then Aphrahat argues that the law was not given for the righteous but for the wicked; therefore, if people had not sinned, there would have been no need for the law, but, he adds, if the law were not given, then "the power of God would not have been made known in all generations and in all the wonders which He showed." He proceeds to show how there was a balance between the sin of man and the revelation of God accompanied by miracles, using the examples of Adam and Noah, etc.

Demonstration V: On Wars

[In his discussion of contemporary international politics, Aphrahat

---

[6] ʾWRYT, *ʾuraita*, revelation.

refers to Dan. 7:27, "The saints of the most high shall receive the kingdom."]

[224] What shall we say concerning this. Perhaps the children of Israel have received the kingdom of the most High? Far be it! Or perhaps that people has come on heavenly clouds? This has passed away from them.

(Parisot I, 224 l. 24—225 l. 3)

Comment: Aphrahat must show that the prophetic promises have not been fulfilled, and cannot be fulfilled, in Israel, but refer to the time to come.

[232, 1.3] 23. And the holy people [= Church] inherited eternal dominion for it was chosen in place of the people [Israel]. For "He provoked them with a people which was no people, and with a foolish people he angered them" (Deut. 32:21). He set free the holy people. Behold the whole covenant [people] of God he set free from the burden of kings and rulers (Hos. 8:10). Even if a man serves pagans, as soon as he draws near to the covenant of God, he is set free. But the Jews serve in bondage among the peoples. Thus he said about the saints, "They will inherit the sovereignty of that which is under the heavens" (Dan. 7:27). Now if he spoke concerning them [namely the Jews], why are they serving in bondage among the peoples? And if they say, it has not yet come about [namely our redemption], but (we reply), Is the sovereignty which will be given to the son of men of heaven or of earth? For behold, the children of the kingdom are inscribed and they have [already] received their freedom from this world . . .

Aphrahat proceeds to trace the gift of sovereignty and its removal by God. He gave the kingdom first to the sons of Jacob and forced the children of Esau to serve them, but he took it away from them and gave it to the children of Esau, and, Aphrahat says, the kingdom will not be taken away from Esau until it will be given to the Giver, "and He himself will preserve it."

Aphrahat tangentially refers to "the holy people," meaning the Christians, who were chosen instead of the people of Israel. A sign that the Jews are no longer the holy people is that they are still subjugated among the gentiles. But the Christians are already recorded, and indeed have already been emancipated from this world. Later on he develops the theme that the Jews' worldly condition testifies against their faith, while that of the Christians confirms it.

I

TRANSLATIONS

CHAPTER TWO

DEMONSTRATION XI

ON CIRCUMCISION

Summary: Israel proudly claims to be the children of Abraham. But when any one of the peoples does righteousness, he is called a child of Abraham, while Israel has already been rejected. Israel has been called Sodom and Gomorrah. Circumcision without faith is useless. It did not avail sinners of old. Furthermore, God has made many covenants, and each of them was signified in a different way. The covenant of circumcision was merely one of these. Abraham's faith, not his circumcision, was reckoned as righteousness. Circumcision actually was widely practiced by the ancients. The Egyptians did so, as did Edomites, Moabites, Ammonites, and others. The purpose of circumcision merely was to distinguish Israel from the unclean peoples of Canaan. They therefore were uncircumcized in the wilderness, but circumcized as they entered the promised land. This furthermore marked them off for punishment if they broke the law. They then could not claim *not* to be Israel, therefore not culpable. Baptism is the Christian circumcision, and Christians are inheritors of Abraham, the first believer.

Pages in Parisot's text are indicated in square brackets [ ], Wright's in parentheses ( ).

I. REBELLIOUS ISRAEL

[468] (202) XI-1. When God blessed Abraham and made him head of all believing, righteous, and upright men, God did not make him father of one people alone, but of many peoples, as he said to him, "Your name will not be called Abram, but your name will be Abraham, for I have made you father of a multitude of peoples" (Gen. 17:5). Now, beloved friend, hear concerning the sign of which he spoke and the foundation about which he gave instruction, what it is right to say against that people which came before us and believes about itself that it is the seed of Abraham. But they do not understand that they have been called rulers of Sodom and the people of Gomorrah (Is. 1:10); their father was an Amorite and their mother a Hittite (Ez. 16:45); [they are] rejected silver (Jer. 6:30); and rebellious children (Is. 30:1).

Moses their leader testified concerning them, saying to them, "You have been rebellious from the day that I knew you" (Deut. 9:24). Furthermore, he reiterated in the hymn of testimony, "Your vine [is] from the vine of Sodom and from the planting of Gomorrah. Your grapes are bitter grapes, and your clusters are bitter for you" (Deut. 32:32). He hinted [469] in that [same] hymn of testimony about the people which is (203) from the peoples [1] when he said to them, "I shall provoke you with a people which is no people, and with a foolish people I shall anger you" (Deut. 32:21). Through Isaiah the Holy One testified, saying, "I have planted a vineyard and have worked it. But instead of grapes, it brought forth wild grapes" [2] (Is. 5:2). Jeremiah the prophet also said concerning the congregation of the people,[3] "I have planted you as a shoot which was entirely a true seed, but you have changed and rebelled against me as an alien vine" (Jer. 2:21). Ezekiel testified about the vine: "Fire has consumed the twig, its middle is dried up, and it is not again useful for anything" (Ez. 15:4). "The shoot was planted, a true seed" [refers to] their original fathers. But the children have turned to the unclean deeds of the Amorites.

When [any] of all the peoples do righteousness, they are called children and heirs of Abraham their father. But when the children of Abraham do an unclean deed of the alien peoples, then they become Sodomites and the people of Gomorrah, as Isaiah testified concerning them, "Hear the word of the Lord, rulers of Sodom and people of Gomorrah" (Is. 1:10).

But show me, O sage, what rulers and people were in Sodom and Gomorrah in the days of Isaiah the prophet? For from the days of Lot, they were wrathfully overthrown and they never will be inhabited. Ezekiel [472] makes manifest the evil of Sodom, and calls her the sister of Jerusalem, as he says to her, "Sodom, your sister, and her daughters have not done evil deeds as you have done, you and your daughters. And this was the evil of Sodom and of her daughters: She did not help [lit: take by the hand] the poor and the needy. So when I saw these deeds among them, I overthrew (204) them" (Ez. 16:48-49). Since Sodom, Gomorrah, and their companions were overthrown from of old, why does Isaiah say, "Hear, rulers of Sodom and people of Gomorrah"? But since they would not mend their ways, he thus called [them], because they used to do the deeds of the Sodomites. They were circumcised and [then] uncircumcised, chosen and [then] rejected. We boast that we are circumcised, chosen, and known from among all the peoples.

---

[1] 'm' dmn 'mm' = the church. Aphrahat consistently refers to the church as "the people which is of the peoples," regarding the "new Israel" as "the people formed from the nations." Since he is careful to use 'm' and 'mm' throughout, I have preserved his exact usage.

[2] ḥrwb' — Payne Smith: husks; Parisot: labruscas; Bert = Herlinge.

[3] knwšt' d'm' — Parisot: synagogam populi; Bert: die Gemeinde des Volkes.

II. CIRCUMCISION-WITHOUT FAITH

XI-2. Anyone who considers [matters] closely knows this: Circumcision without faith has no use nor profits anything, for faith precedes circumcision, and circumcision was given as a sign and a covenant to Abraham, as God said to him, "This is my covenant which you will keep, that you will circumcise every male" (Gen. 17:10).[4] So long as it [circumcision] pleased its Giver, it was observed with the commandments of the law, profited and gave life. But when the law was not observed, circumcision was of no value. Jeroboam [473] the son of Nabat, of the children of Joseph, of the tribe of Ephraim was circumcised as the Holy One commanded Abraham and [as] Moses instructed in the law. All the kings of Israel who walked in the law of Jeroboam were circumcised and [thereby] distinguished. But a good memory was not preserved concerning them, because of their sins. What [then] did Jeroboam profit in his circumcision — he and all the kings of Israel who walked in his footsteps? Or what use and value [from circumcision] did Manasseh the son of Hezekiah have, on account of whose sins, that were many, God was not able again to forgive Jerusalem?

III. THE VARIOUS COVENANTS

XI-3. With all generations and tribes God made his covenants, in each generation as it pleased him, and they [the covenants] were kept in their times but [then] changed. He commanded Adam that he should not eat from the tree of the knowledge of good and evil, but because he [Adam] did not keep the commandment (205) and the covenant, he was condemned. As to Enoch who was pleasing before God, it was not because the commandment concerning the tree was kept by him that he was translated alive, but because he believed. The [act of] pleasing does not seem [to have been keeping] the commandment not to eat from the tree. [God] saved Noah, who preserved his innocence and righteousness, from the wrath of the flood, and made a covenant with him and with his descendants after him, that they should be fruitful and multiply, and [he made] the covenant of the bow in the clouds between God, earth and all flesh. With not one of [476] these covenants was circumcision given.

---

[4] Bert: und die Beschneidung wurde zum Zeichen und Bund dem Abraham gegeben; Parisot: et signaculum circumcisio; data est enim in foedus Abrahae. I have followed Bert, despite the punctuation in Parisot's text, reflected in his translation.

When he chose Abraham, he was not in the circumcision. He called, chose, and named him father for all the peoples. [It was not through circumcision] but through faith. After his believing, then he commanded him to circumcise. But if [men] were living through circumcision, first Abraham should have circumcised and *then* believed. If circumcision were given as an advantage for eternal life, the Scripture should have announced that Abraham circumcised, and *circumcision* was regarded for him as righteousness. But thus it was written, "Abraham believed in God and his *believing* was reckoned as righteousness" (Gen. 15:6).

Thus those who believed even while not circumcised lived, but those who circumcised but did not believe—their circumcision availed them not at all. Abel, Enoch, Noah, Shem, and Japheth were not in the circumcision, [yet] were pleasing before God, for each one of them kept their covenants in their time and believed that one is he who gave his covenants in each generation as he willed. Melchizedek was the priest of God the most high. He blessed Abraham although he was not circumcised, and this matter is known, that the lesser will be blessed by him who is greater than he.

IV. THE PURPOSE OF CIRCUMCISION

XI-4. [477] Now, my beloved, hear and I shall show you in what manner circumcision was given. When Abraham believed, went forth from Ur (206) of the Chaldees, and came to dwell in Haran, God had not [yet] commanded him to circumcise. When he had dwelt in the land of Canaan twenty-four years, he was not circumcised, because he did not have a son, the son of the promise that from him righteous men, kings, priests, and messiahs would be born. But when he was ninety-nine years old, the Holy One informed him that when he had completed one hundred years, a son would be born to him. Then he circumcised himself, so that when he was one hundred years old, Isaac would be born to him.

He commanded him to circumcise the flesh of his foreskin as a sign and signification of the covenant, so that when his seed would multiply, they might be distinguished from all the peoples among whom they would go, so that they might not be mingled with their [the pagans'] unclean deeds. So Abraham circumcised the flesh of his foreskin at the age of ninety-nine years, and he circumcised Ishmael, his son, at the age of thirteen years; and those who were born of his house and purchased of his money did Abraham circumcise on that day, just as God had spoken with him. After he was circumcised, Isaac was conceived, born, and circumcised on the eighth day. Circumcision was observed by the seed of Abraham, [480] by Isaac and Ishmael, by Jacob and his sons, and by Esau and his son, for one hundred ninety years, until Jacob entered Egypt.

In Egypt the children of Jacob kept it [circumcision] two hundred twenty-five years, until they went forth to the wilderness. Also when Lot saw that Abraham his uncle circumcised, he too circumcised his son [Parisot adds: et ipse], after he had separated from him [Abraham], so they retained circumcision as a custom [5] without faith.

v. Circumcision Not Unique to Israel

XI-5. Now if they [Israel] live by circumcision, then the children of Ishmael, the children of Qentura, the children of Lot and the children of Esau also live, for they are circumcised, and though (207) circumcised, they worship many gods. But Jeremiah, the prophet, has shown me quite openly that all those who are circumcised without believing are uncircumcised, and they will not be saved from the wrath through their circumcision. He said, "Lo, I punish all who are circumcised in uncircumsion, the Egyptians, the Jews, Moab, Edom, the children of Ammon, and all those who cut the corner [of their hair] who live in the wilderness, for all these peoples are uncircumcised, and all of the house of Israel are uncircumcised in their heart" (Jer. 9:25-26).

If they derived benefit from circumcision, then why is Judah reckoned with the Egyptians, Edomites, Moabites, Ammonites, and those who cut the corner, who are the children of Hagar and the [481] children of Qentura? But thereby it is known that their circumcision was uncircumcision, for also on Judah he visited wrath, just as on all those others who are circumcised in uncircumcision. For when the Holy One saw that they said, "By this we live, that we are the children of Abraham and are circumcised," and that they did not submit their stiff neck to the servitude of the law, he said to them through the prophet, "Circumcise the foreskin of your heart and do not again stiffen your neck" (Deut. 10:16). So it is known that whoever does not circumcise the foreskin of his heart, then also the circumcision of his flesh is of no value to him,

---

[5] *b'yd' dl' hymnw*—Parisot: circumcisionem infideles in consuetudinem; Bert: die Beschneidung, *die mit der Hand geschah,* ohne den Glauben. Bert is surely wrong.

just as it was of no benefit to whoever was circumcised in his uncircumcision.

XI-6. This should stand firm for you, my beloved, that circumcision is a sign so as to separate [the Jews] from the unclean peoples. Note that when he brought them forth from Egypt, and they walked in the wilderness for forty years, they did not circumcise, for the people was one [alone] and not mixed among other peoples. There he did not mark them because they pastured by themselves. And that he marked out (208) the seed of Abraham, it was not because all the peoples were not his that he separated the seed of Abraham as his own flock. But all the peoples who do evil deeds of idolatry he abandoned because of their deeds.

And as to his marking them as his people, it was not to inform himself that [484] they are the seed of Abraham, for before he marked them, he knew them. But [it was] that they themselves might know one another, so that they might not take refuge through lying. For it might come to pass, if they were not [clearly] marked, that when some of them might be found worshipping idols, or committing fornication or adultery, stealing, or doing anything which was outside of the law, then some of them who were found in these things might deny and lie, [saying] 'We are not the children of Abraham', so that they might not be killed or receive punishment. But the decree of death, which is written in the law, is upon those who do these things. So whoever is found transgressing the law and does any of these odious deeds no longer is able to take refuge through lying, [saying] 'I am not of the seed and a child of Abraham'. For if he is found to deny, they find it out through his circumcision and inflict punishment, as is right according to his transgression.

Now if circumcision were not given for *this* reason, it should have been required even in the wilderness that they circumcise. But because they were set apart from the peoples and pasturing by themselves in the wilderness, they were not marked. But when they crossed the Jordan, the Lord commanded Joshua the son of Nun, saying [485] to him, "Once again circumcise the children of Israel a second time" (Jos. 5:2). And why did he say to Joshua (209) that he should circumcise them a *second* time? Because they were [already] circumcised in their hearts, as he said through the prophet, "Circumcise the foreskin of your heart and do not again stiffen your neck" (Deut. 10:16). Joshua again circumcised them and a second time marked them in their flesh. But how do you understand the saying that Joshua circumcised the people a second time? They were *not* [yet] circumcised in their flesh, for after Joshua circumcised them, Scripture testifies, "Joshua circumcised all those who were born in the wilderness, for no child that was born in the wilderness was circumcised" (Jos. 5:5, 6).

XI-7. See then, my beloved, and be amazed at this, that they who were circumcised who went forth from Egypt died in the wilderness because of their sins, because they tried the spirit of the Holy One and did not believe in him. It is [thereby] known that if they had believed, they would not have been kept from entering the Promised Land. But Joshua the son of Nun and Caleb the son of Yufna of the six hundred thousand who went forth from Egypt lived and entered the land, inheriting it. A child born in the wilderness who believed, though not circumcised, lived and entered to inherit the land. He circumcised them when they were entering the land of the Canaanites, and it [6] was regarded for them as two circumcisions.

VI. EGYPTIAN CIRCUMCISION

XI-8. [488] And why, when he visited wrath on all who were circumcised in their uncircumcision, did he also number the Egyptians, who were not of the seed of Abraham, along with the Ammonites, the Moabites, the children of Lot, the son of Abraham's brother, the Edomites, who were the children of Esau, those who cut the corner [of the hair] who lived in the wilderness, who are the children of Ishmael and the children of Qentura, and with Judah the seed of Jacob? All of these [others] are the seed of the house of Abraham.

(210) The Egyptians received circumcision as a custom without faith from the children of Israel when [the Israelites] dwelt among them. They furthermore received it from Joseph, for when Manasseh and Ephraim were born, and he circumcised them, also they learned from Joseph and began to circumcise, for the command of Joseph in all things was carried out in the midst of Egypt.

And furthermore, my beloved, there are men who say that when the daughter of Pharaoh found Moses, she realized from the covenant which was in his flesh that he was of the children of Israel. But the meaning of the Scripture is not as it appears to be. For the covenant of the circumcision of Moses was in no way different from the circumcision of the children of Egypt. Whoever does not know that the Egyptians were circumcised, let him learn from Jeremiah [above]. For when the daughter of Pharaoh [489] found Moses and saw that he was floating in the river, she [thereby] knew that he was of the children of the Hebrews, because it

---

[6] The believing and the fleshly circumcision.

was not commanded for Egyptians to be thrown into the river as Pharaoh
had commanded concerning the children of Israel, saying, "Every male
child who is born will be cast into the river" (Ex. 1:22). She knew that on
account of fear of the commandment [of Pharaoh] this thing had been
done. When she saw that he had been placed in an ark of wood, she knew
that they had hidden him, made the ark for him, and threw it in the river,
so that his [Pharaoh's] men would not find [him].[7] Now if by means of
circumcision the children of Israel had been distinguished, while the
Egyptians were not circumcised, Moses could not have been brought up
in the house of Pharaoh, because in his childhood at any time the
covenant of his flesh would have been found out. If the daughter of
Pharaoh had transgressed the law and commandment of her father, then
in the whole of Egypt (211) the commandment and law of Pharaoh would
no longer have been carried out.

XI-9. Now, furthermore, my beloved, I shall teach you concerning the
children of Qentura, that they also are neighbors of the children of
Ishmael. When the Midianites (they are the children of Qentura) and the
children of the East (they are the children of Ishmael) gathered together,
and they [all] came to do battle with Israel in the days of Gideon the son of
Joash, in alliance with one another they wished to subjugate Israel. But
they were given into the hands of Gideon with [his] three hundred chiefs.
This [492] I shall explain to you [now] concerning the children of
Qentura, for they and the children of Ishmael were dwelling in the
wilderness. From the time that Abraham sent forth Hagar and Ishmael,
the dwelling of Ishmael and his descendants was in the wilderness. Thus
it is written, "He dwelt in the wilderness and learned the bow. His hand
would be against all, and the hand of all would be against him, and he
dwelt on the border of all his brothers" (Gen. 21:20; 16:12). On his one
side, on the east, dwelt the children of Esau, who are the Edomites, for
when Israel went forth from Egypt, they went around the land of Edom,
the mountain of Esau. Also the Ammonites and the Moabites were
neighbors on the north. And on the east, the children of Qentura were
neighbors of the Edomites, the children of Esau, for when Abraham sent
away the children of Qentura, he sent them forward to the east, and the
children of Hagar possessed all the land of the south.

The Edomites, the children of Esau, dwelt on the east of all of them,
until Bosra. For the Lord also commanded Moses, "You will not draw

---

[7] Bert:". . . erkannte sie, dass sie ihm das Kästchen gemacht und es in den Fluss gesetzt
hatten, damit seine Männer es nicht versenken könnten." I take *str* to be *pa'el*, hence
shelter, protect.

near the land of the children of Esau, for I have not given you their land, not so much as for the sole of the foot to tread on, because I have given to Esau (212) the mountain of Seir. But buy from them bread with money, and eat; and buy from them water [493] with money, and drink" (Deut. 2:5, 6). Moses did as the Lord commanded him. He did not trouble the children of Esau, but when he came to Reqem de Gaya, he sent messengers with words of peace to the king of Edom, saying to him, "Thus says your brother Jacob: You know all the adversity which has befallen us on the way, and how the Egyptians have subjugated us. Now we are at Reqem, the city which is at the limit of your frontier. Now let us pass through your land. By the royal road we shall go. Sell us bread so that we may eat, also water so we may drink, we and our flock. We shall give a fair price." He responded to Israel, "You will not pass through my border. Otherwise with a sword shall I go forth to meet you. Israel turned aside from them, seeing that they were not persuaded" (Num. 20:14-18). When they were passing by their frontier, the children of Israel took Bosra from them, which is in the wilderness, and they inherited it and made it a free city [of refuge].

And whoever wants to accept instruction that Bosra belonged to the children of Esau and that they are Edomites from of old, let him listen to Isaiah, the prophet, who saw that the Holy One, "when he came from Edom and in crimsoned garments from Bosra" (Is. 63:1), trampled and oppressed them, and executed punishment on the children of Esau, because they did not receive their brother, but he forever preserved his wrath.

And whoever will not be persuaded concerning Bosra [496] that of old she served the Edomites, let him listen to Genesis [concerning the time] that kings ruled in Edom: "Jobab the son of Zerah of Bosra ruled" (Gen. 36:33). Further, Isaiah said, "[For my sword has drunk its fill in the heavens], behold it (213) descends on the Edomites, on the people who have been condemned in judgment" (Is. 34:5). David said, "Upon Edom I cast my shoes" (Ps. 60:8, 108:9), "because Esau injured his beloved forever, and forever he bore his grudge and did not permit his brother to pass through his border" (Amos 1:11). On this account he was condemned in judgment, that he should bear his wrath forever.

When Israel turned aside from Esau his brother, they sent messengers to the Moabites, the children of Lot, that they might pass through their borders. They neither listened nor were persuaded, but hired Balaam the son of Beor to curse them. Because he did not let them pass peacefully through their borders, the Holy One commanded that the Ammonites and Moabites should not enter the congregation of the Lord, not until the tenth generation, because they did not present bread and water to Israel on the way, but attacked them while they were afflicted and weary. Concerning the Egyptians and Edomites he commanded that Israel not reject them, the Egyptians — for they had dwelt in their land, and the Edomites — for they were his brethren.

XI-10. All of this I have explained and shown you so that you may know that Ishmael "dwelt on the border of all of his brothers and was a wild ass [497] among men" (Gen. 16:12). Abraham gave gifts to the children of Qentura, and he sent them to Ishmael their brother, so that they might not inherit with Isaac, the son of the promise.

Now if they through circumcision live, also the children of Ishmael, the children of Qentura, the children of Lot, the Moabites, Ammonites, children of Esau, Edomites, and Egyptians, — also they all the more so ought to take pride, for they both circumcise and worship many idols. Now thus it is known that there is no (214) profit in circumcision without faith. But any one who circumcises the foreskin of his heart believes, [thereby] lives and becomes a son of Abraham. So is fulfilled the word which God spoke to Abraham, "I have made you the father of a multitude of peoples" (Gen. 17:5).

XI-11. In all things the law and the covenant have been changed. From of old God changed the covenant of Adam, and he gave another to Noah. Then again he gave it also to Abraham. He changed the one of Abraham and gave another to Moses. Then when that of Moses was not kept, he gave another in the final generation [= that of Jesus], a covenant which will not be changed.

Adam's was the covenant not to eat from the tree. Noah's was the bow in the clouds. Abraham's was at first his choosing him because of his faith, and then was [the covenant of] circumcision, a sealing and a sign [500] for his descendants. Of Moses [the sign of the covenant was] a lamb which was slaughtered on behalf of the people. None of all of these covenants is like the next.

VII. True Circumcision

The circumcision in which he was pleased to give the covenant is that concerning which Jeremiah spoke, "Circumcise the foreskin of your hearts" (Jer. 4:4). Now if the covenant which God gave to Abraham is true, so also is this one true and faithful. And he cannot [again] give a law that is rejected by those outside of the law or by those who are under the law. He gave the law to Moses with his commandments and covenants.

When they did not keep the law and covenants, it was annulled. He determined to give a new testament, and he spoke not like at the first,[8] although the giver of both of them was one and the same. This is the testament which he decided to give: "They should all know me from the least of them even to the oldest" (Jer. 31:34). And in this testament there is no circumcision (215) of the flesh nor a sign of [being a singular] people. We know truly, my beloved, that in every generation God gives laws, and they serve so long as it pleases him, then they are changed, as the apostle said, "In times of old, in all ways the kingdom of God dwelt in all times" (Heb. 1:1).

This is known and explicit to sages and to whoever investigates [501], that every man who is of the covenant [of Christ] and yearns after circumcision, on account of his lust and shamelessness is circumcised, and he does not understand what the apostle said, "I wish that those who frighten you would mutilate themselves" (Gal. 5:12).

Our God is true, and his covenants are very trustworthy, and each covenant in its time was true and trustworthy. They find life who are circumcised in their hearts and who circumcise themselves a second time on the true Jordan, the baptism of the forgiveness of sins.

XI-12. Joshua the son of Nun circumcised the people a second time with knives of stone when he and his people crossed the Jordan.[9] Joshua [Jesus] our redeemer a second time circumcised the peoples who believed in him with the circumcision of the heart, and they were baptised and circumcised with "the knife which is his word that is sharper than the two-edged sword" (Heb. 4:12). Joshua the son of Nun led the people across to the Land of Promise; and Joshua our redeemer promised the land of the living to whoever passed through the true Jordan, believed, and circumcised the foreskin of his heart. Joshua the son of Nun raised up stones as a testimony in Israel; and Joshua our redeemer called Simon the true stone and set him up as a faithful testimony among the peoples. Joshua the son of Nun made a paschal sacrifice in the camp at Jericho in the cursed land [504] and the people ate from the bread of the land; and Joshua our redeemer made a paschal sacrifice with his disciples in Jerusalem, the city which he cursed (216) [saying] "There should not remain in it stone on stone" (Matthew 24:2),

---

[8] Parisot: quod dixit a priori diversum fore. Bert: Und er sprach nicht wie das erste Mal, da doch der Geber von Beiden ein und derselbe ist. This is against the Marcionites, I assume.

[9] tnynwt: Payne-Smith, second rank, second place, second year of age; hence with b, perhaps "in the second year of age"; but I follow Bert: nochmals; Parisot: secundo.

and there he gave the mystery [10] in the bread of life. Joshua the son of Nun condemned the avaricious Achan who stole and hid, and Joshua our redeemer condemned the avaricious Judah who stole and hid money from the purse which he was holding. Joshua the son of Nun wiped out unclean peoples; and Joshua our redeemer threw down Satan and his host. Joshua the son of Nun held up the sun in the sky; and Joshua our redeemer brought on sunset at noon when they crucified him. Joshua the son of Nun was redeemer of the people. Jesus was called redeemer of the peoples. Blessed are those whose hearts are circumcised from the foreskin and who are born through water, the second circumcision, for they are inheritors with Abraham, the head of the believers and the father of all peoples, whose faith was reckoned for him as righteousness.

The demonstration concerning circumcision is completed.

---

[10] *rz* (blḥm* dḥy*) = sacrament.

CHAPTER THREE

DEMONSTRATION XII

ON THE PASCHAL SACRIFICE

Summary: When Israel was in its land, it was lawful to make the paschal sacrifice only in Jerusalem. Now that the Jews are scattered, they celebrate it unlawfully amid unclean peoples. Israel indeed has been rejected, and the church of the peoples has replaced it. Christians are troubled concerning the date of the paschal sacrifice. They should know that Jesus was that sacrifice. The sacraments of blood and flesh marked his death. He was regarded as dead from the time of the last supper, on Thursday. From when he was seized on the night of the fourteenth of Nisan until when he arose on the dawn of the sixteenth, he was among the dead, for three days.

The Jews celebrate the paschal sacrifice on the fourteenth, but for the Christians it is the fifteenth. The Jews eat unleavened bread seven days, but we observe as the festival of unleavened bread the festival of our redeemer. The redemption of Israel contrasts with the redemption of the nations: the former were redeemed through the blood of the lamb and baptized in the sea, the latter through the blood of the redeemer and baptized in the mystery of the passion of our redeemer.

Pages in Parisot's text are indicated in square brackets [ ], Wright's in parentheses ( ).

I. THE JEWISH PASSOVER

[505] (217) XII-1. The Holy One commanded Moses concerning the paschal sacrifice to make it on the fourteenth of the first month. He said to Moses, "Command the congregation of the children of Israel to take for themselves one lamb a year old, a lamb on which there is no blemish. They will take [it] from the sheep and from the goats. And all the children of Israel will make a paschal sacrifice to the Lord" (Ex. 12:3, 5, 6). He said to Moses, Take a lamb from the tenth of the month, and let it be guarded until the fourteenth of the month. They will slaughter it at sunset and sprinkle of its blood on the door of their houses against the destroyer, that he should not come against them as the destroyer passed through the midst of the land of Egypt. The entire congregation will hastily eat the lamb. Thus they will eat it: with their loins bound up, their sandals on their feet, and their staffs in their hands. And he commanded them hastily to eat it. But they should not eat from it raw and also not [508]

boiled in water, but roasted in fire; nor should they take any part of it out of the house, nor break a bone in it. The children of Israel did so, and ate the paschal sacrifice on the fourteenth of the first month which is Nisan, the month of the flowers, the first month (218) of the year.

XII-2. Now consider, my beloved, these mysteries which the Holy One commanded concerning the making of the paschal sacrifice.[1] He commanded them concerning all its laws, saying to them, "It should be eaten in one house, and you should take nothing from it outside of the house" (Ex. 12:46). Thus Moses commanded them, "When you enter the land which the Lord gave you, and you make a paschal sacrifice in its season, you and your household will not permit sacrificing the paschal sacrifice in any one of your cities, but [only] in the place which the Lord your God will choose for himself. You will rejoice in your festal season" (Deut. 16:5-6). Furthermore, he thus commanded them, "A foreigner and a hired hand will not eat from the paschal sacrifice, but as to a slave purchased by money who will be yours, when you have circumcised the flesh of his foreskin, then will he eat of the paschal sacrifice" (Ex. 12:44, 45).

II. JEWISH PASSOVER ILLEGAL

XII-3. Great and wonderful are these mysteries, my beloved. When Israel was in its own land, it was lawful for them to make the paschal sacrifice only in Jerusalem. In our day they are scattered among all peoples and languages, among the unclean [509] and the uncircumcised, and eat their bread in uncleanness among the peoples, just as Ezekiel said concerning them when he [God] made a sign that he [Ezekiel] would eat his bread in uncleanness, and [then] he prayed, saying, "O, Lord of Lords, my soul has not been made unclean, nor has unclean flesh entered my mouth" (Ez. 4:14). Then he said to Ezekiel, "This will be the sign [that] thus shall the children of Israel eat their bread in contamination among the peoples among whom I shall scatter them" (Ez. 4:13). Now if it is as I said above, that when Israel was in its land, it was lawful for him to sacrifice the paschal sacrifice not in any place, but only before one altar in Jerusalem, in our days how is it possible to carry out the mystery of the paschal sacrifice, for behold, they are scattered among the alien peoples? (219) Now they have no ruler [of their own], and through the prophet he

---

[1] Bert = Siehe . . . welche Geheimnisse in dem Gebot des Heiligen, das Pascha zu feiern, verschlossen liegen. Parisot = Vide . . . mysteria quae in paschatis celebratione Sanctissimus instituit.

thus testified concerning them, "Many days will the children of Israel dwell without sacrifices and without an altar, without wearing the ephod and offering the incense" (Hos. 3:4). And again he said to Jerusalem, "I shall put an end to her joys and festivals, her New Moons and Sabbaths" (Hos. 2:11). And concerning the ark of the testament he said, "They shall no longer say 'the ark of the testament of the Lord', nor will they remember it, nor will it be made again" (Jer. 3:16). Now that he said that they will not remember it, nor will it be made, and it will not come to mind, how is it that they dare to do it?

Moses earlier said concerning them, "I shall provoke them [512] with a people which is not a people, and with a foolish people I shall anger them" (Deut. 32:21). Now I ask you, O wise debater of the people, who does not examine the words of the law: Show me when this [Scripture] was fulfilled, that God will provoke his people by a people which is not a people. When did he outrage them by a foolish people? If you are provoked by the people which is from among the peoples, you fulfill the Scripture which was written, which Moses first set down for you in Scripture. If you make the paschal sacrifice anywhere in your settlement, you do it in transgression of the commandment.

III. JEWS REJECTED AND REPLACED

XII-4. For a bill of divorce is written for you,[2] and if you are not persuaded, then listen to Jeremiah the prophet who said, "I have abandoned my house. I have abandoned my inheritance. I have given the beloved of my soul into the hand of his enemies. My inheritance has become for me like a painted bird [of prey]" (Jer. 12:7-9). What is this painted bird [of prey]? I ask you. This painted bird [of prey] is the church of the peoples. See how he calls it (220) 'painted,' for from many nations has it been gathered together, and from distant peoples has it been brought near.

But if you are not persuaded that the peoples are the inheritance of

---

[2] Bert = Und wenn du das Pascha feierst. . . so feierst du es mit Übertretung des Gebots. (3) Denn euch ist der Scheidebrief geschrieben. Und wenn du dich nicht überzeugen lassen willst . . . Parisot = Et si pascha ubilibet . . . illud celebras contra praeceptum; etenim conscriptus est adversum vos libellus repudii. The difference is surely in the text. Bert understands the phrase beginning *mtl dktyb* as the start of the following paragraph. Parisot's text (and translation) attaches the phrase to the foregoing. Ideally, it would read "you do it in transgression of the commandment, on which account a bill of divorce . . ." But this would require *mtl hn'* or equivalent, rather than *mtl d*, which must yield, "because a bill of divorce is written for you." Bert follows Wright's paragraphing (p. 219), as given here.

God, then further hear how Jeremiah calls the peoples and rejects Israel, saying, "Stand by the ways and look, and ask the wayfarers of the world and see which is the good way, and walk [513] in it. But you said we shall not walk [in it]." Again he said, "I raised up over you watchmen, that you might hear the sound of the trumpet. But they said, We shall not hearken" (Jer. 6:16, 17). Then, when the children of Israel did not listen to him, he turned to the church which is of the peoples saying, "Hear, O peoples, and know, O church which is among them" (Jer. 6:18).

David said, "Remember your church which you acquired from of old" (Ps. 74:2). Isaiah said, "Hear, O *peoples*, the thing which I have done, and know, O *distant ones*, my power" (Is. 33:13). Isaiah further said of the church which was destined to come into existence among the peoples, saying, "It shall be in the last days that the mountain of the house of the Lord will be established at the head of the mountains and higher than the heights, and all of the peoples will flow to it" (Is. 2:2). Why did Isaiah say, "Hear, O peoples, the thing which I have done, and know, O distant ones, my power. The sinners in Zion are afraid, trembling has seized the pagans" (Is. 33:13-14)? Now what is this which he makes known, the thing which he did, announcing his power to those who are far away, causing the sinners in Zion to fear, and bringing trembling upon the pagans? He calls the peoples, and by means of them he provokes the people. He informs of his power those who are distant from him when he brings wrath, judging his people. And he frightens the sinners in Zion (221), the name of which was the Holy City (Is. 52:1). As to the trembling which has fallen on the pagans, they are the false [516] prophets, as he says concerning the prophets of Jerusalem, "From them has gone forth idolatry into all the land" (Jer. 23:15).

IV. THE CHRISTIAN PASSOVER

XII-5. You have heard, my beloved, concerning this paschal sacrifice, that I said to you that it was given as a mystery to the prior people, and its truth is today made known among the peoples. Greatly troubled are the minds of foolish and unintelligent folk concerning this great day of festival, as to how they should understand and observe it. Our redeemer is the true "lamb a year old, on whom is no blemish," as the prophet said concerning him, "There was no iniquity in him, nor was evil found in his mouth. But God wanted to humble him and to give him over unto suffering" (Is. 53:9, 10). They called him a year old, for he was a child as to sins, as he said to his disciples, "If you do not turn and become like these children, you will not enter the kingdom of heaven" (Matthew 18:3). Isaiah said concerning the righteous, "A child who sins will die like [3] a hundred-year-old, and be cursed" (Is. 65:20).

XII-6. Our redeemer ate the paschal sacrifice with his disciples on the watch-night of the fourteenth. He made for his disciples the sign of the paschal sacrifice in truth. After Judah left them, he took bread, blessed, and gave it to his disciples, saying to them, "This is my body. All of you take and eat from it." He also thus blessed the wine, saying to them, "This is my blood, [517] [Wright: of] the new testament, which in behalf of many is shed for the forgiveness of sins. Thus you shall do in my memory whenever you are gathered together" (Matthew 26:26, 28). Before our Lord was seized, (222) he said these things. Our Lord arose after he had made the paschal sacrifice and had given his body to be eaten and his blood to be drunk. Then he went with his disciples to that place where he was seized.

Now whoever eats his body and drinks his blood is reckoned with the dead. Our Lord by his own hands gave over his body to be eaten; and before he was crucified, gave his blood to be drunk. Then he was seized on the night of the fourteenth and judged before the sixth hour. At the sixth hour they declared him guilty and raised him up and crucified him. When they judged him, he did not speak, nor did he say a word to his judges. He was able to speak and make reply, but it is not possible that one who is reckoned with the dead should speak. From the sixth hour to the ninth there was darkness. He gave up his spirit to his father at the ninth hour. He was among the dead [520] in the night before [lit.: of the dawn of] the fifteenth, the Sabbath night, the whole day, and three hours of the evening. At the dawn's light of Sunday, at the time that he had given his body and his blood to his disciples, he rose from the abode of the dead.

XII-7. Now show us, O sage, what are these three days and three nights that our redeemer was among the dead? For lo, we see the three hours of the evening, and the night before the Sabbath, and then the entire day [Sabbath], and on the night [before] Sunday he arose. Now tell me, these three days and three nights, what are they? For lo, the day and the night were truly complete, as our redeemer said, "Just as Jonah, the son of Matai, was in the belly of the fish three days and three nights, so the Son of Man shall be (223) in the heart of the earth" (Matthew 12:40). From the

---

[3] *kd* for *br.* Parisot: Infans qui peccaverit, filius centum annorum morietur ut maledicatur.

time that he gave his body to be eaten and his blood to be drunk, there were thus three nights. It was night-time when Judah left, and those eleven disciples were eating the body of our redeemer and drinking his blood. Now behold: the night before Friday until the sixth hour [of Friday] when they judged him equal one day and one night. Then [came] three hours when there was darkness, from the sixth to the ninth hour; and then [came] three hours [521] after the darkness, — equal to two days and two nights. Then [came] the whole night before the Sabbath and the whole day of the Sabbath. Thus for our Lord among the dead were completed three days and three nights. And on the night of [= before] Sunday he arose from the abode of the dead.

v. The Old Passover and the New

XII-8. The paschal sacrifice of the Jews is the day of the fourteenth, night and day. But for us the day of the great passion is Friday, the fifteenth [of Nisan], night and day. Then after the paschal sacrifice Israel eats unleavened bread seven days until the twenty-first of the month. But we observe as the festival of unleavened bread the festival of our redeemer. They eat unleavened bread with bitter herb. But our redeemer rejected that cup of bitterness and removed all bitterness from the peoples when he tasted but did not wish to drink. The Jews recall [4] concerning themselves their own sins from festal season to festal season, but we recall [5] the crucifixion and the pain of our redeemer.

They on the paschal sacrifice went forth from the slavery of Pharaoh, but we on the day of his crucifixion were redeemed from the slavery of Satan. They sacrificed a lamb from the flock, and with its blood they were saved from the destroyer, but we through the blood of the chosen son were redeemed from the works [524] of destruction which we were doing.

Moses was their leader, but for us Jesus was leader and redeemer. Moses divided the sea for them (224) and caused them to pass through. Our redeemer divided Sheol and broke its doors, when he went into its midst and opened them, and besought a way before all those who believed in him. Mana was given to them to eat. Our Lord gave us his body to eat. For them he brought forth water from the stone. For us our redeemer brought down living waters from his belly. For them he promised the land of Canaanites as an inheritance. For us he promised

---

4. *dkr.*
5. *'hd.*

the land of the living in the promise. For them Moses raised the copper snake, so that whoever looked at it might live from the bite of the snake. For us Jesus raised up himself, so that when we look toward him, we shall be saved from the bite of the snake, which is Satan. For them Moses made the temporal tabernacle so that they might offer on it sacrifices and offerings and be forgiven for their sins. Jesus raised up the tabernacle of David which had fallen, is now arisen.

Again he said to the Jews, "This temple, which you see, if it is destroyed, in three days I shall raise it up" (John 2:19), and his disciples understood that he was speaking concerning his own body, for when they would destroy it, he would raise it up in three days. In that very tabernacle he has promised us life, and in it [525] our sins are forgiven. Theirs is called the *temporal* tabernacle, because it was used for a little while. But ours is called the temple of the Holy Spirit which is forever.

XII-9. Be persuaded, my beloved, concerning this lamb of the paschal sacrifice about which the Holy One commanded that it should be eaten *in one house* and not in many houses: *That one house is the Church of God*. Again he said, "A *hired hand* and an *alien* should not eat from it" (Ex. 12:45). And who are these *hired hands and aliens if not those who teach evil?* It is not lawful of them to eat (225) of the paschal sacrifice, for our redeemer has said concerning them, "When he who is a hireling and to whom the flock does not belong sees that a wolf is coming, he leaves the flock and flees" (John 10:12).

He said, "You should not eat from it raw or boiled in water" (Ex. 12:9). This will be known and interpreted as *the sacrifice which is offered in the Church of God by fire*. This is to be burned in fire, and not boiled nor offered raw.

He said, "Thus you will eat it: with your loins bound up, your sandals on your feet, and your staffs in your hands" (Ex. 12:11). These are certainly great mysteries. Whoever eats from the true lamb, the Messiah, binds up his loins *in faith*, and sets his feet *in the preparation of the Gospel*, and holds [528] in his hand *the spiritual sword* which is the word of God (Heb. 4:12).

Again he said, "A bone should not be broken in it" (Ex. 12:46). And this was fulfilled on the day on which they crucified him, when they broke the bones of those who were crucified with him, but *his they did not break*.

And it says, "So is fulfilled the word which is written, A bone will not be broken in him" (John 19:36).

And it says, "When the flesh of the foreskin of the servant bought for money is circumcised, then will he eat of the paschal sacrifice" (Ex. 12:44). Now the servant who is bought is the *man who sins, but repents and is bought with the blood of the messiah.* After he circumcises his heart from evil deeds, then he progresses to baptism, the fulfillment of the true circumcision, is joined with the people of God, and added to the body and the blood of the messiah.

As to the saying, "You should hastily eat it" (Ex. 12:11), that is (226) observed in the Church of God, who eat the lamb hastily, in fear and trembling, as they stand on their feet, for they *hasten to eat life* from the spiritual gift which they have received.

XII-10. Israel was baptised in the midst of the sea on that night of the paschal sacrifice, on the day of redemption. Our redeemer washed the feet of his disciples on the night of the paschal sacrifice, [which is] the mystery of baptism. You should know, my beloved, it was on that night that our redeemer gave the true baptism, [529], for so long as he was wandering with his disciples, they were baptised with the baptism of the law of the priests, the baptism of which John spoke, "Repent from your sins" (Matthew 3:2). On that night he showed them the mystery of the baptism of the passion of his death, as the apostle said, "You were buried with him in baptism unto death, and you rose with him by the power of God" (Romans 6:3, 4; Col. 2:12). So know, my beloved, that the baptism of John does not effect the forgiveness of sins but only penitence. The Acts of the Twelve Apostles reports (Acts 19:3) concerning this, that when the disciples asked those who were called from the peoples and from Israel, and said to them, "Are you baptised?" they replied, "We are baptised in the baptism of John." Then they baptised them with the true baptism, the mystery of the passion of our redeemer. Also our redeemer testified to this when he said to his disciples, "John baptised in water, but you will baptise in the Holy Spirit"(Acts 1:5).

Then our redeemer took water and poured it into the basin, and he took a cloth, girded his loins, and began to wash the feet of his disciples. When (227) he came to Simon Kephas, he said to him, "Are you, my Lord, washing my feet? you for me? Never will you wash my feet for me" (John 13:4-15). Jesus said to him, "But if I do not wash for you, you have no portion with me." Simon said [532] to him, "In that case, my Lord, not my feet alone shall you wash for me, but also my hands and head." Jesus said to him, "He who has bathed has no need but to wash the feet alone." When he had washed the feet of the disciples, he took his garments, seated himself, and said to them, "What do you call me? *Rabban* and *Maran.* And so be it. But if I, your Rabbi and your Master, am washing your feet, how much [more] is it appropriate for you to wash the feet of one another. This example I have shown to you, so that as I have done, thus will you do." And after he had washed their feet and had resumed his place, then he gave them his body and his blood, and not as Israel who, after eating the paschal sacrifice, then were baptised in the clouds and the sea, as the apostle said, "Our fathers were all under the cloud, and all passed through the sea" (I Cor. 10:1).

XII-11. These few words of instruction I have written to you as a response to the Jews, on account of their observing the time of the paschal sacrifice in transgression of the commandment, unlawfully. They make the ark and testament of the covenant not as they were commanded, for they do not understand the prophet, who said, "You will not again say 'the ark of the covenant of the Lord,' and it will not come to mind nor be mentioned, nor should they remember it, nor should it be done again" (Jer. 3:16). And now that he said that it should not be done [533] again or come to mind (228) nor should they remember it, then know, my beloved, that whoever does it transgresses the commandment. Jeremiah further said, "The children of Israel and the children of Judah have annulled my testament" (Jer. 11:10).

Concerning the testament which was given to the people, thus he pronounced, "I shall complete with the house of Israel and with the house of Judah a new testament, not like the testament which I gave to their fathers on the day that I took them by the hand and led them out of Egypt, for, because they have cast off my testament, I also reject them" (Jer. 31:31, 32). Now if they should say, "Lo, to Israel and to Judah he said that he would give a *new* testament" — the One who called Israel "rulers of Sodom and people of Gomorrah" (Is. 1:10) [also] called Abraham and chose him, when he blessed him, saying, "Your name will not be called Abram any longer, but your name will be Abraham. For I have made you father of a multitude of peoples" (Gen. 17:5). And again he said to him, "Through your seed will all the peoples of the earth bless themselves" (Gen. 22:18).

XII-12. Now you will be persuaded, and you will persuade the brethren, the members of your church who are vexed concerning this time of the paschal sacrifice. For the people who hold correct opinions these things will not be difficult to comprehend. Now if it should happen to us that the day of the paschal sacrifice of the passion of our redeemer should fall on the first day of the week, according to the law it is appropriate that we should make it [536] on the second day, so that the entire week should be kept in his passion and his unleavened bread. For after the paschal sacrifice, there are seven days of unleavened bread until the twenty-first. If on another day of the days of the week the passion should fall, we have no reason to be vexed by these things, for our great day is Friday. According to the days of the month, the day of the crucifixion, on which our redeemer suffered and was among the dead, night and day, (229) is the fifteenth, from the sixth hour on Friday until the midst of Sunday; and on Sunday, the sixteenth, he rose. For on Friday the fourteenth he ate the paschal sacrifice with his disciples according to the law of Israel. And on that very Friday the fourteenth was he judged until the sixth hour, and he was crucified three hours; he descended to the abode of the dead on the night before the dawn of the fifteenth; on the Sabbath day, which is the fifteenth, he was among the dead. And the night before Sunday, which is the sixteenth, he arose and appeared to Miriam Magdelita and to two of his disciples as they were walking on the way. Now let anyone that happens to be vexed concerning these days understand that from the midst of the fourteenth our Lord [537] made the paschal sacrifice, ate and drank with his disciples. Then, from the time that the rooster called, he ate and drank no more, for they seized him and began judging him, and, as I explained to you above, on the day of the fifteenth, the night and the day, he was among the dead.

XII-13. But as for us, it is required that we keep the festival in its time from year to year, fasting in purity, praying firmly, praising diligently, saying psalms as is appropriate, giving the sign [of the cross] and the baptism as is right. The blessings of the Holy One in their time and all his wishes in their time may be fulfilled. For our Lord suffered, rose, and again will not die; and death does not rule over him. One who dies for sin dies one time; but the one who lives lives unto God. And also as to us who were dead, he has given us life with him.[6]

Now if we are vexed about these things and about the fourteenth alone, then let us be diligent, but not concerning (230) a season, or from one season to another. But let us take delight to keep the fourteenth of *every* month, and on the Friday of every week shall we mourn. But thus it is appropriate for us: *All* the days of the week we should do what is right [540] before the Lord our God.

Now be persuaded by this small essay which I have written to you, for you are *not* commanded to be vexed with word-games, matters in which there is no profit, but [to preserve] a pure heart which keeps the commandment and the festival and the times of the observances of each day.

The demonstration concerning the paschal sacrifice is completed.

---

[6] Parisot: Nos etiam qui mortui eramus, secum ipse vivificavit.

CHAPTER FOUR

DEMONSTRATION XIII

ON THE SABBATH

Summary: The Jews take pride in the Sabbath and hold that through it they find life. But the Sabbath was given not to mark off righteousness and sin, but merely to provide for rest from work. It has no salvific value, but only signifies the Creator's concern for the welfare of his creatures. Cattle are expected to keep the Sabbath, and when they do, they sin, for they take the occasion to fornicate with their blood relatives. Cattle do not need justification and the Sabbath does not bring them merit.

If the Sabbath were given for righteousness, then Adam should have had the opportunity to be justified through it. Noah likewise should have kept it, but Noah's righteousness was that he did not marry in the generation of destruction, but only after God had spoken with him. Noah did not keep the Sabbath or practice circumcision; neither did the patriarchs or Joseph. The Sabbath serves merely as a day of rest.

As to God's "resting" on the Sabbath, the meaning is that he *completed* his works of creation, not that he was fatigued. Joshua and the Maccabees made war on the Sabbath; the priests in the Temple conducted the Temple business, and no one was regarded as a sinner on that account.

I. SABBATH AND SALVATION

[541] (231) XIII-1. The Lord commanded Moses his servant that the children of Israel keep the Sabbath Day. He thus said to them, "Six days will you do your work, and the seventh is the Sabbath, a rest holy to the Lord your God, for in six days the Lord made heaven, earth, the seas, and all which is in them, and he rested and had repose on the seventh day. On this account God blessed the seventh day and sanctified it, for on it he rested from all his works which he had done" (Ex. 20:9-11). Thus he commanded them, "You, your man-servant, your maid-servant, your oxen, and your ass should rest" (Deut. 5:12-14). And he further added and commanded them, "The hired hand, the alien, and the whole herd which labors and works in bondage should rest."

Now concerning this Sabbath Day, my beloved, the Jewish people take pride and find glory, saying, "By this we live, that we keep the Sabbath and the tradition." As best as I am able, I shall explain in a few words, as I have explained to you concerning circumcision and the paschal sacrifice.

[544] XIII-2. The Sabbath has not been placed between death and the living, or between (232) righteousness and sin,[1] but has been given for rest. [It is not] like other commandments, by which men live, or, if they do not do them, die.[2] For at the time the Sabbath was observed, it was given so that people might rest, and not that people alone might rest, but also cattle.

He said, "Your ox, your ass, and all your flock should rest" (Ex. 20:10, 23:12). Now if the Sabbath were placed between death and the living, and between righteousness and sinners, what profit is there for cattle that keep the Sabbath? Or what punishment will they have if they do not keep it? For we see that on other days on which cattle work in bondage and in wearisome labor, they are more righteous than on the Sabbath Day. On the days of work cattle labor and work in carrying and in burden, and the oxen bear the yoke, and because they are wearied by labor, there is no occasion that they should commit sins. But on the Sabbath Day, the asses, oxen, and all cattle are idle, and each kind is not kept away from mixing among its mothers, sisters, and all its kinfolk. There is no sin, and they are not censured that they do these sins on the Sabbath Day, for this is the law [545] of all cattle.

Know that just as there is no sin pertaining to cattle that do such things, there also is no righteousness, for the retribution [reward] of righteousness in the new world will be in the resurrection of the dead for whoever does deeds of righteousness. But cattle do not participate in the resurrection, that they should be punished with regard to the keeping of the Sabbath, nor will they come to judgment. Just as the law does not set another commandment for cattle to keep, so likewise the Sabbath (233) gives no benefit to them. The Holy One commanded in his law, "You shalt not commit adultery" (Ex. 20:14), but cattle publicly commit adultery, and in the open they fornicate. The law commanded and admonished, "Cursed is anyone who takes his sister and the rest of all who are near unto his flesh" (Lev. 20:17). But all these things do cattle do. Further it is written, "You shalt not kill" (Ex. 20:13). But cattle on account of ignorance kill their fellow and eat of his flesh. Further it is written, "All things you may slay and eat, but the blood you shall not eat" (Deut. 12:15-

---

[1] Bert = Der Sabbath ist nämlich nicht eingesetzt, dass er denen, die das Leben haben, zum Tode, gereiche, und auch nicht zur Rechtfertigung von der Sünde, sondern er est zur Ruhe gegeben.

[2] Both Parisot and Bert read *not*: Bert = Es ist nicht wie bei anderen Geboten. Parisot = sicut praecepta cetera per quae vivunt homines, si autem ea non observant moriuntur; he notes that the second *I* has been added by another hand between he lines.

16). But cattle lick up their own blood, and eating unclean flesh is very pleasing to them. Now if there is any profit for cattle in keeping the Sabbath, then the law ought first to have restrained them from these unclean things, and then it should have justified them if they kept the Sabbath.

XIII-3. I have written you this argument that the Sabbath was given for rest [548] for every creature that does labor. If it were not given for rest for each laboring body, then it would have been appropriate that in earlier times creatures which do not labor also should have kept the Sabbath, so that they might be justified. But we see that the sun moves; the moon wanders; stars run; winds blow; clouds fly; birds wander; springs gush forth luxuriantly; waves rise up; lightening runs and illuminates creation; thunder in its season loudly rumbles; trees bear their fruit; and the profit of everything waxes strong. We see nothing that rests on the Sabbath, except for men and cattle, which are bound under (234) the burden of labor.

II. ANCIENT WORTHIES DID NOT KEEP SABBATH

XIII-4. Now if the Sabbath were given for righteousness, then [even] before Israel it would have been appropriate that it should have been given to Adam that he might keep it and be justified through it, and God would not have given [3] him the commandment that he should not eat of the tree of knowledge of evil and good and so not die. But because Adam was not given over to labor before he had transgressed the commandment, he did not give the Sabbath to him. Only after he transgressed the commandment, then he received the judgment to do labor and to work [549] on the earth as a sinner and a criminal, and he [God] decreed death on him [Adam].

III. NOAH JUSTIFIED BY VIRGINITY, NOT BY THE SABBATH

XIII-5. Now if in the Sabbath were righteousness, Enoch and all the generations after him would have excelled in it. Noah also did not keep the Sabbath, that through it he might be called perfect and lacking in sins. But thus God said to Noah, "You have I seen righteous and innocent in this generation" (Gen. 7:1). It was not in keeping the Sabbath that he was justified, but because he kept his innocence in the generation of

---

[3] Parisot: *neque* imposuisset ei Deus legem . . . . Bert: so hätte er . . . vor Israel . . . und Gott hätte ihm nicht das Gebot gegeben das . . . .

destruction, as the force of the Scripture makes clear. It is not written that he took part in the world [= married]. Noah was five hundred years old when God spoke with him and said to him, "You have I seen righteous and innocent before me in this generation." And his innocence—so, it seems to us—was in this regard: When he saw that the generation of Seth was intermingled with the house of Cain, which was cursed, he determined that he would not marry a wife nor have children, so that they should not be intermingled and cursed with the house of Cain, the cursed seed. When God saw that his heart was pure and innocent, he wanted that from him should go forth the replacement for the world which he was planning to blot out (235) because of their sins. Then he [God] spoke with him, when he was five hundred years old, saying to him, "You have I seen innocent before me in this generation." Now as yet he had no son, [552] as history tells us and as I explained above, for Noah had not married a wife in that entire time before God spoke to him and said to him, "You have I seen perfect before me in this generation. Now make for yourself an ark of wood that you may take shelter in it" (Gen. 7:1). Now when Noah heard these things, that God commanded him to make an ark, saying to him, "I am surely going to destroy mankind from off the face of the earth, for they have corrupted their way" (Gen. 6:7), then, in his five hundredth year, Noah took a wife from the daughters of Seth, the blessed seed of the righteous. He fathered Shem, Ham, and Japheth, these three. Noah commanded his sons not to take wives from the children of Cain. But he gave them wives from the seed of the righteous, so that seed would be preserved from them on the face of the earth, and so that from them the world might be reestablished. That you will know that these things are so, I shall demonstrate for you from the reckoning of the years.

XIII-6. Shem, the first-born of Noah, two years after the flood had a son, Arpakhshar.[4] And Shem was one hundred years old when he fathered Arpakhshar, two years after the flood. From these things the fact is known to us that Noah was five hundred two years old when he fathered Shem. From this calculation it is clear that Noah had not married a wife [553] before God spoke with him, (236) nor had he taken wives for his sons until the time that he went into the ark. If he had taken a wife in his youth, he would also have fathered sons like Adam, who at the age of one hundred thirty years fathered Seth. Seth at the age of one hundred five years fathered Enosh. Enosh at the age of ninety years

---

4 Arpachshad.

fathered Kenan. Kenan at the age of seventy years fathered Mahallel. Mahallel at the age of sixty-five years fathered Jared. Jared at the age of one hundred sixty-two years fathered Enoch. Enoch at the age of sixty-five years fathered Methuselah. Methuselah at the age of one hundred eighty-seven years fathered Lamech. Lamech, the father of Noah, at the age of one hundred eighty-two years, fathered him.

XIII-7. Now if he had taken a wife before God spoke to him, he would have fathered [children] like his fathers, for barrenness did not bear sway over him, for at that time the children of Adam were blessed to be fruitful and multiply in their generations, so that from them the earth might be filled. Noah who preserved his innocence did not have to fear concerning himself lest he be intermingled with the cursed seed of the house of Cain, but lest, when he took a wife and fathered children, the children transgress [556] the law, and take wives from that seed. But when he saw that God spoke with him, saying to him, "I am destroying the children of men from off the face of the earth, but you alone am I going to save," then he took a wife so that he might have seed from which the world might be rebuilt, and so that he might be the father of righteous and upright men. The Holy Spirit chose him so that even the Messiah, the life-giver of the world, (237) who would annul the curse of Adam, would be born from his seed.

Then he forthwith took a wife from the blessed seed and fathered Shem, father of righteous men, in the five-hundred-and-second year of his life, and in the second year of God's speaking with him. When he had fathered three sons, he began to make the ark. He commanded his sons not to take wives until the time that they should go into the ark, lest they have sons who might pervert their way and on account of whose sins might not be saved before the wrath which was about to come. He guarded his sons ninety-seven years. Then he took for them wives from the blessed seed of his fathers. Then, in the six hundredth year of the life of Noah, God spoke with him saying, "Go into the ark, you, your wife, your sons, and the wives of your sons with you." Noah went [557] into the ark at the age of six hundred years. Shem, his son, was ninety-seven years old when he went into the ark. Then came the flood, and the generation of destruction perished. Noah and his sons were in the ark, before they went forth, for twelve months and ten days. From Noah came a second world, because he preserved his innocence in the generation of destruction. But he did not keep the Sabbath, nor was he justified through circumcision — but this matter I have already explained to you.

From Noah was born the faithful man, the head of the righteous,

Abraham, who kept the law [even] before the law was given. He fathered Isaac, the son of the promise, and Jacob, the head of the people. These righteous fathers did not keep the Sabbath, but it was through faith they were justified, as it is written, "Abraham believed in God, and it was reckoned for him (238) as righteousness" (Gen. 15:6). Isaac, Jacob, and their sons walked in the commandment and law of their father, and they were justified through faith, and *not* through the Sabbath. Joseph in the midst of the land of Egypt was not a Sabbath-observer, [but] was justified by his righteousness, for when the wife of his master raised her eyes to him so that he might do with her an unclean thing, he spoke, saying to his mistress, "How shall I do this great and evil thing, and sin against God?" (Gen. 39:9). In this way was Joseph justified, and *not* by the Sabbath.

iv. Sabbath for Rest, Not Salvation

[560] XIII-9. Now if it were between death and the living, between iniquity and righteousness, then to these righteous men whose names I have mentioned above the Sabbath should have been given, so that they might keep it and live. But on this account was the Sabbath given for observance: so that man-servants, maid-servants, hired hands, aliens, and dumb cattle might find rest, so that those who work should rest from labor. God cares for all his creation, living things and cattle, birds and beasts of the field. Moses said when he taught the law to the people, "Six years you will sow your land and gather its fruits, but in the seventh year you will work it and leave it, so the needy of your people will eat. The beast of the field will eat the remnant" (Ex. 23:10-11).

Also concerning the bird, the Holy One thus commanded through Moses his servant, "When you find a nest of birds before you in any tree or on the earth, and the mother and the children or the eggs are there, and the mother is sitting on the children or the eggs, you will not take the mother with her babes. But you will certainly let the mother fly (239) away, and take the babes for yourself. On account of these things the Lord your God will bless you" (Deut. 22:6-7). David said, "The children of the raven who call to him does he sustain" (Ps. 146:9). Again David said, "You, O Lord, redeem men and cattle" (Ps. 36:6). Job also said, "Who has let the wild ass go free, who has loosed [561] the bonds [of the swift ass]? To whom have I given the steppe for his home and the salt land for his dwelling place?" (Job 39:5-6). Job further said, "He prepares food for the eagle's children" (Job 39:30; 38:41). And he [David] further said, thinking of the birds and the cattle, "They all look to you, and you give them their food in its season [lit.: their time]. You give them, and they are nourished. You open your hand, and they are satisfied. But if you turn away your face, they are frightened" (Ps. 104:27-29). Also Isaiah said, "There shall the owls gather together. And he commanded with his mouth, and his spirit gathered them, and his hand divided them the measures of an inheritance" (Is. 34:15, 17). Now see from these things that God is concerned for all his creation, and nothing escapes him; on this account he has admonished and commanded that there should be rest, the Sabbath Day.

v. God Not Wearied by Creation

XIII-10. Now again hear what he says: "In six days God made heaven and the earth; he rested and had repose from all his works. On this account God blessed the seventh day and sanctified it." (Gen. 2:1-3). Now what shall we say about this matter, that God rested on the seventh day? Now hear and I shall explain to you concerning this: God was *not* (240) wearied by the work of these six days, that because of weariness he rested on the seventh day. Far be it from us that we should say God was weary. But the force of the Scripture is this: God *completed* in six days [564] all of his works, and he rested [desisted] on the seventh day from all his works which he had done. Hear the proof that God was not weary, for David said, "The guardian of Israel does not slumber nor sleep" (Ps. 120:4). Now whoever does not slumber and does not sleep is also not weary. Isaiah said to the children of Israel, "Thus says the Lord: Because the thought has entered your mind that God is unable to redeem us (— he spoke to them through Isaiah —), is my hand shortened that it cannot redeem? Or do I not have power to save? Behold by my rebuke, I dry up the sea. I make the rivers as a desert, and their fish stink from lack of water and die. I clothe the heavens in darkness, and I make sackcloth as their covering" (Is. 50:1-3). Just as I dried up the sea of reeds in the days of your fathers, and I split the Jordan and caused them to pass through, so now I have sufficient power to redeem you. "But on account of your sins you have been sold, and on account of your transgression, your mother was divorced" (Is. 50:1). And although I was not tired, *you* made me tired, as Malachi the prophet says, "You have fatigued the Lord by your words" (Mal. 2:17).

XIII-11. Now hear and be persuaded that God created all his works with neither fatigue nor exertion. He said, "With the word of the Lord, the heavens were made and with the breath (241) of his mouth all of their

hosts" (Ps. 33:6). [565] Man alone he made with his hands. It is not written
that he was tired when he made him. When he made all the creatures,
with a word of his mouth he spoke, and they came into being [5] —without
labor and without tiredness. But thus is to be understood this matter that
God rested from all his works, and God took repose on the seventh day: if
God, who is not fatigued, rested and took repose from his labors, how
much the more so for one who is under the burden and the yoke is it
appropriate to rest! So also Isaiah said concerning God, "He is not
wearied, and he does not sleep. Nor is there any searching out of his
understanding" (Is. 40:28). And in another place, on account of the sins
of the people, he said, "You have burdened me with your sins, and with
your iniquities you have tired me" (Is. 43:24). See how first it is written
that he is not weary and does not sleep, but on account of their sins he
[then] said to Israel, "You have burdened me, and you have tired me." All
these words are written truly, and are to be heard by the wise with
understanding, as the apostle said, "The law is good if a man read it with
understanding" (I Tim. 1: 8). Again the prophet said, "The ways of the
Lord are right. The sinners stumble in them. But the righteous go upright
and walk in them" (Hos. 14: 9). Now similarly this matter that God rested
from his works, by fools thus is understood, as if he were fatigued,
[568] just as when he wanted to wipe out man because of their sins, that
were many, he said, (242) "I regret that I made them." [6] But hear the
apostle, who says, "If things were thus, how should God judge the world?"
(Rom. 3:6).

VI. HEROES OF ISRAEL VIOLATED SABBATH

XIII-12. But hear then, my beloved, concerning the Sabbath, and I
shall explain to you, just as I have explained to you concerning
circumcision in which the children of Israel vainly take pride. Likewise
concerning the Sabbath I shall explain that vainly do they take pride in
keeping it. Joshua the son of Nun did not permit them to rest on the
Sabbath when he made war against Jericho, as the glorious apostle said,
"If Joshua had permitted them to rest, it would not again have been

---

[5] *bmlt pwmh 'mr whwy.*

[6] Bert = Es ist aber mit der Stelle, dass Tott ruhete von seinen Werken, was von den
Thoren so verstanden wird, also ob er müde würde, ähnlich wie mit der andern, in welcher
er die Menschen wegen ihrer vielen Sünden vertilgen wollte, und sprach . . . Parisot =
Simile autem illud est: Requievit Deus ab oberibus suis (quod ab insipientibus eodem sensu
intelligitur ac si fatigatus fuisset), huic quod dixit cum voluit homines propter plurima
eorum peccata delere . . .

spoken regarding the day of the Sabbath. So now the Sabbath of God endures" (Heb. 4:8-9).

Also when the Maccabees' enemies came against them to do battle with them on the Sabbath day, they wanted to keep the Sabbath according to the law. When they kept it, their enemies came against them on the Sabbath and slew many of them. When they saw that they contrived against them, so that while they were keeping the Sabbath, they would once again do battle with them, they profaned the Sabbath, made war on that day, and conquered their enemies. They were not censured that they broke the Sabbath. These were not [569] the only ones who broke the Sabbath, for also the priests in the Temple profaned the Sabbath, but they were not sinning, because on the Sabbath day the priests were offering the sacrifice. They slaughtered; they flayed; they cut the wood; they carried fire. But it was not reckoned for them as a sin that they broke the Sabbath, for thus it was commanded for them to do. Now if the priests, (243) who would admonish the people against sinning, were violating the Sabbath — and would that it were in only a minor place, but it was a place in which all sins were atoned for — and if they did no wrong, nor was sin accounted to them, then why are they so very proud in keeping the Sabbath, which was given for rest [alone], as I have already explained to you?

VII. THE SABBATH OF GOD

XIII-13. Now hear concerning the Sabbath in which God is pleased. Isaiah said to them, "This is my rest: To bring comfort to the disturbed" (Is. 28:12). And again he said, "They who keep the Sabbath without profaning it are they who are strengthened in my covenant and choose the things which I want" (Is. 56:2). To those who do not profane the Sabbath, which is the rest of God, he said that he has decided to give to them [a reward], for he said, "I shall give to them in my house and in my walls a name which is better than sons and daughters" (Is. 56:4-5).

The Sabbath is of no value, therefore, for sinners, [572] killers, or thieves, but for those who choose the things which God wants, keeping their hands from that which is evil. Among them God dwells, and with them he lives as he said, "I shall dwell with them, and I shall walk with them" (II Cor. 6:16). In the days of Isaiah they were keeping the Sabbath, but they were walking in the deeds of the unclean peoples, and they were doing [deeds] like the deeds of Sodom and Gomorrah, and they were telling the peoples, "Keep back from me, for I am holy" (Is. 65:5).

Concerning these things Isaiah said, "These are smoke in my wrath and a fire which burns all day long" (Is. 65:5). He took and threw them out of his land, and scattered them among all (244) peoples, because they did not keep the rest of the Lord, but they observed the Sabbath in a [merely] fleshly sense.

But we shall keep the Sabbath of the Lord in a way in which his will is pleased, so that we may go into the Sabbath of rest, on which the heavens and the earth will keep the Sabbath, and all creatures will rest and take repose. And fugitives will not be there, as our Redeemer said, "Let your flight not be in the winter or on the Sabbath" (Matthew 24:20). The apostle said, "Still stands firm the Sabbath of the Lord" (Heb. 4:9).

This small argument I have written to you concerning the Sabbath against those who take pride in it.

The demonstration concerning the Sabbath is completed.

CHAPTER FIVE

DEMONSTRATION XV

ON MAKING DISTINCTIONS AMONG FOODS

Summary: Food renders a man neither clean nor unclean, but is neutral. The Jews, nonetheless, do not eat food of pagans. The real purpose of the dietary laws was to separate Israel from its former idolatry, for the Jews had worshipped the gods of the Egyptians, particularly the calf. They therefore were told not to eat what they had eaten in Egypt, but to eat what they had worshipped there; not only to eat, but also to sacrifice to God the gods of the Egyptians. The commandment to do so came only after Israel worshipped the golden calf. God does not actually need sacrifices, which were commanded only on account of Israel's sin. In fact, supposedly unclean birds and animals served the purposes of the ancient worthies, Samson and Elijah.

I. KASHRUT AND SALVATION

[728] (306) XV-1. Greatly vexed are the minds of simple and ordinary folk concerning things which go into the mouth, which are unable to defile man. So say those who are perplexed by these matters: God distinguished and explained to Moses his servant concerning unclean and clean foods. He admonished Moses, These are appropriate to eat and those are worthy of being declared unclean. And he commanded him concerning the living things, birds, and fish which are in the sea, according to their species. Concerning these things, my beloved, as best as I am able, I shall give you a little instruction, that foods in no way avail those who keep them, also in no way injure those who make use of them. The mouth of the Holy One has testified. "It is not the thing which goes into the man which makes him unclean, but the thing which comes out of the man, that it is which renders him unclean" (Matthew 15:11). This our redeemer has said to put in their places the Pharisees and the Sadducees, for they were taking pride in their baptism, [729] purity, (306) washing of hands, and the making of distinctions among foods. Then he reproved them, saying to them, "O blind Pharisees, why do you wash the outside of the cup and the plate, while the inside is full of evil and rapaciousness? You are like sepulchres which on the outside are made white and appear beautiful, but the insides are full of the bones of the

dead and every sort of uncleanness" (Matthew 23:25, 27). Then he taught and showed them that in no way do they profit in their baptisms and purifications, saying to them, "In the heart are evil thoughts, and these evil thoughts which are in the heart make a man unclean, but not foods. For foods go to the belly, and from there they are cast out in the excrement, so therefore a man is not made unclean by them" (Matthew 15:17-20). Now if of all tastes which are pure and pleasant for the gums, and for scent, appearance, and taste, a man should eat, his gums alone sense their pleasant tastes. From there, his stomach receives them, whose power divides among them for all his arteries and the parts of [his] body. When the food goes down, in place of a pleasant odor it is changed and becomes a stink. Instead of the good taste and beautiful appearance it is changed to a bad appearance and is cast out in the excrement. If a man should eat black bread [732] which is not of good appearance, does not have a pleasant taste, and does not have a desirable odor, by the very same path it goes into the man, and his power sends it (308) through all his arteries and parts. From there it is cast out in the excrement. And it so comes about that that pleasant food is changed more to stink than that which is not pure and pleasant. In these matters is neither sin nor righteousness.

XV-2. The glorious apostle also replied to those who take pride in foods. He said to them who boast in this opinion, who reject and distinguish [among] foods, "Foods will not establish us before God. Neither if we eat are we enhanced, nor if we do not eat are we diminished" (I Cor. 8:8). For if a man eats all foods and varieties of nourishment and is firm in righteousness and does not avariciously make use of the creation of God, and in faith he receives his gift, in no way does he suffer sin and unrighteousness. And if he eats dirt like a snake and is poisoned by the venom of the snake, in no way does he gain advantage or profit, for all the creations of God are splendid, and there is no reason to reject them. They are sanctified by the word of God and by prayer (II Tim. 4:4, 5).

This word which the apostle said, my beloved, against the children of his people did he say [it] when he saw that they declared unclean the foods of the peoples. [733] The children of Israel have nothing whatever to do with the foods which the peoples prepare, and no wine which the peoples tread will they drink. For over all which they tread and over all which they thresh, the pagan peoples sacrifice and make mention of the names of their idols. (309) On this account the children of Israel will not make use of their foods. And this is an infirm conscience (I Cor. 8:7). The apostle replied to those who hold this opinion, saying. "All foods are sanctified by the word of God and by prayer" (I Tim. 4:5). When a man makes use of the creatures of God, before he tastes of them, he remembers, praises, blesses, and sanctifies the name of the one who made the creatures, and he prays. Then they are sanctified and the power of the evil one flees from them. The apostle furthermore stated, "If any pagan invites you to dinner and you want to go, then whatever he sets before you, eat on account of conscience" (I Cor. 10:27).

II. PURPOSE OF DIETARY DISTINCTIONS

XV-3. Concerning these things, my beloved, as best as I am able, I shall teach you. That the Holy One, our God, distinguished foods for the children of Israel was not in any way so that there should be righteousness for them. But on account of their lust and avariciousness, he found this way to restrain them from the worship and the sins which they were doing in the land of Egypt. From of old, when he made man, God thus [736] commanded Adam and his descendents, Noah and his seed: "Behold, I have given to you the living creatures, the birds, and all flesh. Pour out the blood upon the earth, and eat, and it will be regarded for you as a vegetable. But the blood you should not eat. Pour it out on the ground like water, for the blood is the soul" (Gen. 1:29, 30; 9:3, 4; Lev. 17:13, 14; Deut. 12:16).

These things did God command those early generations, but he did not (310) distinguish foods for them. Now if in any way sin or transgression of the law pertained to foods, from of old he would have distinguished for Adam and for Noah the unclean from the clean things, just as he admonished, saying to them, "You should not eat the blood; but all flesh slay and eat, and as a vegetable it will thus reckoned for you." And Abraham and his descendents he furthermore commanded not to make use of an unclean thing. But we know that all righteous and upright men who were in the former generations until Moses, who distinguished foods for Israel, all those generations without sinning would make use of the foods which the soul does not loathe.

But as to his commanding the children of Israel and distinguishing for them among foods, it was because the children of Israel had turned aside to the worship of the Egyptians and abandoned the God of their fathers. The Egyptians worshipped oxen and calves. Now I shall [737] instruct you on this matter. When the brothers of Joseph came to him, he commanded his steward to make them a meal. "When the time came to recline," it is written, "they set for him by himself, and for his brothers by themselves, and for the Egyptians who were eating with him by themselves. For the Egyptians cannot eat bread with the Hebrews, because it is unclean for them" (Gen. 43:32). From of old, before the children of Israel entered Egypt, they ate all [kinds of] meat. But the Egyptians did not eat the meat of sheep and oxen, for these were their gods. Also when Jacob went down to Egypt, Joseph chose from among his brothers five men, and he set them before Pharaoh (311) and commanded them, "When Pharaoh will ask you and say to you, What is your work? You will say to him, Your servants are shepherds of sheep, and we are masters of herds, so also [were] our fathers. When you say this to him, he will honor you, for shepherds are those whom the Egyptians honor,[1] and he will give you as a good pasture the land of Goshen, and will abhor you, so that none of you will be led away and set to work in his labor," as is written. "The Egyptians abhor all those who pasture flocks" (Gen. 46:34).

Further it is written that when Moses said before Pharaoh, "We shall go and sacrifice for the Lord our God in the wilderness," Pharaoh said to him [740], "Serve the Lord your God in the land of Egypt." Moses said to him, "We are not able to carry out this word, for if we sacrifice the animals of Egyptians before their very eyes, they will stone us" (Ex. 8:20, 25, 26). Further it is written, "The Lord also carried out judgment on the gods of the Egyptians" (Num. 33:4) when he wiped out herds of sheep and herds of oxen by means of hail-stones and pestilence. For the Egyptians possessed herds of sheep and oxen according to their needs. They did not eat them, because they worshipped them. But the food of the Egyptians even to our day is the flesh of pigs with fish, which are numerous in their land, as the children of Israel said when they desired food: (312) "We remember the fish which we ate for nothing in Egypt, with the smell of onions, garlic, leeks, cucumbers, and melons" (Num. 11:5). The children of Israel ate their food and worshipped their gods according to the custom which the Egyptians followed.

III. JEWS' IDOLATRY IN EGYPT

XV-4. So that you will know that they practiced idolatry in the land of Egypt and worshipped their gods, [listen to the following]: When the time came for Joshua the son of Nun to die, he called the children of Israel and said to them, "Choose you this day whom you will serve, either

---

[1] Parisot: (pascebant enim ipsa numina Aegyptiorum). Bert: (denn sie waren Hirten dessen, was die Aegypter verehrten).

the gods whom your father Terah, the father of Abraham and Nachor, worshipped on the other side [741] of the river, or the gods whom you served in the land of Egypt. But I and the children of my house will serve the Lord God." He further admonished them, "Choose you this day whom you will serve." They said to him, "The Lord shall we worship, and him shall we serve, for he is our God." He said to them, "Behold, perhaps you will not be able to serve the Lord." They said, "We shall be able to do so." Then he said to them, "Do you bear witness by your lives that you have chosen for yourselves to worship the Lord?" And they said, "We bear witness" (Joshua 24:15-22). Now, that you should be more certain that they were worshipping sheep and oxen in Egypt, note that when Moses tarried on the mountain, and they turned aside from the Lord and worshipped idols, no other images did they make for themselves as an idol but the image of the calf, the thing which they were accustomed to worship in the land of Egypt. So they roared and celebrated before the calf which they had made.

Also when Jeroboam the son of Nabat turned them aside, he made for them as an idol a calf, the thing which they had worshipped in Egypt.

When the Holy One saw (313) that they were not purified from the leaven of the Egyptians, but remained in that very opinion of paganism, then he commanded Moses to distinguish foods for them. He made unclean for them those very things [744] which had been clean for them to eat in the land of Egypt, and he commanded them to eat those very things which they had worshipped in the land of Egypt and of which they had [formerly] not eaten. On account of their evil impulse, he commanded that they even bring as an offering before him that thing which they had worshipped. They should eat the flesh of sheep and oxen, which they had not wanted to eat because they were sacrifices. And note that when he separated for them many animals for purity, from all of them he did not command that they offer a sacrifice except from sheep and oxen alone. Now be persuaded, my beloved, that vain is the pride of Israel in distinguishing among foods.

IV. HEROES OF ISRAEL DID NOT DISTINGUISH AMONG FOODS

XV-5. Tell me, O scribe, wise debater of the people, if it was an uncleanness for Israel to offer, or make use of, anything which the law has made unclean, then why did Samson the Nazirite, the hero of Israel, take honey from an unclean beast, from the skeleton of the lion, eat [it] and pour [it] on his hands? He did not incur sin or evil on account of this deed, nor is it written that he was made unclean. Also when he had achieved victory by the jaw-bone of an ass, and had heaped up a pile [of the bodies] of Philistines, he was thirsty, and prayed before his God saying, "O Lord, God, you have made this great victory through the hand of your servant. [745] Now shall I die of thirst?" (Judges 15:18). God heard the prayer of Samson, and he brought forth for him water from the bone (314) of the ass, so he drank, and his thirst was assuaged. Now if there were any matter of uncleanness or sin in the bones of the ass (for it is unclean according to the law), then why did he bring forth for his Nazirite a well of water from the bone for him to drink? If there were any uncleanness, he should have brought forth for him water from a stone, just as he brought forth water from the stone for the children of Israel in the wilderness, or from the earth, just as he brought forth [water] for Hagar, so Ishmael drank.

If then there were uncleanness in food, among all the birds there is none more unclean and filthy than the ravens, which bore bread and meat to Elijah, the holy prophet, when he dwelt by the brook of Kerith. And from whence were the ravens bringing the food of Elijah, but from Jerusalem? The portion which belonged to him the priests would set aside, and in faith they would give it to the ravens. They took and brought it to Elijah according to the commandment of the Most High, his God. The food of Elijah, which he received from the mouth of the ravens, from the bird which the law had declared unclean, was pure.

V. SACRIFICES NOT NEEDED BY GOD

XV-6. You should know, my beloved, that because [748] he determined concerning them that they should not worship calves, the gods of the Egyptians, he distinguished for them among foods and commanded them to sacrifice offerings of the very thing they had feared in the land of Egypt. For God had no need for sacrifices and offerings. But in order to restrain them from sacrifices, so that they should not worship the gods of the peoples, when they would go in and be mixed (315) among them, as they had worshipped the gods of the Egyptians when they had gone in and had been mixed among them—on this account he forbade and restrained them thus: Before *his* altar they should bring their offerings and sacrifice their sacrifices. When he had greatly admonished them, they turned aside from him and worshipped and served the gods of the peoples, and perverted their way, as Moses had said to them, "I know that after I die, you will be corrupted, and you will turn aside from the way which I have commanded you. And many evils will happen to you in the end of days" (Deut. 31:29).

XV-7. You may be persuaded that God had no need of sacrifices, offerings, whole offerings, and incense, but [commanded these things] so that they might be restrained. When they had turned away from him and had begun to offer to idols the sacrifices which he had given to them, then through the prophet he said to them, "I have no use for the multitude of your sacrifices, [749] says the Lord" (Is. 1:11). And he said to them, "Your whole-offerings are rejected by me, and my soul hates your New Moons and your seasons" (Is. 1:13, 14). David also said, "I do not eat the flesh of calves, and the blood of lambs I do not drink, but instead of these things, sacrifice to God thanksgiving, and carry out your vows to the Most High. And when you have done this, then call on me in the day of need, and I shall save you, and you will praise me" (Ps. 49:13-15). It is again written in the prophet, "I hate, I reject your festivals. I shall not smell your burnt-offerings" (Amos 5:21). Again it is written, "Even though you bring me offerings, (316) I will not look upon the multitude of your fat animals" (Amos 5:22). Again he said, "Did you, children of Israel, offer me sacrifices and offerings in the forty years in the wilderness?" (Amos 5:25). "And if you eat and drink, do you not eat and drink for yourselves, says the Lord?" (Zech. 7:6). Isaiah said, "He who sacrifices a lamb is like the one who sacrifices a dog. He who offers an ox is like the one who slaughters a man. And the one who offers incense is as though [he offered] the blood of the pig; and the one who prays before me is like the one who blesses idols" (Is. 66:3).

Samuel said to Saul when he heard the sound of the sheep and the oxen which had come from the Amalekites, "What is this noise which I hear?" Saul said to him, "The people saved the best of the flock to sacrifice [752] to the Lord your God." Samuel said to him, "Lo, listening is better than sacrifices, and obedience [is better] than a multitude of fatted beasts" (I Sam. 15:14, 15, 22). Again it said, "The Lord does not want the sacrifices of sinners" (Prov. 15:8). Again it is written, "The sin of the house of Eli will not be forgiven through sacrifices and through offerings forever" (I Sam. 3:14). And again it is written, "The Lord has no pleasure in males, nor in multitudes of hosts of anointed [beasts]. But in place of these things, I shall show you, O man, the thing which helps, which the Lord demands of you: You should do justice, and seek faith, and be ready to go after your God" (Micah 6:7-8).

Also, when he rejected sacrifices and offerings in the days of Isaiah, he said, "I shall show you the thing which I want: Depart from evils, and learn to do good. Cleave to justice and do good (317) to the oppressed. Judge the orphans, and judge the widows. When you have done these things, come, let us speak together, says the Lord. And if your sins shall be as crimson, as snow they will be whitened. And if they shall be as red as vermillion, they shall be like wool" (Is. 1:16-18). Malachi said, "Do not offer up on my altar freely, for I am not pleased with you, says the Lord" (Mal. 1:10). Daniel said to Nebuchadnezzar: "Wipe out your sins through righteousness and your iniquities through mercy on the poor" (Dan. 4:27)[753]—and *not* with sacrifices and offerings. He rejected Israel and rejected its sacrifices, as Jeremiah said. "He called them 'rejected silver,' for the Lord has rejected them" (Jer. 6:30). And again he said, "I shall throw them from before me, and they will go out. If they say, Where shall we go? say to them, Those to the sword, to the sword; those to famine, to famine; those to captivity, to captivity" (Jer. 15:1-2). Again it is written, "He will not continue to look at them" (Lam. 4:16). Isaiah [sic!] also said, "Keep afar from them and call them unclean" (Lam. 4:15). Jeremiah also said, "I have abandoned my house. I have abandoned my inheritance. I have given the beloved of my soul into the hands of his enemies" (Jer. 12:7).

Again it is written, "I have given the daughter of my people a bill of divorce" (Jer. 3:8). Again it is written, "The Lord will cause festivals and Sabbath to be forgotten from Zion" (Lam. 2:6). Also in Ezekiel, the prophet, he explained and showed them that because (318) of their contentiousness, he gave them sacrifices and offerings, so that perhaps on their account, they might be restrained from their sins. He said above, "I have given them commandments and judgments, and I have informed them that if a man does them, he will live through them" (Ez. 20:11). Again he said, "I have given to them commandments which are not excellent, and judgments through which they will not live. And I defiled them through their very gifts when they bring offerings" (Ez. 20:25, 26).

vi. Kashrut Not Good

XV-8. Be persuaded O lying scribe of the law, teacher of the people! For now the mouth [756] of the Holy One has testified that the commandments and the judgments which are given to you are not useful and are not excellent. How then do you raise up your face and hasten to disputation? Lo, it was on account of your sins that he gave you offerings and distinguished foods for you. Concerning which commandments and judgments did Ezekiel say that whoever did them would live in them?

And concerning which ones did he say that 'I have given you commandments which are not excellent and judgments through which one may not live'? The commandments and judgments which give life are those which have been written above. The righteous and just judgments which he placed before them are the ten holy commandments which he wrote with his hand and gave to Moses to teach. When they made for themselves the calf and turned away from him, *then* he gave them commandments and judgments which are not excellent: sacrifice, the purification of lepers, of discharge, of menstruation, and of childbirth; and that a man should not come near the dead, the grave, bones, and those who have been killed; that for all sins one must bring a sacrifice and for all uncleanness in man. Concerning each one of them he said, "You [Parisot: He] should be unclean until the evening" (Lev. 15:5), even though he has washed in water. Truly through these matters (319) which are written, Israel has not a single day of purity from sins, but all their days are spent in sins and in uncleanness. By the law they are unable to be justified, as [757] the apostle said, "A man is not justified through the law, but whoever does the things which are written will live through them" (Gal. 3:11, 12). And this is known: A man is unable to do them and cannot keep them.

When our Lord saw they were so hard, he called us and said to us, "Come to me, those who are weary and burdened, and I will give you rest. Take my yoke upon you, for my yoke is easy and pleasant" (Matthew 11:28-30). We confess the mercies that took from us a difficult and hard yoke and placed upon us his, which is light and pleasant.

These few remembrances I have written to you, my beloved, because the Jewish people is exulting and taking pride, boasting that they declare unclean and distinguish among foods. In these three things they boast: in circumcision, in keeping the Sabbath, and in making distinctions among foods, among other things. On these three things I have written to you briefly, as well as I could, and I have instructed you. On the others,[2] as best as God gives me to do, from time to time I shall write and instruct you.

The demonstration on making distinctions among foods is completed.

---

[2] I assume Aphrahat here refers to other matters about which Jews boast and indicates his intention of writing on the Messianic hope, the election of Israel, etc. If so, the present order of the Judaic Demonstrations follows the chronology in which they were actually composed.

CHAPTER SIX

DEMONSTRATION XVI

ON THE PEOPLES WHICH ARE IN THE PLACE OF THE PEOPLE

Summary: The people Israel was rejected, and the peoples took their place. Israel repeatedly was warned by the prophets, but to no avail, so God abandoned them and replaced them with the gentiles. Scripture frequently referred to the gentiles as "Israel." The vocation of the peoples was prior to that of the people of Israel, and from of old, whoever from among the peoples was pleasing to God was more justified than Israel: Jethro, the Gibeonites, Rahab, Ebedmelech the Ethiopian, Uriah the Hittite. By means of the gentiles God provoked Israel.

I. VOCATION OF THE GENTILES

[760] (320) XVI-1. The peoples which were of all languages were called first, before Israel, to the inheritance of the Most High, as God said to Abraham, "I have made you the father of a multitude of peoples" (Gen. 17:5). Moses proclaimed, saying, "The peoples will call to the mountain, and there will they offer sacrifices of righteousness" (Deut. 33:19). And in the hymn of testimony he said to the people, "I shall provoke you with a people which is no people, and with a foolish nation I shall anger you" (Deut. 32:21). Jacob our father testified concerning the peoples when he blessed Judah, saying to him, "The staff shall not depart from Judah, the lawgiver from between his feet, until there shall come he who possesses dominion, and for him the peoples will hope" (Gen. 49:10).

Isaiah said, "The mountain of the house of the Lord will be established at the head of the mountains and high above the heights. All the peoples will look to it, [761] and (321) many peoples from a distance will come and say, Come, let us go up to the mountain of the Lord, to the house of the God of Jacob. He will teach us his ways, and we shall walk in his paths. For from Zion law will go forth, and the word of the Lord from Jerusalem. He will judge among peoples and will correct all the distant peoples" (Is. 2:2-4). When he judges and corrects them, then will they accept instruction, be changed, and be humbled from their hardheartedness. "And they shall beat their swords into ploughshares, and their spears into pruning hooks. No longer will a nation take the sword against a nation; no longer will they learn how to make war" (Is. 2:2-4). From of old, those peoples who did not know God would do battle against robbers and against wrong-doers with swords, spears, and lances. When the redeemer, the Messiah, came, "he broke the bow of war and spoke peace with the peoples" (Zech. 9:10). He had them turn "their swords into ploughshares, and their spears they made into pruning hooks," so that they would eat from the works of their hands, and not from spoil.

Furthermore, it is written, "I shall turn chosen lips for the peoples, so that they will all of them call upon the name of the Lord" (Zeph. 3:9). From of old the nations did not have chosen lips, nor did they call on the name of the Lord, for with their lips they would praise the idols which they had made with their hands, and on the name of their gods [764] they would call, but not on the name of the Lord. Furthermore, also the prophet Zechariah said,"Many and strong peoples will adhere to the Lord" (Zech. 2:11). Jeremiah the prophet publicly and clearly proclaimed concerning the peoples, when he said, "The peoples will abandon their idols, and they will cry and proclaim, saying, The lying idols, which our fathers left us as an inheritance, are nothing" (Jer. 16:19).

II. REJECTION OF ISRAEL

(322) XVI-2. To his people Jeremiah preached, saying to them, "Stand by the ways and ask the wayfarers, and see which is the good way. Walk in it." But they in their stubbornness answered, saying to him, "We shall not go." Again he said to them, "I established over you watchmen, that you might listen for the sound of the trumpet." But they said to him again, "We shall not hearken." And this openly, publicly did they do in the days of Jeremiah when he preached to them the word of the Lord, and they answered him, saying, "To the word which you have spoken to us in the name of the Lord we shall not hearken. But we shall do our own will and every word which goes out of our mouths, to offer up incense-offerings to other gods" (Jer. 44:16-17). When he saw that they would not listen to him, he turned to the peoples, saying to them, "Hear O peoples, and know, O church which is among them, and hearken, O land, in its fullness" (Jer. 6: 18-19). And when he saw that they rashly rose against him and impudently responded to him, then he abandoned them as he had prophesied, saying [765], "I have abandoned my house. I have abandoned my inheritance. I have given the beloved of my soul into the

hands of his enemies. And in his place a painted bird has become my inheritance" (Jer. 12:7-9). And this is the church which is of the peoples, which has been gathered together from among all languages.

XVI-3. So that you will know he has truly abandoned them (323)[listen to this]: Isaiah further said concerning them, "You have abandoned your people, the house of Jacob" (Is. 2:6). He called their name Sodomites and the people of Gomorrah, and in their place he brought in the peoples and he called *them* 'House of Jacob.' For Isaiah called the peoples by the name of the House of Jacob, saying to them, "O House of Jacob, come and let us go in the light of the Lord" (Is. 2:5-6), for the people of the house of Jacob has been abandoned and they have become "the rulers of Sodom and people of Gomorrah" (Is. 1:10). "Their father is an Amorite and their mother is a Hittite" (Ez. 16:3, 45); "they have been changed into a strange vine" (Jer. 2:21). "Their grapes are bitter and their clusters are bitter for them" (Deut. 32:32). [They are] rebellious sons (Is. 30:1), and rejected silver (Jer. 6:30). [They are] "the vine of Sodom and the planting of Gomorrah" (Deut. 32:32); "a vineyard which brings forth thorns instead of grapes" (Is. 5:2). [They are] "a vine whose branches the fire has consumed, they are good for nothing, they are not serviceable, and they are not wanted for any use" (Ez. 15:4).

Two did he call Jacob, one to go in the light of the Lord, one [768] to be abandoned. In place of Jacob they are called "rulers of Sodom." By the name of Jacob [now] are called the people which is of the peoples. Again the prophet said concerning the peoples that they shall bring offerings in place of the people, for he said, "Great is my name among the peoples, and in every place they are offering pure sacrifices in my name" (Mal. 1:11). Concerning Israel the prophet said, "I am not pleased by your sacrifices" (Jer. 6:20). Again he said (324), "Your sacrifices do not smell good to me" (Jer. 6:20).

Furthermore Hosea also said concerning Israel, "In lying they seek the Lord" (Hos. 5:7). Isaiah said that his heart is distant from his God, for he said, "This people honors me with its lips, but its heart is distant from me" (Is. 29:13). Hosea said, "Ephraim has encircled me in lying, and the house of Israel and Judah in deceit until the people of God go down" (Hos. 11:12). And which people [of God go down], if not the righteous and faithful people? If then he said concerning Israel, "He has surrounded me with lying and deceit," and concerning Ephraim, "Lo, the sinning kingdom of Ephraim has arisen in Israel," — since the name of Judah is not mentioned in this saying, [then] they respond, *Judah* is the holy and faithful one that has gone down and [still] adheres to the Lord. But the prophet openly and articulately declared, "Ephraim *and* Israel have surrounded me with lying, [769] for Jeroboam the son of Nabat has publicly turned them aside after the calf." "And Judah in deceit" (Hosea 11:12)—for in deceit and in concealment they were worshipping idols, as he furthermore showed Ezekiel their uncleanness (Ez. 8:10ff). Concerning them Hosea preached when he called them a licentious and adulterous woman. He said concerning the congregation of Israel, "Remove her licentiousness from her face," and concerning the congregation of the house of Judah he said, "Remove her adultery from between her breasts" (Hos. 2:2). Now, so that you should know that the prophet spoke concerning both of their congregations and called them [both] licentious and adulterous, he said at the end of the verse, "If she does not remove her licentiousness from before her face and her adultery from between her breasts, (325) then I shall throw her out naked, and I shall abandon her as on the day on which she was born, and as on the day on which she went forth from the land of Egypt" (Hos. 2:2, 3, 15). [These are] *both* their congregations, one of Israel and one of Judah. The one of Israel has played the whore, and the one of Judah has committed adultery. And the people which is of the peoples is the holy and faithful people which has gone down and adhered to the Lord. Now why does he say that it has gone down? Because they have gone down from their pride. Ezekiel moreover called them by the name of Ohola and Oholibah, and *both* of their congregations he called two shoots of the vine which the fire has eaten (Ez. 23:4). David further proclaimed and said concerning the peoples, "The Lord will count the peoples in a book" (Ps. 87:6), [772] and concerning the children of Israel he prophesied, saying, "They shall be blotted out of your book of the living. With your righteous they will not be inscribed" (Ps. 69:28).

XVI-4. You should know, my beloved, that the children of Israel were written in the book of the Holy One, as Moses said before his God, "Either forgive the sin of this people, or blot me out from the book which you have written." He [God] said, "Him who sins against me shall I blot out of my book" (Ex. 32:31-33). When they sinned, David said concerning them, "They are wiped out of your book of the living. With your righteous will they not be inscribed" (Ps. 69:28). But concerning the peoples he said, "The Lord will number the peoples in the book" (Ps. 87:6). For the peoples were not recorded in the book and in the Scripture.

See, my beloved, that the vocation of the peoples was recorded before the vocation of the people. When (326) they sinned in the wilderness, he

said to Moses, "Let me blot out this people, and I shall make you into a
people which is greater and more worthy than they" (Ex. 32:10). But
because the time of the peoples had not come, and another was [to be]
their redeemer, Moses was not persuaded that a redeemer and a teacher
would come for the people which was of the peoples, which was greater
and more worthy than the people of Israel. On this account it is
appropriate that we should name the son of God [with] great and
abundant praise, as [773] Isaiah said, "This thing is too small, that you
should be for me a servant and restore the scion of Jacob and raise up the
staff of Israel. But I have made you a light for the peoples, that you may
show my redemption until the ends of the earth" (Is. 49:6). Isaiah further
preached concerning the peoples, "Hear me, O peoples, and pay
attention to me, O nations, for the law has gone forth from before me,
and my justice [1] is the light of the peoples" (Is. 51:4). David said, "Alien
children will hear me with their ears," and these alien children, "will be
kept back and will be lamed from their ways" (Ps. 18:45, 46), for the
peoples have heard and have been lamed from the ways of the fear of
images and of idols.

XVI-5. If they should say, "Us has he called alien children," they have
not been called *alien* children, but sons and heirs, as Isaiah said, "I have
raised up and nurtured children, and they have rebelled against me" (Is.
1:2). The prophet (327) said, "From Egypt I have called him my son"
(Hos. 11:1). And the Holy One said to Moses, "Say to Pharaoh, let my son
go that he may serve me" (Ex. 4:23). Further he said, "My son, my first
born [is] Israel" (Ex. 4:22). But the peoples are those who hearken to God
and were lamed and kept back from the ways of their sins. Again Isaiah
said, "You will call the peoples who have not known you, and peoples
who do not know you will come to you [776] and turn" (Is. 55:5). Again
Isaiah said, "Hear, O peoples, the thing which I have done, and know, O
distant ones, my power" (Is. 33:13). Concerning the church and the
congregation of the peoples, David said, "Remember your church which
you acquired from of old" (Ps. 74:2). Again David said, "Praise the Lord all
peoples, and praise his name, O nations" (Ps. 117:1). Again he said,
"Dominion belongs to the Lord, and he rules over the peoples" (Ps.
22:28). Again the prophet said, "At the end of days I shall pour my spirit
over all flesh, and they will prophesy. No longer will a man teach his
fellow-citizen nor his brother, and say, 'Know our Lord,' for all will know
me from the least of them even to the oldest" (Jer. 31:34).

---

[1] *dyny.*

Concerning the children of Israel he said, "I shall send a famine in the land, not that they shall hunger for bread, nor that they shall thirst for water, but (328) for hearing the word of the Lord. They shall go from the west to the east and from the south to the north to seek the word of the Lord, but they shall not find it, for he has withdrawn it from them" (Amos 8:11, 12). Moses earlier wrote about them, "When in the end of days many evil things will happen to you, you will say, Because the Lord is not in my midst, these evil things have happened to me" (Deut. 31:17). So it was that they said in the days of Ezekiel, "The Lord has abandoned the land, and the Lord no longer sees [777] us" (Ez. 8:12). Isaiah said about them, "Your sins have separated between you and your God, and your iniquities have held back good things from you" (Is. 59:2). Again he said, "You will call in my ears with a loud voice, but I shall not hear you" (Ex. 8:18). Concerning the people which is from the peoples David said, "All you peoples clap hands, and praise God with the sound of praise" (Ps. 47:1). Again he said, "Hear this, all of you peoples, and pay attention, all who dwell on earth" (Ps. 49:1).

III. ISRAEL AND THE NATIONS

XVI-6. Even from of old, whoever from among the peoples was pleasing to God was more greatly justified than Israel. Jethro the priest who was of the peoples and his seed were blessed: "Enduring is his dwelling place, and his nest is set on a rock" (Num. 24:21).

And [to] the Gibeonites from among the unclean peoples Joshua gave his right hand, and they entered, took refuge in the inheritance of the Lord, and were hewers of wood and drawers of water for the congregation and the altar of the Lord. When Saul wanted to kill them, (329) the heavens were closed up from [giving] rain until the sons of Saul were slaughtered. Then the Lord turned toward the land and blessed its inheritors.

Rahab, the prostitute who received the spies, and the house of her fathers received an inheritance in Israel.

Obededom of Gath of the Philistines, into whose house the ark of the Lord entered and by whom it was honored more [780] than by all Israel, and his house were blessed by the Lord. Ethai, the Gathite, fed David when he was persecuted, and his name and seed were honored.

Ebedmelech the Ethiopian, the man of faith, raised up Jeremiah from the pit when the children of Israel his people imprisoned him. This is the matter concerning which Moses said concerning them, "The stranger that is among you will be higher, and you will be lower" (Deut. 28:33). They imprisoned and lowered Jeremiah the prophet into the lowest pit, but Ebedmelech the sojourner from Ethiopia raised up Jeremiah from the pit.

Ruth the Moabite, from the people smitten with wrath, came and was assimilated with the people of Israel, and from her seed arose the leader of kings, from whom was born the redeemer of the peoples.

Uriah the Hittite, from an unclean people, was chief among the men of David. Because David killed him with deceit in the war with the children of Ammon, desired his wife, and married her, David received the judgment that the sword would never depart from his house (II Sam. 12:10).

XVI-7. Furthermore Isaiah said concerning our redeemer, "I have set you as a covenant for the people and as a light for the peoples" (Is. 42:6). Now how was this covenant for the people? From the time that the light and the redeemer (330) [781] of the peoples came, from that time Israel was restrained from the worship of idols, and they had a true covenant. Concerning this matter Moses said, "I shall provoke you with a people which is no people, and with a foolish people I shall anger you" (Deut. 32:21). By us they are provoked. On our account they do not worship idols, so that they will not be shamed by us, for we have abandoned idols and call lies the thing which our fathers left us. They are angry, their hearts are broken, for we have entered and have become heirs in their place. For theirs was this covenant which they had, not to worship other gods, but they did not accept it. By means of us he provoked them, and ours was the light and the life, as he preached, saying when he taught, "I am the light of the world" (John 8:12). Again he said, "Believe while the light is with you, before the darkness overtakes you" (John 12:35). And again he said, "Walk in the light, so that you may be called the children of light" (John 12:36). And further he said, "The light gave light in the darkness" (John 1:5). This is the covenant which the people had, and the light which gave light for all the peoples, and lamed and hindered them from crooked ways, as it is written, "In his coming the rough place will be smooth, and the high place (331) will be plain, and the glory of the Lord will be revealed, and all flesh will see the life of God" (Is. 40:4, 5; Luke 3:5, 6).

XVI-8. This brief memorial I have written to you concerning the [784] peoples, because the Jews take pride and say, "We are the people of God and the children of Abraham." But we shall listen to John [the Baptist] who, when they took pride [saying], 'We are the children of Abraham', then said to them, "You should not boast and say, Abraham is father unto us, for from these very rocks can God raise up children for Abraham" (Matthew 3:9). Our redeemer said to them, "You are the children of Cain, and not the children of Abraham" (John 8:39, 44). The apostle said, "The branches which sinned were broken off. We were grafted on in their place and are partners in the fat of the olive tree. Now let us not take pride and sin so that we too may not be broken off. Lo, we have been grafted onto the olive tree" (Rom. 11:17, 18). This is the apology against the Jews, because they take pride saying, "We are the children of Abraham, and we are the people of God."

The demonstration on the people and the peoples is completed.

CHAPTER SEVEN

DEMONSTRATION XVII

ON THE MESSIAH, THAT HE IS THE SON OF GOD

Summary: The Jews blaspheme concerning the "people which is of the peoples," that is, the church, accusing them of worshipping a man and calling a son of man God, although God has no son. But it is not strange that Christians do so, for the Jews themselves know that the title of divinity was applied to righteous men. Moses was called God. Israel was called the son of God. Nebuchadnezzar was called the king of kings. Jews pay worship to infidel rulers and see no sin in doing so. It is all the more appropriate for us to worship Jesus who taught us to worship one God. Daniel worshipped Nebuchadnezzar, and Joseph worshipped Pharaoh. We worship Jesus in whom we know the father. Jesus was moreover foretold beforehand by the prophets, and his passion was foreseen as well. The messianic Scriptures were not fulfilled in Saul, David, or others, but only in Jesus.

I. Judaic Critique of Christian Worship of Jesus

[785] (332) XVII-1. This apology is against the Jews who blaspheme concerning the people which is of the peoples, for thus they say, You worship and serve a man who was born, a son of man who was crucified, and you call a son of man God. Although God has no son, you say concerning this crucified Jesus that he is the son of God. They offer as an argument that God said, "I, I am God and there is none else beside me" (Deut. 32:39). Again he said, "You will not worship other gods" (Ex. 34:14). Then you stand against God and call a son of man God.[1]

XVII-2. Now concerning these things, my beloved, as best as I am able to understand in my insignificance, I shall expound for you. While we grant them that he is a man, and [still] we honor and call him [788] God and Lord, it is not strange that we thus call him, and we do not give him a strange name, (333) something which they themselves do not make use of. We are, however, certain that Jesus our Lord is God son of God, the King son of the King, Light of the Light, Creator and Counsellor, Guide

---

[1] In addition to Bert and Parisot, I followed John Gwynn, "Selections . . . from the Demonstrations of Aphrahat the Persian Sage," in Philip Schaff and Henry Wace, eds., *Select Library of Nicene and Post-Nicene Fathers*, Second Series, Vol. XIII, Part II (Repr. Grand Rapids, 1956), pp. 387-392.

and Way, Redeemer, Shepherd, Gatherer, Gate, Pearl, and Lamp. With many names is he called. We shall leave them all, and we shall argue concerning him that he who came from God is son of God and God.

XVII-3. The honored title of divinity also has been applied to righteous men, and they have been deemed worthy to be called by it. Men whom God approved he called my sons and my friends. When he chose Moses as his friend and beloved and made him the head, teacher, and priest of his people, he called him God. He said to him, "I have set you as God for Pharaoh" (Ex. 7:1). And he gave him his priest as a prophet: "Aaron, your brother, will speak for you with Pharaoh, and you will be for him as God and he will be for you as an interpreter" (Ex. 7:2). It was not alone for Pharaoh, who was evil, that he made Moses God, but also for Aaron, the holy priest, he made Moses God.

[789] XVII-3. Further hear concerning [the fact that] we call him son of God. They say that while God has no son, you make this crucified Jesus into the son and the first-born of God. But he [himself] called Israel "my son, my first born," when he sent to Pharaoh by the hand of Moses, saying to him, "My son, (330) my first born [is] Israel. I say to you, Send my son to serve me. But if you do not want to send him, lo, I shall kill *your* son, *your* first born" (Ex. 4:22, 23). By the hand of the prophet, he also gave testimony concerning this matter, and he reproved them, saying to the people, "From Egypt I have called him my son. As I called to them, thus they went and worshipped Baal, and offered incense to idols" (Hos. 11:1, 2). Isaiah said concerning them, "I have raised and nurtured sons, but they have rebelled against me" (Is. 1:2). Again it is written, "You are the sons of the Lord your God" (Deut. 14:1). Concerning Solomon he said, "He will be for me as a son, and I shall be for him as a father" (II Sam. 7:14).

So we also call this Messiah the son of God, for by him we know God, just as he called Israel "my son, my first born," and just as he said concerning Solomon, "He will be a son to me." And we call him God, just as he called Moses by his own name. David also said concerning them, "I said, You all are Gods and the sons of the Most High" (Ps. 82:6). But when they did not make themselves worthy [792], then he said concerning them, "You will die like men, and like one of the princes you shall fall" (Ps. 82:7).

II. TITLE OF DIVINITY APPLIED TO GREAT MEN

XVII-5. The title [name] of divinity is given in this world for great honor, and to the one whom God wills, he gives it. But the names of God are many and honored, as he gave his names to Moses, saying to him, "I am the God of your fathers, God of Abraham, God of Isaac, God (335) of Jacob. This is my name forever, and this is my memorial for generations" (Ex. 3:6, 1, 4, 15). He called his name, "I am that I am, God Almighty" (Ex. 3:15); and "the Lord of Hosts" (Jer. 32:18). By these names God is called. And while great and honored is the title of divinity, he did not withhold it even from his righteous men. While he is the great king, the great and honored name of dominion he ungrudgingly gave to men, who are his creatures.

XVII-6. By the mouth of his prophet, God called Nebuchadnezzar, the evil king, "king of kings," for Jeremiah said, "Every people and kingdom which does not put its neck in the yoke of Nebuchadnezzar, the king of kings, my servant, with famine, sword, and pestilence shall I punish that people" (Jer. 27:8). Although he is a great king, the title of sovereignty he did not withhold from men. Although he is the great God, the title of divinity [793] he did not withhold from the children of flesh. Although his is all fatherhood, he also calls men fathers. He said to the congregation, "Instead of your fathers will be your children" (Ps. 45:16). Although his is rulership, he gave men authority over one another. Although his is worship unto honor, he permitted a man to honor his fellow in the world. Even though a man may honor evil and wicked men and those who deny his goodness, he is not censured by God.

Concerning worship he commanded his people, "You will not worship the sun, moon, and all the host of the heavens, nor any creatures which are on the earth will you desire to worship" (Deut. 4:17f.). Now see the goodness and the mercy of our good Maker, who did not withhold from men the title of divinity, (336) the title of worship, the title of sovereignty, and the title of rulership, for he is the father of the creatures which are on the face of the earth. More than all his creatures has he honored, exalted, and praised the sons of man; for with his holy hands he formed them, and from his spirit he breathed into them, and he was a dwelling place for them from of old. With them he abides and among them he walks (Lev. 26:12, II Cor. 6:16). He said through the prophet, "I shall dwell with them, and I shall walk with them" (Lev. 26:12). And further Jeremiah the prophet [796] said, "You are the Temple of the Lord, if you will improve your ways and your works" (Jer. 7:4-5). From of old David said, "O Lord, you have been a dwelling place for us for generations. Before the mountains were conceived, before you formed the earth, before the world was established, from of old until eternity, you are God" (Ps. 90:1-2).

XVII-7. Now how do you understand this matter? One prophet said, "Lord, *you* have been a dwelling place for us," while another said, "*I* shall dwell among them, and I shall walk among them." At first he was for us a dwelling place, and afterwards he dwelt and walked among us. For sages both matters are true and simple. David says, "O, Lord, you have been a dwelling place for us for generations. Before the mountains were conceived, before the earth travailed, and before the world was established." You know, my beloved, that all the creatures which are above and below were first created, and after all of them, man [was created]. When God gave thought to create the world with all its embellishments, in the first place he conceived and formed (337) man in his mind. After man had been conceived in his thought, then he conceived the creatures, as it said, "Before the mountains were conceived and the earth travailed." For [797] man is older and prior in conception to the creatures, but in birth the creatures [Wright: on the earth] are older and prior to man. Man was conceived and dwelt in the thought of God, and while in conception he was held in his mind, by the word of his mouth he created all the creatures. When he had completed and adorned the world, and nothing was lacking in it, then he gave birth to man from his thought, and he shaped the son of man with his hands. Adam saw that the world was completed.[2] He [God] gave him [man] authority over everything that he had made, like a man who has a son and wishes to make him a marriage feast. [First] he betrothes for him a woman, then builds him a house, prepares and adorns all that is needed for his son. Then he makes him a wedding feast and gives his son authority over his house.

So after the conception of Adam, he gave birth to him and gave him authority over all his creation. Concerning this matter, the prophet said, "O Lord, you have been for us a dwelling place for generations, before the mountains were conceived, and before the earth travailed, and before the world was established, from of old until eternity, you are the Lord." So that no one should suppose that there is another God either from of old or afterward, he said, "From of old even unto eternity," [800] as Isaiah said, (388) "I am the first and I am the last" (Is. 44:6). After God brought forth Adam from his thought, he shaped him, blew into him of his breath, and gave him knowledge of discernment, so that he might distinguish good from evil and know that God had made him. And as he knew his Maker, God was formed and conceived in the midst of the thought of man. So he

---

[2] *mtqn* = established.

[man] became a temple for God his Maker, as it is written, "You are the Temple of God" (I Cor. 3:16). And he said, "I shall dwell in them, and I shall walk among them" (Lev. 26:11-12). But if the sons of man do not know their maker, he is not formed in their midst, does not dwell with them, and is not conceived in their thought. But they are regarded before him like the beasts, like the rest of the creatures.

XVII-8. By these facts stubborn men will be persuaded that it is not strange for us to call the Messiah the son of God. For lo, all men he conceived and brought forth from his thought. And they will have [to admit] that also the title of divinity belongs to him, for even to his righteous men he gave the name of God.[3] And as to this, that we worship Jesus through whom we know God, let them be ashamed, for even before the evil men who hold power, who are from among [801] the unclean peoples, they fall down, worship, and honor, and there is no evil in the matter, for this honor of worship God gave to men by it to honor one another and also those of them that excel and are honorable. (339) Now if they worship and honor with the name of worship the evil men, those who in their iniquity even deny the name of God, but they do not worship them as their maker, as though they worshipped them alone, and so do not sin, how much the more is it appropriate for us to worship and honor Jesus who turned our stubborn minds from all our worship of vain error and taught us to worship, serve, and work for one God, our father and our maker. We know that the kings of the world call themselves god by the name of the great God, deny [God], force others to deny [him], fall down and worship before them, and they serve and honor them as graven images and idols. But the law never censured them, nor is there sin involved.

Even Daniel worshipped Nebuchadnezzar, who denied and forced others to deny [God], and was not censured on that account. Joseph worshipped Pharaoh, and it is not written that this was a sin for him. For us [804] it is certain that Jesus is God the son of God, and in him we know the Father, and he has restrained us from all our [other] worship. Now we cannot pay back the one who has borne these things for us, but through worship we pay him honor on account of his sufferings which are on our behalf.

---

[3] Gwynn: For He (God) associated the righteous also in the name of God. Parisot: cum ipse iustos suos deorum nomine appellaverit. Bert: dass auch der Gottesname auf ihm ruht, da er (Gott) auch seinen Gerechten den Namen Gottes beilegt.

III. JESUS CHRIST FORETOLD BY PROPHETS

XVII-9. Further it is appropriate for us to prove that beforehand this Jesus was promised from ancient times by the prophets and was called the son of God. David said, "You are my son, and today (340) I have begotten you" (Ps. 2:7). Again he said, "In the glories of holiness, from the womb, from of old, have I begotten you, O child" (Ps. 110:3). Isaiah said, "A child is born for us, a son is given to us. His authority will be upon his shoulder. His name will be called wonderful, counsellor, mighty God of the ages, and peaceful ruler. To the increase of his authority and his peace there is no limit" (Is. 9:6-7).

Now tell me, O wise man, teacher of Israel: Who is this one who is born, whose name is called a child, son, wonderful, counsellor, mighty God of the ages, peaceful ruler, and to the increase of whose authority and power he said that there is no limit? Now if we call the Messiah the son of God, David has taught us so. And as to our calling him God, from Isaiah we have heard it. And his authority is set [805] upon his shoulder, for he took his cross and went out of Jerusalem. And as to the child that is born, Isaiah further said, "Lo, a virgin shall conceive and give birth, and his name will be called Emanuel, for with us is our God" (Is. 7:14).

XVII-10. But if you should say that the Messiah has not yet come, I will grant this also to your contentiousness. For when he comes, it is written, "Peoples will hope in him" (Gen. 49:10). Lo, I who am of the peoples have heard that the Messiah has come. And before he had yet come, I went ahead and believed in him. And through him I worship the God of Israel. Perhaps when he comes, he will censure me that before he came, I already believed in him?

(341) But, O fool, the prophets have not permitted you to say that the Messiah has not yet come, for Daniel confutes you, saying, "After sixty-two weeks the Messiah will come and be killed. And when he comes, the Holy City will be destroyed, and her end will be in a flood. Until the completion of the things which are decided, she shall remain desolate" (Dan. 9:26-27). Now you hope and expect that when the Messiah comes, through it [his coming] Israel will be gathered together from all regions, and Jerusalem will be rebuilt and inhabited. But Daniel bore witness that when the Messiah comes and is killed, Jerusalem will be destroyed and will continue in desolation until the completion of the things which have been decided forever.

Concerning [808] the passion of the Messiah, David said, "They pierced my hands and my feet, and all my bones cried out. They gazed and looked at me. They divided my garments among them, and for my clothing they cast lots" (Ps. 22:17-18). Isaiah said, "Lo, my servant will be known, revealed, and raised up, so that many will be astonished at him. As for this man, his appearance will be marred more than that of man, and his aspect more than that of the sons of man" (Is. 52:13-14). He said, "He will purify many nations, and kings will be surprised at him" (Is. 52:15). In that passage he said, "He came up before him as a child, and as a root from the dry land" (Is. 53:2). He said at the end of the passage, "He will be killed on account of our sins, humbled on account of our evil. The chastisement of our wholeness is upon him, and in his bruises we shall be healed" (Is. 53:5).

By what wounds [then] were men healed? David was not killed, for he died in good old age, (342) and was buried in Bethlehem. And if they say [that it] concerns Saul, Saul died on the mountains of Gilboa in battle with the Philistines. And if they say that they pierced his hands and his feet when they hung up his body on the wall of Bethshean, it has not been fulfilled in Saul, for when the limbs of Saul were pierced, his bones [809] did not feel his suffering, for he was dead. After Saul died, they hung up his body and the bodies of his sons on the wall of Bethshean.

When David said, "They pierced my hands and my feet, and all of my bones cried out," he said in the next verse, "God, abide for my help. Deliver my soul from the sword" (Ps. 22:17, 18). Now the Messiah was delivered from the sword; he went up from the midst of Sheol, lived, and rose after the three days. God abode as his help. Saul cried out to the Lord, but he did not answer him. He asked by means of the prophets, but a word was not given to him. He disguised himself, asked the soothsayers and learned. He was conquered by the Philistines and killed himself by his own sword when he saw that the battle had overcome him. David said in this passage, "I will declare your name to my brothers, and in the midst of the church I shall praise you" (Ps. 22:23). How can these things have been fulfilled concerning Saul? And again David said, "You did not give your holy one to see corruption" (Ps. 16:10). But all of these things are fulfilled in the Messiah. When he came to them, and they did not receive him, they wickedly judged him by false witness. By their hands was he hung upon the tree. They pierced his hands and his feet with the nails (343) which they had fastened in him, and all his bones cried out.

[812] On that day there was a great miracle: the light was darkened at the middle of the day, as Zechariah had prophesied, saying, "The day is known to the Lord. It is not day, and it is not night. At the time of evening there will be light" (Zech. 14:7). Now what is the day which was

distinguished by the miracle that it was not day nor night, but at the evening time there was light? But it is the day on which they crucified him, for there was darkness in the middle of the day, and toward evening there was light. Again he said, "On that day there shall be cold and frost" (Zech. 14:6). As you know, the day on which they crucified him was cold, and they made a fire so that they might warm themselves, when Simon came and stood with him. Again he said, "The spear shall rise against the shepherd and against the sheep, [or, man], my beloved, and it will smite the shepherd, and the sheep of his flock will be scattered. I shall turn my hand against the pastors" (Zech. 13:7).

David further said concerning his passion, "They gave for my food gall, and for my thirst they gave me vinegar to drink" (Ps. 69:21). He further said in that same verse, "They have persecuted him whom you have smitten, and they have added to the affliction of him that was slain" (Ps. 69:21, 26). They added to him many things which were not written concerning him, cursings and revilings, things which even Scripture was unable to reveal, [813] for their revilings were hateful. "But the Lord wanted to humble and afflict him" (Is. 53:10). He was killed on account of our iniquity, humbled on account of our sins, and sin was placed in his soul (II. Cor. 5:21).

(344) XVII-11. We worship these mercies. We bow the knee before the majesty of his Father, who turned our worship to him. We call him God like Moses, first born and son like Israel, Jesus like Jesus the son of Nun, priest like Aaron, king like David, great prophet like all of the prophets, shepherd like the shepherds who watched and tended Israel.

He called us sons, as he said, "Alien sons will hearken to me" (Ps. 18:44). He has made us his brothers, as he said, "I shall declare your name to my brothers" (John 15:15), and we became his friends as he said to his disciples, "I have called you my friends" (John 15:15), just as his father called Abraham "my friend." And he said to us, "I am the good Shepherd, the Gate, the Way, the Vineyard, the Sower, the Bridegroom, the Pearl, the Lamp, the Light, the King, God, Lifegiver, and Redeemer." By many names is he called.

[816] XVII-12. This brief argument I have written to you, my beloved, so you may reply to the Jews on account of their saying that God has no son, and [on account of] our calling him God son of God, King, first-born of all creatures.

The demonstration which is on the Messiah, the son of God, is completed.

CHAPTER EIGHT

DEMONSTRATION XVIII

AGAINST THE JEWS
and on Virginity and Sanctity

Summary: The Jews accuse Christians of unnatural living and violating God's will by refraining from marriage and procreation. But mere numbers avail nothing before God; rather, obedience by a few is better. Virginity and sanctity were preferable even in ancient times. Moses refrained from marital life after he was called by God. The priests could marry only virgins. Joshua, Elijah, Elisha, Jeremiah—none of them married. God made Ezekiel a widower. Marriage is good, but celibacy is better, for a celibate honors God with undivided love.

I. JUDAIC CRITIQUE OF CHRISTIAN CELIBACY

[817](345) XVIII-1. I wish to instruct you, my beloved, also about this matter which distresses me, this holy covenant, the virginity and sanctity in which we endure, for, because of their lasciviousness and the immodesty of their bodies, the Jewish people stumble therein. They change and weaken the minds of those simple and ordinary folk who are attracted and captivated by their disturbing argument. They say, When God created Adam, he thus blessed him, saying to him, "Be fruitful and multiply. Procreate and fill the earth" (Gen. 1:28). Also to Noah in the same way he said, "Be fruitful in the earth and procreate in it" (Gen. 9:7). He blessed Abraham, saying to him, "Look to the heavens and count the stars if you can." He said to him, "Thus shall your seed be (346)" (Gen. 15:5). And to Israel [820] in the blessings, he said, "There will not be among you a barren male and a barren female" (Deut. 7:14). Again he said. "There shall not be a sterile man and a barren woman in your land" (Ex. 23:26). In the blessing Isaac was given to Abraham, and Isaac prayed for Rebecca that she might give birth. He blessed Jacob that his seed might multiply. Hannah beseechingly asked for Samuel; numerous was the procreation of the barren through the promise, and all the righteous received seed and blessing.[1]

---

[1] Parisot reads *bmwldh*, in her generation; the variant, followed by Bert, is *bmwlkn'*, promise. Parisot: et sterilis [mulieris] proles generatione multiplicata est. Bert:. . . und es ward zahlreich die Nachkommenschaft der Unfruchtbaren durch die Verheissung. . .

But you do a thing which was not commanded by God, for you have received a curse and have multiplied barrenness. You have prohibited procreation, the blessings of righteous men. You do not take wives, and you do not become wives for husbands. You hate procreation, a blessing given by God. Concerning these matters, my beloved, as best as I can, I shall instruct you.

ii. Procreation No Blessing

XVIII-2. When God blessed Adam, he said to him, "Procreate and be fruitful on the earth" (Gen. 1:28). For this reason he blessed them, so that the world might be filled by them, and that from his children there might be fruit. But when they were numerous, they were corrupted and sinned, until on account of their sins they sickened and annoyed the spirit of their Creator, so that he said, "I regret that I made them" (Gen. 6:7). In a torrent of wrath and harsh judgment [821] he blotted them out with the water of the flood.

Now tell me, O debater of Israel, how did the blessing of Adam help? For they corrupted their way and were blotted out by the water of the flood. (347) They corrupted the nature of marriage and were condemned, and the blessing was extinguished by the sins of iniquitous men. Noah with a small number, though not numerous, built the altar and aroused the compassion of the Holy One. Noah was better in his few numbers than the whole generation of destruction, and from him was founded a second world. Furthermore, Noah was blessed that his descendants should multiply, so that the world might be filled, and men might be numerous. But when they were numerous and strong, and had multiplied in procreation, they transgressed against God, and all the peoples and the tongues who were of his seed worshipped idols. So they were reckoned before God as if they were nothing, like a drop from the bucket, like dust from the scales (Is. 40:15). Only the seed of the righteous lived and were delivered before God. What then did the blessing avail the ten generations who were before the flood? And what was the advantage for the Sodomites, whose lives were snuffed out by the fire and the sulfur, whose blessing was extinguished by the sins of iniquitous men? And what profit and advantage did the blessing provide for the six hundred thousand who went out of Egypt, who perished [824] in the dry wilderness, having angered the Holy One? And what advantage and profit were in the blessing of procreation for the unclean peoples whom Joshua destroyed? What was the advantage for Israel in the blessing that his seed should be multiplied like the stars, when war and the sword have finished them off?

III. FAITH, NOT MERE NUMBERS

XVIII-3. To God one man who does his will is more excellent and distinguished before his majesty than myriads and thousands of those who do evil. Noah was more excellent and distinguished before God than the ten generations of destruction who preceded him. Abraham was reckoned before God (348) more than the ten generations that were before him; also he was more excellent than those that were after him. Isaac and Jacob, children of the promise, were better and more excellent before God than all of the Amorites among whom they dwelled. Joseph was reckoned before God more than the whole evil people of the house of Pharaoh. Moses, the great prophet that was in Israel, was better and more excellent before God than the six hundred thousand whom he brought forth from Egypt, whose rebellion angered God so that they were unable to enter the Promised Land.

IV. HEROES OF ISRAEL DID NOT MARRY: MOSES

XVIII-4. I shall show you that virginity and sanctity were worth more before God among that people, that prior people [825], than much procreating, which profited naught. From the time that his master spoke with the man Moses, the great prophet, the leader of all Israel, he loved sanctity and served the Holy One. He held himself back from the world and from procreating, and abided by himself, so that he might please his master.

But show me: What do you say, O wise debater of the people? From the time that God spoke with Moses did he perform the duties natural to marriage? And if you bring against us a perverse argument, I shall not be tricked by your provocation, for you want to render the Holy One unclean on account of your licentiousness. If he had carried out the duties of marriage, he would not have been able to serve the majesty of his master, as Israel was unable to receive the message of the Holy One and the living words which the Holy One spoke with Moses on the mountain, until he had sanctified (349) the people for three days. Then Holy One spoke with them. He said to Moses, "Go down to the people and sanctify them for three days" (Ex. 19:10). Thus Moses openly declared to them, "You should not draw near to a woman" (Ex. 19:15). When they had been sanctified these three days, then, on the third day, the Holy One revealed himself in powerful radiance, in great glory, with a mighty noise, [828] with frightful thunder, with a loud trumpet, with strong lights, and with brilliant lightening. The mountains trembled. The hills were moved. The sun and the moon changed from its [their] course. Moses went up to Mount Sinai, arose on the cloud, and received the commandments. Moses saw the glorious splendor, was made to tremble, and was frightened. Trembling gripped him, for he saw the *Shekhinah* of the Most High which drew near to the mountain, the great power of the throne of God, to which the myriads and thousands minister, covering their faces from its [his] glorious splendor. They run and swiftly fly with their wings, call, sanctify, and exalt his majesty. Alert and ready, swiftly running, beautiful, lovely, worthy, desirable, they run, sanctifying, completing his commandment, going up and coming down in the air, like swift flashes of lightening.

XVIII-5. Moses was speaking and God was answering him with a voice. Israel stood on that day in fear, trembling, and dread. They fell on their faces, for they were not able to bear [it], and said to Moses, (350) "Let not God speak with us so, that we may not die" (Ex. 20:19). O stubborn man, who is vexed by these things and stumbles! [2] If the people of Israel, with whom God spoke only one hour, [829] were unable to hear the voice of God until they had sanctified themselves three days, even though they did not go up to the mountain and did not go on the dense cloud, how was it possible for the man Moses, the prophet, the clear eye of the entire people, who was standing all the time before God, speaking with him mouth to mouth, to be married? And if God spoke with Israel, that had sanctified itself for only three days, how much better and more beloved are those who through all their days are sanctified, alert, prepared, and standing before God! Should God not all the more love them and his spirit dwell among them, as he said, "I shall dwell among them and I shall walk among them" (Lev. 26:12). Isaiah said, "Upon whom shall I look and with whom shall I dwell, if not with the peaceful and the humble who fears my word" (Is. 66:2).

XVIII-6. I shall show you that virginity is very desirable and beloved before God. The Holy One commanded the priests, the children of Aaron, who serve before him, that not one of them should marry a woman who was a widow, divorced, or unclean through prostitution, but he should marry a virgin of his people, one who was not made unclean by

---

[2] Parisot: O [homo] indocillis, qui contra ista contendis, et scandalizaris! Bert: O du Unverständiger, der du hierin Schwierigkeiten findest und Anstoss daran nimmst!

another man. So you see that a widow is more unclean than a virgin. [832] If marriage were better than virginity and sanctity, why was it necessary (351) for him to admonish Israel that they sanctify [themselves] those three days and then he would speak with them? And why was it necessary that the priest marry a virgin and not draw near to a widow or a divorce? And why did Moses sanctify and restrain himself from his wife for forty years, so that he did not have other children beside Gershon and Eliezer?

It furthermore seems to me that it would have been better if Zimri had not been born on account of his licentiousness, for in one hour twenty-four thousand of Israel fell. Also [it would have been better] had Achan not been formed in the belly of his mother, who made an anathema of the camp of Israel. Eli should have abided in his sanctity and not fathered Hophni and Phineas, who troubled the priesthood and behaved avariciously. And why for Samuel were sons necessary, who did not keep the law and did not go in his ways? There are many like these, for whom it would have been better had they not procreated, indeed had they not been born.

v. Joshua, Jeremiah, Elijah, Elisha Were Celibate

XVIII-7. Moses loved sanctity and was beloved before the Holy One, who showed him his glory. Joshua the son of Nun loved virginity and dwelt in the tabernacle, the place [833] in which the Holy One was served. Elijah was distinguished by virginity and dwelt in the wilderness, in mountains and caves. The Holy One brought him to the place of the sanctities, a place in which those who love filth have no authority. Elisha remained solitary and chaste. He did astounding works of power through the power of God.

(352) Jeremiah furthermore said, "I do not love the birthday of a man" (Jer. 17:16). Furthermore, his Lord commanded him, saying to him, "You will not take for yourself a wife, nor will you have sons and daughters" (Jer. 16:2). The Jews respond concerning this matter, that he commanded Jeremiah not to take a wife and not to have sons and daughters in this place. On this account the Lord commanded concerning the sons and daughters that would be born in this place, because they would suffer a lingering death through famine. On this account he said to him not to take a wife. O men who lack intelligence, who hold this opinion! The one who gave Jeremiah a good standing in the eyes of the king of Babylonia, if he had fathered any sons, would also have saved them from sword and famine.

Also his master did Ezekiel good and took away from him the delight
of his eyes in a sudden plague. He took and threw off from him the
injurious yoke.

But show me, O teacher! concerning Joshua [336] the son of Nun, that
he took a wife and gave birth to sons! And persuade me also concerning
Elijah and Elisha, his disciple, what house was their possession in this
world? For lo, in the wilderness, in mountains and caves, they dwelt in
want and in persecution. With none of them was there a wife. They were
served by their disciples. See that when Gahazi, the disciple of Elisha, was
perturbed concerning this world and desired property, a wife and sons,
Elisha said to him, "At *this* time will you acquire possessions (353)
vineyards and olive trees? Because you have done this thing the leprosy
of Naaman will clothe Gahazi and all of his descendents forever" (II
Kings 5:26-7).

Now if you can bring me proof from Scripture concerning any one of
these I shall accept it from you. But I shall not listen to anything you have
made up in your mind and spoken, for you want to render the Holy One
unclean through your perverse proof.

vi. Marriage Is Good, Celibacy Better

XVIII-8. Far be it from us that we should attribute anything shameful
to marriage which God has placed in the world, for thus it is written,
"God saw all that he had made, and it was very good" (Gen. 1:31). But
there are some things which are better than others. God created heaven
and earth, and they are very good, but the heaven is better than the earth.
He created darkness and light, and light is much better [837] and more
distinguished than darkness. He created night and day. Day is much
better and more distinguished than night. He created the sun and the
moon. The sun is much better and more distinguished than the moon.
He created the stars of the heaven, and one star is much better and more
distinguished in its light than another star. He created Adam and Eve,
and Adam is much better and more distinguished than Eve. He created
marriage, worldly procreation, and it is very good; but virginity is more
excellent than it.

XVIII-9. When the earth was virgin, it was not rendered unclean, but
after rain fell on it, it brought forth thorns. Adam in his virginity was
beloved and good. After he gave birth to Eve, he erred and transgressed
the commandment. The sons of Seth in their virginity were worthy, but
when (354) they became mixed up with the daughters of Cain, they were

blotted out with the water of the flood. Samson was excellent in his Naziriteship and in his virginity, but by his licentiousness he destroyed his Naziriteship. David was beloved in his youth, but in his desire for Bathsheba, he transgressed the law and violated three commandments of the ten: Thou shalt not covet, Thou shalt not kill, Thou shalt not commit adultery. Amnon was excellent in his virginity, [840] but by reason of his unclean lust for his sister, Absalom killed him. Solomon was worthy and beautiful in his virginity, but in his old age through his desire for women his heart turned away from God.

VII. CELIBACY FOSTERS PIETY

XVIII-10. We have heard in the law, "A man should leave his father and his mother and cleave to his wife, and they shall be one flesh" (Gen. 2:24). In truth this prophecy is great and honorable. Does a man after he takes a wife abandon his father and his mother? This is the explanation: When a man has not yet taken a wife, he loves and honors God, his father, and the holy spirit, his mother, and has no other love. But when a man takes a wife, he abandons his father and his mother, [namely] those things which are mentioned above, and his mind is captivated by this world. His mind, heart, and thought are turned aside from God into the world. He adores and loves it as a man adores the wife of his youth, and separate is the love for her from that for his father and his mother.

XVIII-11. And it says, "The two of them should be one flesh" (Gen. 2:24). And this is true, for just as a man and woman become one flesh and one mind, and (355) his mind and thought separate from his father and his mother, so also a man [841] who has not yet taken a wife but remains solitary is in one spirit and one thought with his father.

XVIII-12. I have written to you, my beloved, concerning virginity and sanctity, because I have heard about a Jewish man who shamed one of our brethren, the children of our church, saying to him, "You are unclean, for you do not take wives. But we are holy and excellent, who procreate and increase seed in the world." On this account, lo, I have written you this argument.

But concerning virginity and sanctity I have written to you above, and have instructed you in the Demonstration on the Children of the Covenant, how worthy and desirable is virginity, even when a man accomplishes it in necessity, as our Lord said, "Not every man but he to whom it is given is able to accomplish it" (Matthew 19:11). The apostle said, "On account of necessity which is in the world, it is good for a man to remain as he is" (I Cor. 7:26). For this portion there is a great reward, because in our freedom we accomplish it, but not in bondage or compelled by the commandment, for we are not bound to it under the law. Its model and its image have we found in Scripture. We have seen that this likeness of the watchers which are in heaven [= angels] is found with reference to the victorious [martyrs], and on earth it is acquired as a gift. This (356) is a possession which, if a man loses it, will not [844] be found [again], nor can a man acquire it with money. No one who has it and loses it again finds it. No one who does not have it and runs will overtake it.

My beloved, love this gift for which there is no equivalent in the whole world. With this matter which I have written to you, respond to the Jews who in their licentiousness do not grasp the power of virginity and sanctity.

The demonstration of virginity and sanctity is completed.

CHAPTER NINE

DEMONSTRATION XIX

AGAINST THE JEWS

on account of their saying that they are
destined to be gathered together

Summary: The Jews expect to be gathered together by the Messiah, but this expectation is in vain. God was never reconciled to them but has rejected them. The prophetic promises of restoration were all fulfilled in the return from Babylonia. Daniel's prayer was answered, and his vision was realized in the time of Jesus and in the destruction of Jerusalem. It will never be rebuilt.

I. EARLY REDEMPTIONS

[845](357) XIX-1. The voice of the Holy One was heard by Moses. He sent him to take his people out of Egypt, out of the house of Pharaoh, the bondage of the Egyptians, saying to him, "Say to Pharaoh: My son, my first-born is Israel. I say to you: Send out my son to worship me" (Ex. 4:22-3). When he took them forth from Egypt with signs and wonders, with a mighty hand, with a high arm, and with great visions, he brought them through the wilderness and led them there forty years. He led them to the Promised Land, took them across the Jordan, and caused them to inherit it, having destroyed its inhabitants from before them. They dwelt in it four hundred and forty years before Solomon built the holy house, and then four hundred [848] years before the king of Babylonia conquered them.

On account of their sins, which were many, he uprooted and scattered them among every nation, for they did not listen to his prophets, whom he had sent to them. When they had been in Babylonia seventy years, he again gave thought in their behalf to the covenant of their fathers. He proclaimed concerning them through his prophets that they should go up from Babylonia (358) at the end of seventy years. When the seventy years were fulfilled, as Jeremiah had prophesied, Daniel prayed and offered supplication that he should restore their captivity and have mercy upon them. "And the Lord aroused the spirit of Cyrus, and he issued a proclamation through his entire kingdom. He announced to them saying, Whoever remains of all of the people of the Lord, may his God be with him. Let him return and go to Jerusalem which is in Judah" (Ezra 1:1, 3).

But because they were assimilated among the peoples, had built, planted, and acquired [property] in the place of their captivity, not all of them entirely wanted to go up, but some of them went up, and some of them remained. Because God knew their evil impulse, he did not force them to go up from Babylonia, but without compulsion did Cyrus the king of Persia proclaim to them. For even when he brought them out of Egypt by the hand of Moses, if the bondage of Pharaoh were not strong on them, they would not have wanted [849] to go out of Egypt, as they said to Moses when they were rebelling against him in the wilderness, "This is the word which we spoke to you in Egypt: You should let us serve the Egyptians, for it was good for us in Egypt" (Ex. 14:12). So see that even when they were oppressed by bondage, they did not want to go out of Egypt until the Egyptians forced them to go out of their land when they saw that their first-born were dead, saying, "We are all dead" (Ex. 12:33). It is written, "The Egyptians forced the people to go out of their land" (Ex. 12:33). And also from Babylonia, if (359) the persecuters had gathered together [1] against them, they all would have gone forth.

II. Jews' Hope

XIX-2. I have written this to you because even today they hope an empty hope, saying, "It is still certain for Israel to be gathered together," [2] for the prophet thus spoke, "I shall leave none of them among the nations" (Ex. 39:28). But if all of our people is to be gathered together, why are we today scattered among every people?

Concerning these things, my beloved, as best as I am able, I shall instruct you: Israel *never* is going to be gathered together. For they depend on this: All of the prophets gave Israel hope. Hear, O debater of Israel: [852] No law has been imposed upon God, nor is there anyone above him to censure him for anything that he does. He said, "If I declare concerning a people and a kingdom to be built and to be planted, and afterward it will do that which is evil before me, I shall make my word into a lie and shall turn away from it the good which I promised for it. In

---

[1] Variant: *'stkhw*. Bert: wenn sich Bedränger über ihnen versammelt hatten.

[2] Bert: Es ist für Israel noch bestimmt, dass es versammelt wird. Parisot: . . . fore ut Israel adhuc congregetur . . . Note also T. Nöldeke, *Compendious Syriac Grammar*, trans. James A. Chrichton (London, 1904), p. 225, "It still remains appointed for Israel to be brought together."

its iniquity and sins I shall destroy it. If again I shall declare concerning a people and a kingdom to be built and planted, and afterward to be uprooted, overthrown, destroyed, and wiped out, and it will do that which is right before me, then I shall turn away from it the evil which I promised for it" (Jer. 18:7-10). Isaiah also said, "Woe unto him who despoils. You will not despoil. A liar shall not lie among you. When you want to despoil, you will be despoiled, and when you want to lie, there will be lying among you" (Is. 33:1). And with regard to these things there is none who censures the will of God.

III. GOD NEVER RECONCILED TO ISRAEL

XIX-3. I shall write and show you that never did God accept (360) their repentence [through] either Moses or all of the prophets. For Moses said to them, "You were rebellious before the Lord from the day I knew you" (Deut. 9:24). Again he said, "It is a people whose mind is lost, among whom is no understanding" (Deut. 32:28). Further he said, "They have outraged me with their idols, and with their gods they have provoked me. So shall I provoke them with a people [853] which is no people, and with a foolish people I shall anger them" (Deut. 32:21). And Moses further said to them, "I know that after my death you will certainly become corrupt, and you will turn aside from the way which I have commanded you. Many evil things will happen to you at the end of days. And lo, while I am still alive with you, you are rebelling against the Lord" (Deut. 31:29).

Hosea said, "I have cut off my prophets and have killed them with the word of my mouth" (Hosea 6:5). "And you, O children of Israel, have not turned from your evil, from the days of your fathers" (Mal. 3:7). Again he said to them, "Your goodness is like the clouds of the morning and like the dew which first passes" (Hosea 6:4). And again he said, "Woe to them who wander from me. Evil is upon them" (Hosea 7:13). And again he said, "Go to Baalpeor and become a Nazirite unto its disgrace" (Hosea 9:10). And again he said, "Like a bird has their honor flown from them. If they raise sons, I shall then wipe them out from among men, and I shall smite the delight of their bowels" (Hosea 9:11, 12).

Further, Jeremiah said, (861) "They are called rejected silver, for the Lord has rejected them" (Jer. 6:30). Hosea said, "I shall drive them out of my house, and I shall no longer continue to have mercy on them" (Hosea 9:15). Now that he said, "I shall no longer continue to have mercy on them," what do they have to say? [856]

Again he said, "The Lord has rejected them because they did not listen to him" (Hosea 9:17). Again he said, "They shall be wandering among the peoples" (Hosea 9:17). Again he said concerning them, "According to the good of their land, they have multiplied altars and built high places" (Hosea 10:1). Again he said, "Ephraim will receive shame, and Israel will be confounded in its opinion" (Hosea 10:6). Again he said, "Ephraim has surrounded me with lying, and Judah and the house of Israel with deceit" (Hos. 11:12). Again he said, "I have destroyed you, O Israel. Who will help you?" (Hos. 13:9). Again he said, "I have given to you a king in my anger, and I have taken him away in my wrath" (Hosea 13:11). Micah said, "Do not raise up your face, and do not go standing up straight" (Micah 2:3). Again he said, "Rise up, go, for this was not my rest" (Micah 2:10). Again he said, "Those who see visions will be confounded, and those who divine will be shamed, all their lips will be covered, for God does not answer them" (Micah 3:7).

XIX-4. And why did he say concerning the diviners and those who see visions that they will be confounded, and that their lips will be covered? For this is a plague for which there is no healing. It is written in the law, "When there shall be a leper in Israel, his lips (362) shall be covered, and his clothes shall be ripped, and his head will be disheveled. His dwelling will be outside of the camp. He will call himself unclean all the days he is a leper" (Lev. 13:45-46). [857] On this account the prophet who proclaims with lying lips will receive the plague of leprosy, cover his lips all the days, and sit in confusion, like Uzziah, the king of the house of Judah. Because he wanted to rob the priesthood, a leprosy went out from before the presence of the Holy One and smote him between the eyes, and he dwelt in the house in secret, for he was confounded all the days. There was a great movement [earthquake] [3] in the whole people, as Zechariah said, "You will flee as you fled in the earthquake which was in the days of Uzziah, the king of the house of Judah" (Zech. 14:5).

IV. ISRAEL REJECTED

XIX-5. See, then, they have never accepted correction in their lives. He said, "I smote you with a hot wind and with hail stones, and the canker-worm has consumed the multitude of your orchards. But you did not return to me, says the Lord" (Amos 4:9). And again he said, "I overthrew you, as God overthrew Sodom and Gomorrah" (Amos 4:11). I announced that they have no further hope, for "the virgin of Israel has fallen and will no longer continue to rise" (Amos 5:2). Again he said, "She

---

[3] zw⁰ = Bert: Bewegung; Parisot: terrae motus.

is abandoned upon the ground, and there is none to raise her up" (Amos 5:2). Again he said, "In all of their markets are lamentations, and in all of their streets they will say woe, woe" (Amos 5:16). He rejected and cast them from before him, saying, "I hate and I reject [860] your festivals. I will not smell your offerings" (Amos 5:21). (363) Again he said, "I am not pleased by your offerings, and upon the beauty of your fatted beasts I shall not look" (Amos 5:22). Again he said to them, "For the forty years in the wilderness did you offer to me sacrifices and offerings, O children of Israel?" (Amos 5:25). And concerning his abandoning them Jeremiah said, "I have abandoned my house, I have abandoned my inheritance" (Jer. 12:7). Again he said, "I have given to the daughter of my people a writ of divorce" (Jer. 3:8). Because they take pride [saying] that we are the people of God, the prophet called, saying to them, "Lo, you are like the children of Ethiopians unto me, O children of Israel. Thus the children of Israel I brought forth from the land of Egypt, the Philistines from Cappadocia, and Aram from Kyr. The eyes of the Lord of Lords are upon the sinning kingdom, and I will destroy it from off the face of the earth" (Amos 9:7, 8). Know that he reckoned them like the Philistines. Jeremiah said concerning the congregation of Israel, "I planted you a root which was entirely a true seed. But you have turned and rebelled against me like an alien vine" (Jer. 2:21). Moses said, "Their vine is from the vine of Sodom and from the planting of Gomorrah. Their grapes are bitter grapes, and their clusters are bitter for them" (Deut. 32:32).

David said, "You have brought forth a vine from Egypt [861] and looked upon it, and have planted its root" (Ps. 80:8). He said, "You have destroyed peoples and planted it" (Ps. 80:9). When they had sinned, he said, (364) "The pig of the forest has eaten it, and the wild beasts of the field have pastured in it" (Ps. 80:13).

Ezekiel said concerning the vine, "The fire has consumed the two branches and laid waste their inside" (Ez. 15:4). He said, "When the vine was without blemish, it was good for nothing. And now that the fire has consumed and destroyed it, how shall it be good for anything?" (Ez. 15:5). Concerning the entire vineyard Isaiah prophesied saying, "My beloved had a vineyard on a hill which was a fertile place. He worked it, surrounded it with a fence, and planted in it vines. But when the vineyard brought forth thorns, he tore down its fence, threw over its watch towers, left it unworked, and restrained his clouds from bringing down rain upon it" (Is. 5:1-6).

Concerning the false prophets, he said, "Woe unto those who build Zion in deceit, and Jerusalem in iniquity" (Hab. 2:12; Micah 3:10). He further said concerning them, "From the prophets of Jerusalem has gone forth pollution into all the land" (Jer. 23:15).

v. Peoples Called in Place of People

Concerning the vocation of the peoples Isaiah said, "It shall come to be in the last days that the mountain of the House of the Lord will be established at the head of the mountains and high above the heights. Peoples will come together to it, and many peoples will go and say, Come, let us go up to the mountain of the Lord, to the House of the God of Jacob. He will teach us his ways, and we shall walk in his paths. [864] For from Zion the law will go forth, and the word of the Lord from Jerusalem" (Is. 2:2, 3). Now when the law went forth from Zion, where did it go? He said, "He will judge between peoples and will chastise many nations who are at a distance" (Is. 2:4). Concerning them [the Jews] Isaiah said, "Separate (365) from them, and call them unclean, for the Lord has rejected them" (Is. 52:11; Lam. 4:15; Jer. 6:30). Again the prophet said, "Their goodness is rejected like a piece of tattered cloth which the moth has eaten" (Micah 7:4, 17). Further he said, "They are enraged by their ways, and by the Lord our God they are terrified and frightened" (Micah 7:17). Again he said, "I shall burn with smoke your gathering places, and your young lions the sword will consume" (Nahum 2:13). Again he said, "Woe unto the city of blood, which is entirely filled with lying, in which destruction is not attended" (Nahum 3:1). Micah [sic] said, "Judah has lied, and pollution has been done in Israel and in Jerusalem, for Judah has polluted the sanctity of the Lord" (Malachi 2:11). He said, "You have turned away from the way and have caused many to stumble from the law, and you have corrupted the covenant of Levi. I also have made you contemptible and humiliated among every people, because you did not keep my ways" (Malachi 2:8, 9). Concerning the peoples he said, "I shall turn to them a chosen lip" (Zeph. 3:9). Concerning them [the Jews] Malachi said, "You have wearied the Lord with your words" (Malachi 2:17). [865] Again he said, "You, children of Jacob, have not passed from your evil, and from the days of your fathers you have not kept my commandments" (Malachi 3:6, 7).

vi. Israel's Redemption in the Past, Not Future

XIX-6. Now hear, my beloved: Two times only did God save Israel: Once from Egypt, the second time from Babylonia; from Egypt by Moses, and from Babylonia by Ezra and by the prophecy of Haggai and

Zechariah. Haggai (366) said, "Build this house, and I shall have pleasure in it, and in it I shall be glorified, says the Lord" (Hag. 1:8). Again he said, "Act, for I am with you, and my spirit endures among you. Do not fear, for thus says the Lord almighty: One more time shall I shake the heaven and the earth, the sea and the dry land, and I shall shake all the peoples, and they will bring the treasure of all the peoples and will fill this house with glory. The latter glory of this house will be greater than the former" (Hag. 2:5-8, 10). All of these things were said in the days of Zerubbabel, Haggai, and Zechariah. They were exhorting concerning the building of the house.

Zechariah said, "I have turned to Jerusalem in mercy, and my house do I set in its midst" (Zech. 1:17). Again he said, "Cities will be emptied of goods. The Lord will build Zion and choose Jerusalem again" (Zech. 1:17). Again he said, "I am jealous for Zion [868] and for Jerusalem with great jealousy. I am angry with great wrath against the peoples who are in commotion" (Zech. 1:14-15). Again he said, "In great estates will Jerusalem dwell, with the multitude of men and beasts which are in its midst, and I shall be in it like a wall of copper, and for glory will I be in its midst, says the Lord" (Zech. 2:4, 5). Again he said, "O, O, flee from the land of the North, says the Lord, for to the four winds of heaven have I scattered you. O Zion, escape, [you who] dwell with the daughter of Babylonia" (Zech. 2:6, 7). Again he said, "The Lord will inherit Judah as his portion on (367) his holy land, and he will again take pleasure in Jerusalem" (Zech. 2:12). Again he said, "The hands of Zerubbabel laid the foundations of this house, and *his* hands are going to complete it" (Zech. 4:9). All these things did Zechariah prophesy, and with the gathering of Israel from Babylonia they were fulfilled and completed. It is *not* as they say, that Israel is still destined to be gathered together.

XIX-7. Hear then, my beloved, I shall show you that Israel was saved two times, once from Egypt, the second time from Babylonia. Isaiah said, "The Lord will stretch his hand a second time to acquire the remnant of his people that remains in the land of Assyria, Egypt, Tyre, Sidon, Hamath, and from the distant islands" (Is. 11:11). Now if they were destined to be [869] gathered together and redeemed, why did Isaiah say that the Lord would stretch out his hand a *second* time and acquire the remnant of his people that remained? If there were still [to be] salvation for them, Isaiah should have said, "God will stretch out his hand a *third* time to possess the remnant of his people," and not say a *second* time.

VII. Daniel's Vision and its Meaning

XIX-8. Further hear and I shall instruct you concerning the prayer which Daniel prayed before his God, pled and made supplication concerning the children of his people so that they might be brought back and return from Babylonia. Daniel was the beloved man, to whom the hidden things were revealed and the last thing made known, for he was a prophet, building upon the words of the prophets. When his people was exiled to Babylonia, there arose among them false prophets who were prophesying in deceit (368) and lying, saying, "Thus says the Lord: After two years I shall break the yoke of Nebuchadnezzar, the king of Babylonia, from off the neck of all the peoples" (Jer. 28:11). Then, when Jeremiah had heard the prophecy of the false prophets, he wrote a letter and sent it to Babylonia: "Do not listen to the false prophets who are among you, who promise you, saying, After two years you will return from Babylonia. For thus says the Lord: Build houses and dwell [in them], plant vineyards and eat [872] their fruit. Acquire for your sons wives, and your daughters give to husbands. For after seventy years are completed for Babylonia, then will you return from there" (Jer. 29:8, 5, 6, 10).

Daniel, who was cloaked in the spirit, knew that the prophecy of Jeremiah was true. When the seventy years were completed, then he prayed, pled and supplicated before God: "In the first year of Darius the son of Ahasuerus, of the seed of the Medes, who reigned over the kingdom of the Chaldaeans, in the first year of his rule, I, Daniel perceived in the book, in the number of the years, and I saw that thus was the word of the Lord, which Jeremiah the prophet said when the seventy years will have been completed from the destruction of Jerusalem. I [then] raised up my face before the Lord God to beseech in prayer, supplication, fast, sack cloth and ashes. I prayed before the Lord my God, and I confessed and said in supplication: Lord God, great and revered, keeping the covenant and the blessing (369) for those whom he loves, for those who keep his commandments: We have sinned, we have done evil, we have transgressed, we have rebelled, we have turned away from your commandments and from your laws. We did not listen to your servants, the prophets who spoke in your name concerning our kings, princes, fathers, and all of the people of the land.

[873] "Yours, O Lord, is the victory, but ours is confusion of face, as it is this day for the men of Judah, for the inhabitants of Jerusalem and for all Israel which are near and which are far, in all of the lands where you have

scattered them on account of their evil, for they have rebelled against you, O Lord. Shame belongs to us, to our kings, princes, and fathers, for we have sinned against you. Mercies and forgiveness of sins belong to the Lord God, for we have rebelled against him and have not hearkened to the voice of the Lord our God, to walk in his law, which he set before us through his servants, the prophets. All Israel have transgressed your law and turned aside, and they have not hearkened to your voice. So you brought upon them the curses and plagues which are written in the law of Moses, the servant of God. Because we sinned before him, he has carried out his words which he spoke against us and against our judges who judged, by bringing upon us the great evil, the like of which was never done under the heavens as was done in Jerusalem, as written in the law of Moses, 'All this evil which has come upon us' (Deut. 28:15, 31:17, 29).

"We did not pray before the Lord our God to repent of our sins and confess your faith. So the Lord aroused evil and brought it upon us, for the Lord our God is righteous in all [876] his deeds which he has done, for we did not hearken to his voice. (370) Now Lord our God, who brought your people out of the land of Egypt by a mighty hand and high arm and made for yourself a name as of this very day: We have sinned and done evil, O Lord. According to all your righteousness which you have done with us, turn aside your anger from your city, Jerusalem, and from your holy mountain, for on account of the sins and the evil of our fathers your people has been scattered in every place. Jerusalem has become a shame before all the peoples. Now, hear, O God, the prayer of your servant and our supplication, and shine the light of your face on your sanctuary which has been destroyed. For your name's sake, O Lord, turn your ear, O my God, and listen. Open your eyes, and see our destructions and our desolations and the city upon which your name is called. It is not upon our righteousness that we trust and pray before you, but upon your many mercies. Lord, hear. Lord, have mercy upon us. Lord, take notice. Do and do not tarry, because of your name, O my God, because your name is called upon your city and upon your people" (Dan. 9:1-19).

XIX-9. When Daniel had completed his prayer, he said, "While I was praying, confessing my sins and the sins of my people Israel, and was presenting my supplication before the Lord my God [877] concerning the holy mountain of my God, while I was speaking in prayer, the man Gabriel, whom I had seen at the first, flew, fluttered, came down from heaven, and drew near me at the time of the evening offering. He came, spoke with me, and said to me: Daniel, now I have come forth to teach you so that you may know. At the beginning of your prayer, the word went forth, and I have come to instruct you (371) because you are beloved. Consider the word, and understand the vision. Seventy weeks will press heavily [4] upon your people and upon your holy city, to fulfill the debts, to finish the sins, to forgive iniquity, to bring righteousness which is of eternity, and to fulfill the vision and the prophets, until the Messiah, the Holy of Holies. Know and be informed: From the going forth of the word to restore and rebuild Jerusalem until the coming of the Messiah, the King, [are] seven weeks and sixty-two weeks. He will restore and build Jerusalem, its markets and palaces, at the completion of time. After sixty-two weeks, the Messiah will be killed, and shall have nothing,[5] and the Holy City will be destroyed with the king that is coming. Its end shall come with an overwhelming flood, and to the end there will be wars, for desolations have been decreed.[6] And he shall strengthen the covenant for many for one week and for half a week, and he shall abolish sacrifice [880] and offerings, and upon wings of pollution he will make desolation" (Dan. 9:20-27).[7]

XIX-10. Behold then, my beloved, and consider the prayer which Daniel prayed and the vision which was laid before him. At the completion of seventy years of the destruction of Jerusalem, he prayed and confessed, in the first year of Darius. When he had confessed his sins and the sins of his people Israel, then Gabriel, who receives prayers, came and said to him, "At the beginning of your prayer a word has gone forth." The word which was at the beginning of his prayer is this: The exile will return from Babylonia. Again Daniel gave thought (372) to what should happen to the people after its return. Then Gabriel said to him, Because you are beloved, I shall show you what shall happen to your people at the end of days. Now look into the word and understand the vision. Seventy weeks will press upon your people and upon your holy city to make recompense for the transgressions, to finish the sins, to forgive iniquity, to bring righteousness which is eternal, and to fulfill the vision and the prophecies, until the Messiah, the Holy of Holies. Know and understand that after the going forth of the word to restore and build Jerusalem until the coming of the Messiah, the king, [are] seven weeks and sixty-two weeks. He will restore [881] and rebuild Jerusalem, its marketplaces and

---

[4] *nttnyḥwn* = Parisot: immorabuntur; Bert: wird . . . Ruhe sein; RSV: Seventy weeks of years are decreed concerning your people and your holy city, to finish the transgression. . .

[5] Parisot: et non erit ei. MT: ואין לו

[6] So RSV. Parisot: et usque ad finem in vastatione, et usque ad finem belli sententiae desolationis.

[7] Parisot: . . . et super extrema abominationis vastatio. It seems to me Aphrahat has translated the passage following the MT more or less closely.

palaces, at the fulfillment of time. After sixty-two weeks the Messiah will be killed, and he shall have nothing, and the Holy City will be destroyed with the king who is coming. Its end shall come with an overwhelming flood and to the end shall be war, for desolation has been decreed. He shall strengthen the covenant for many for one week and half of a week. He will annul sacrifice and offerings. Upon wings of pollution he will make desolation.

XIX-11. He said to him, "Seventy weeks will press upon your people and upon your Holy City." The seventy weeks are the four hundred ninety years from the time that Daniel prayed until Jerusalem was destroyed in its final destruction and again will not be resettled. He said, "For seven weeks he will restore and build Jerusalem," for, when the exile went forth through Ezra and began building the house, from the days of Cyrus and Darius they laid the foundations of the house. But their enemies prevented them (373) in the days of Darius, Artaxerxes, and other Persian kings. So they did not let them build and complete [it].

I shall show you the implications of the word. Thus it is written in Zechariah the prophet, "I saw the candelabrum and seven lamps were on it with seven [884] mouths on each of the lamps" (Zech. 4:2). The forty-nine which are there are the seven weeks. Then he said in this same prophecy, "This is the word of the Lord concerning Zerubbabel: Not by power and not by might, but by spirit" (Zech. 4:6). And earlier he said, "The hands of Zerubbabel have laid the foundations of this house, and *his* hands are going to complete it" (Zech. 4:9). Now all the days, from the day on which the foundations of the house were laid until the building of the house was completed, were forty-nine years. These are seven weeks out of the seventy.

The vision of the candelabrum of seven lamps and their forty-nine mouths and this word of the Lord which was concerning Zerubbabel — these are forty-nine years. After these seven weeks of the building of the Temple which was in the days of Zerubbabel, then Jerusalem was inhabited sixty-two weeks, that is, four hundred and thirty-four years. Why did he say earlier, "Seventy weeks of years shall press upon your people and upon your Holy City," and later on, "They had seven and sixty-two" which are altogether sixty-nine? But later he said, "A week and half a week he will abolish sacrifice (371) and offerings." This is one [885] week of the seventy in which the sacrifice ceased. Thus it was reckoned concerning them as those seventy years in which they dwelt in Babylonia, during which the land had rest in its captivity, all the days of its desolation.

Now understand that after these weeks, the Messiah came and was killed in fulfillment of the vision and the prophets. Jacob our father also said when he blessed Judah, "The staff will not move from Judah, and the legislator from between his feet, until there shall come one who possesses dominion" (Gen. 49:10). Understand, my beloved, and perceive, that the weeks were fulfilled; the visions and the prophets have ceased. Sovereignty has been cut off from Judah. Lo, Jerusalem is destroyed, and its people is scattered among every people. The children of Israel dwell without sacrifices and without an altar. Until the completion of the things which have been decided, Jerusalem is desolate and remains in its desolation. The vineyard has been destroyed and brings forth thorns (Is. 5:2, 5). The fire has consumed its two branches (Ez. 15:4). The fence of the vineyard is thrown down, its watch tower is overthrown, and its winepress has been destroyed. The silver is rejected and is of no use (Jer. 6:30). A writ of divorce is written for Jerusalem (Jer. 3:8).

Now this brief exposition which I have written for you is so that you may respond when [888] it is necessary to give an answer, and so that you may strengthen the mind of whoever listens [to you], so that he will not be deceived by their seditious arguments. They will not accept persuasion, (375) for the Scripture has imprisoned them [8], so they will not hearken and be persuaded that God will have mercy for all men. He said concerning them, "This people honors me with their lips, but their heart is far from me" (Is. 29:13). They say to Jeremiah, "To the word which you have spoken to us in the name of the Lord we shall not hearken" (Jer. 44:16).

XIX-13. Concerning these visions of Daniel, beloved, as best as I could, I have written to you. But you should know that after Gabriel explained to him what would happen to his people, then, "in the third year of Cyrus, the word was revealed to Daniel, saying, The word is true, and with great power he had understanding of the vision" (Dan. 11:1). And he said, "I was sitting in mourning for three weeks. I did not eat desirable bread, nor did meat or wine enter my mouth" (Dan. 10:2-3). See, in the third year of Cyrus Daniel saw this vision, on the twenty-fourth day of the first month, that is Nisan, two years after he [Cyrus] had caused the word to pass through his kingdom that the exile should return [889] to Jerusalem.

In the first year of Darius the son of Ahasuerus he prayed before God, and [it was] at the completion of seventy years, in fulfillment of the words of Jeremiah, and, as matters make clear, it was the first year of the reign of Darius the Mede. When he had killed Belteshazzar, he ruled in his place.

---

[8] *dḥbš 'nwn ktb'*

A little while he exercised dominion, and [then] Cyrus the Persian received it. Now why did Darius receive dominion first? But it was, as the matter appears to us, so as to fulfill (876) the vision which Daniel explained to Belteshazzar, saying to him, "This is the interpretation of the word and the reading of what is written: MENE TEQEL and PARSIN. MENE: God has numbered the days of your dominion and given it [to another]. TEQEL: You have been weighed in the balance and have been found wanting. PERES: Your kingdom has been divided and given to Medea and to Persia" (Dan. 5:25-28). On this account Darius earlier arose to dominion, so that the vision might be fulfilled. After him Cyrus the Persian received it, at the completion of the seventy years, at the time that Daniel prayed that the captivity might be restored through him [Cyrus], just as Isaiah prophesied concerning him: "He will build my city and send forth my captivity" (Is. 45:13). That same Cyrus said, "God has given us dominion over the earth and commanded me to build [892] for him a house in Jerusalem which is in Judah" (Ezra 1:2).

See that the fast of Daniel after his prayer was for this: He fasted because for seventy weeks Jerusalem would be inhabited, and afterward it would be destroyed and would remain in destruction forever, until the completion of the things which have been decided.

The demonstration against the Jews is completed.

CHAPTER TEN

DEMONSTRATION XXI

ON PERSECUTION

Summary: Gentiles and Jews reproach the Christians who are being persecuted. They say that if the Christians had a God, he would save them and exact vengeance from their enemies. The Jews recall that faith is supposed to move mountains, yet cannot save the Christians. In truth, the Jews hope for the restoration of Zion, but like Sodom and Gomorrah, destroyed of old and never rebuilt, so Jerusalem will never be rebuilt. Furthermore, the Jews were persecuted, and many years passed before they were delivered. The truth of the matter is that those who were persecuted were superior to their persecutors and enjoyed divine favor. Even more, the persecutions of heroes of old prefigure those of Jesus and thus also of his followers. These heroes include Joseph, Moses, Joshua the son of Nun, Jephthah, David, Elijah, Elisha, Hezekiah, Josiah, Daniel, Hananiah and his brothers, Mordecai, the Maccabees. Jesus is the model for the martyr, and he in turn is modeled on the martyrdom of the heroes of Israel of old.

I. Judaic Critique of Persecuted Christians

[932] (394) XXI-1. I have heard a reproach which has greatly troubled me, for the unclean [men] say, This people which is gathered together from all the peoples has no God. Thus say the evil [men], If they had a God, why does he not exact the vengeance of his people? Darkness still more thickens upon me when even the Jews reproach us and magnify themselves over the children of our people.

It happened that one day a man who is called "the sage of the Jews" met me, and asked, saying, Jesus who was called your teacher has written to you "If there shall be in you faith like one seed of mustard, you will say to this mountain, 'move,' and it will move from before you; and [you may say] even, 'be lifted up,' and it will fall into the sea, for it will obey you" (Matthew 17:19; 21:22). Thus [he continued] there is not [to be found] among your entire people one wise man, whose prayer is listened to, who seeks from God that [933] your persecutions should cease from you. Thus it is written to you in the word, "There is nothing which you will be unable to do" (Matthew 17:19).

XXI-2. When I saw that he was blaspheming and talking much against the [Christian] way, (395) my mind was disturbed, for I knew that he would not accept the explanation of the words he was quoting to me. Then I also questioned him concerning words from the law and the prophets. I said, You thus hope, that even though you are scattered, God is with you. He agreed with me: God is with us, for thus God said to Israel, "Even in the lands of your enemies I have not abandoned them [var.: you], and my covenant which is with them [var.: you] has not been annulled" (Lev. 26:44). Again I said to him, Very good is that which I hear from you, that God is with you. Against your words I also shall say [something] to you. Isaiah the prophet said to Israel [speaking] as from the mouth of his God, "If you pass through the sea, I am with you, and rivers will not overflow you. And if you walk in fire, you will not be burned, and the flame will not scorch you, for the Lord your God is with you" (Is. 43:2-3). Thus there is not a single man who is righteous, good, and wise among your entire people, who may pass through the sea and not be drowned [936], [or pass through] a river but it would overflow him. Let him walk on fire, and let us see whether he would not be scorched, or whether the flame would not burn him. Now if you should bring me an explanation, I shall not be persuaded by you, just as you will not accept from me the explanation of the words concerning which you questioned me.

II. ISRAEL AND SODOM

XXI-3. I further questioned him concerning another passage written in Ezekiel, which he said to Jerusalem: "Sodom and her daughters (396) will be built up as of old, and you and your daughters will be as of old" (Ez. 16:55). Now explain to me this word. He began to respond, saying to me, This is what God said through the prophet to Jerusalem: "Sodom and her daughters shall be rebuilt as of old, and you and your daughters shall be as of old." This is the force of the expression: Sodom and her daughters will be in their place as of old and shall be subjugated by Israel, and Jerusalem and her daughters will be in the splendor of dominion as of old.

When I heard from him this defense, he was very contemptible in my eyes, and I said to him, When the words of the prophets are spoken in anger, is the entire expression of wrath, or perhaps part is of wrath and part is of grace? He said, A wrathful passage is altogether wrath, and there is no peace in it. Then I said [937] to him, Now that you have instructed me that there is no peace in that wrathful passage, hear without contention and without blaspheming, and I shall explain to you concerning this word. From the beginning [of the passage] to the end, the entire Scripture was spoken in wrath. He said to Jerusalem, "As I live, says the Lord God, Sodom and her daughters did not do as you and your daughters have done" (Ez. 16:48). He said to her, "Be ashamed and receive your ignominy, for you have overcome your sisters in your sins, and they are more righteous [justified] than you" (Ez. 16:52). Now that (397) he said that Sodom and her daughters are more righteous than Jerusalem and her daughters, and Jerusalem has overcome Sodom in her sins, it is right that when Israel will be gathered together, its settlement should be in Sodom and Gomorrah, for "Their vine is of the vine of Sodom and their planting is of Gomorrah, their grapes are bitter and their clusters are bitter for them" (Deut. 32:31). Isaiah also called them "rulers of Sodom and people of Gomorrah" (Is. 1:10). If, then, Israel will be gathered together, it is appropriate that they should dwell in Sodom and Gomorrah with the rulers of Sodom and the people of Gomorrah, on the vine of Sodom and the planting of Gomorrah, and that they should eat the bitter grapes and gather clusters [940] of gall, eat the eggs of the basilisk and clothe themselves with spider webs (Is. 59:5), should be used with the thorns of the vineyard (Is. 5:2), and should be turned into rejected silver (Jer. 6:30). Sodom and her daughters which were more righteous than Jerusalem should be rebuilt as of old, and Jerusalem which vanquished Sodom in her sins should continue in her sins and will remain desolate "until the completion of the things which have been decided, forever" (Dan. 9:27).

XXI-4. Ezekiel said, "This is the iniquity of Sodom and her daughters, that they did not take by the hand the needy and the poor, and when I saw these things among them, I overthrew them" (Ez. 16:49). Now reckon and see that from the time that Sodom was overturned until Jerusalem was built, (398) there were eight-hundred and ninety-six years. From the time that Abraham was informed by God through the angel, "This time next year I shall return to you, and Sarah your wife shall have a son" (Gen. 18:14), from that time until Jacob went down to Egypt were one hundred and ninety-one years [Wright: two hundred and four]. The children of Israel were in Egypt two hundred and twenty-five years. All the years from the conception of Isaac and the overthrow of Sodom were four hundred and sixteen years [Wright: four hundred and nineteen]. From the exodus of Israel from Egypt [941] until the building in Jerusalem of the great building by Solomon and the building of the Temple were four hundred and eighty years. Now all of the years from the conception of Isaac and the overthrow of Sodom until the great building in Jerusalem were eight hundred and ninety-six years. From the great building in Jerusalem until the destruction of Jerusalem were four hundred and twenty-five years.

III. Sodom and Israel Will Never Be Rebuilt

The sum of all the years from the overthrow of Sodom to the destruction of Jerusalem is one thousand three hundred twenty-one years. These are all the years that Sodom and her daughters were destroyed before [the destruction of] Jerusalem. She that was more righteous than Jerusalem has not yet been resettled.

Now the entire reckoning of the years from the overthrow of Sodom until the six hund ed (399) and fifty-fifth year of the kingdom of Alexander the son of Phillip of Macedon [= 344 A.D.] is two thousand, two hundred and seventy-six years.

From the time that Jerusalem was destroyed by the Babylonians until this time are nine hundred and fifty-five years. Jerusalem was inhabited after the Babylonians destroyed it these seventy weeks concerning which Daniel gave testimony. Then it was laid waste in the last destruction by the Romans, and again [944] it will not be inhabited forever, for it remains "in desolation until the completion of the things which have been decided" (Dan. 9:7). But all of the years of the destruction of Jerusalem, both the former and the latter [years] are four hundred and sixty-five years, and when you deduct from them the seventy years of the Babylonian exile, they are three hundred and ninety-five years.

XXI-5. I have written to you this whole argument, because the Jews take pride: "We are destined to be gathered together." Now if Sodom, whose iniquity was not so much as that of Jerusalem, has not yet been resettled, and if we say thus, that it will *never* be resettled, Jerusalem whose iniquity was greater than that of Sodom and her daughters, how will it [ever] be resettled? As for Sodom, for two thousand two hundred and seventy-six years God has not had mercy on it. Shall we say that he will have mercy on Jerusalem? Up to the present time it is three hundred and ninety-five (400) years since it was destroyed, according to that calculation which is written above.

But now with reference to this fact, that he said, "Sodom and her daughters shall be established as of old," and that he said to Jerusalem, "You and your daughters shall be as of old" — this is the force of the expression: They [both] shall *never* more be inhabited. For the Lord has thus [945] cursed that land with which he was angry: "It shall not be sown and shall not produce, nor shall any herb spring up in it, but it shall be like Sodom and Gomorrah against which the Lord was wrathful and towards which he was not appeased" (Deut. 29:33).

Now be persuaded, O hearer, that Sodom and her daughters will never be resettled, but will be as of old, [that is] as [they were at] that time before which they were settled, and as the time that the Lord was angry against them and would not be appeased towards them. Jerusalem and her daughters will be as of old, as at the former time that the mountain of the Amorites lay in desolation, on which Abraham built the altar, binding Isaac his son upon it; and as it lay desolate when David bought the threshing-floor from Araunah the Jebusite and built there an altar. Now understand and see that that mountain on which Abraham offered up his son is the very same mountain of the Jebusite, and that is Jerusalem. This place of the threshing-floor which David bought from Araunah is that upon which the Temple was built. Thus Jerusalem shall be in desolation as of old. Understand that when Ezekiel prophesied this word, Jerusalem was still established in its greatness, and those who were in her were rebelling against the king of Babylonia. The word (401) which the prophet spoke, in wrath and in shame did he speak [it] against Jerusalem.

[948] XXI-6. [Now] consider and see, O hearer, that if God had given hope to Sodom and her companions, he would not have overturned them in fire and in brimstone, the sign of the last day of the world. But he would have given them over into the hands of one of the kingdoms to be chastised, as it is written that when Jeremiah caused the peoples and the nations to drink the cup of wrath, he said concerning each one of the states, "After they shall drink the cup, I shall turn back the captivity of Elam, Tyre, Sidon, the children of Ammon, Moab, and Edom" (Jer. 25:15-27; 48:47; 49:6, 39). Concerning each one of these kingdoms he said, "At the end of days I shall restore her captivity" (Jer. 48:47, 49:6, 39). We see that Tyre was inhabited and was opulant after she had wandered for seventy years, and had received the reward of her harlotries, and after she had committed prostitution with all the kingdoms. She took the harp, played it well, and sang many songs (Is. 23:15-16). The country of Elam also was settled and opulant. Concerning Babylonia Jeremiah said, "Babylonia shall fall and not rise" (Jer. 51:64). Lo, until our times and even forever it will remain desolate. Also concerning Jerusalem he said, "The virgin of Israel will fall and not continue to rise. She is left upon the ground [949] and there is none to raise her up" (Amos 5:1-2). Now if this prophesy is true (402) which Jeremiah spoke concerning Babylonia, also the one concerning Jerusalem is true and faithful. Isaiah said to Jerusalem, "I shall no longer be angry against you, and I shall not rebuke you" (Is. 54:9). It is quite true that he will no longer be angry against her, nor will he ever again rebuke her, for that which is in desolation he does not reprove, nor will she enrage him.

IV. ISRAEL WAS ALSO PERSECUTED

XXI-7. Now concerning those who reproach us: You are persecuted, but you are not delivered, — let them be ashamed of themselves, for at every period *they* were persecuted, and for many years they were not redeemed. They were subjugated in Egypt two hundred and twenty-five years. The Midianites subjugated Israel in the days of Barak and Deborah. The Moabites ruled over them in the days of Ehud, the Ammonites in the days of Jephthah, the Philistines in the days of Samson, also in the days of Eli and Samuel the prophet, the Edomites in the days of Ahab, the Assyrians in the days of Hezekiah, and the king of Babylonia uprooted them from their place and scattered them. After he had greatly tried and persecuted them, they did not improve, as he said to them, "In vain have I smitten your sons, but they did not take correction" (Jer. 2:30). Again he said, "I have cut off the prophets, and I have killed [952] them with the word of my mouth" (Hos. 6:5). To Jerusalem he said, "By afflictions and by plagues be instructed, O Jerusalem, lest my soul depart from you" (Jer. 6:8). But they abandoned him and worshipped idols, as Jeremiah said concerning them, "Go to the distant islands, and to Kedar send. Consider well, and see if (403) there has been such a thing as this: Have the peoples changed their gods, which are no gods, but my people has changed its glory for that which is of no value. Be astonished, O heavens, about this, quake and greatly fear, says the Lord. Two evil things have my people done: They have abandoned me, the source of living waters, and have gone and dug for themselves pits, broken pits which are unable to hold water" (Jer. 2:10-13). The "broken pits" are the fear of images and idols. It is heaven which is to be astonished at them, for they worshipped the hosts of the heavens, and the heavens received a penalty, to be rolled-up as a scroll "and all the hosts of them will fall down" (Is. 34:4).

XXI-8. This entire word above I have written to you, my beloved, because a Jewish man reproached the children of our people. Now as best as I am able, I shall instruct you about those who are persecuted, that they [953] received a good reward, but the persecutors came into scorn and contempt.

V. HEROES OF ISRAEL WERE PERSECUTED

XXI-9. Jacob was persecuted, and Esau was the persecutor. Jacob received the blessings and the birthright, but Esau was rejected of both. Joseph was persecuted, and his brothers were persecutors. Joseph was raised up, and those who persecuted him worshipped him, and his dreams and visions were fulfilled.

Joseph who was persecuted was the likeness of Jesus who was persecuted. Joseph's father clothed him in a cloak of many colors [Parisot: tunica fimbriata] and Jesus' father clothed him in a body from a virgin. Joseph's father loved him (404) more than his brothers, and Jesus was the beloved and precious one of his father. Joseph saw visions and dreamed dreams, and Jesus fulfilled visions and prophets. Joseph was a shepherd with his brothers, and Jesus is the chief of shepherds. When Joseph's father sent him to visit his brothers, they saw that he was coming and took council together to kill him; and when Jesus' father sent him to visit his brothers, they said, "Here is the heir. Come, let us kill him" (Matthew 21:38). Joseph's brothers threw him down into a pit, and Jesus' brothers cast him into the abode of the dead. Joseph ascended from the pit, and Jesus arose from the abode of the dead. [956] After Joseph arose from the pit, he ruled over his brothers, and after Jesus arose from among the dead, his father gave him a great and honored name, so that his brothers should serve him, and so that his enemies should be placed under his feet.

When Joseph made himself known to his brothers, they were ashamed, feared, and were amazed at his majesty; and when Jesus will come at the end of time so that he will be revealed in his majesty, his brothers who had earlier crucified him will be ashamed, will fear, and be dismayed. By the council of Judah, Joseph was sold into Egypt, and by the hands of Judah Iscariot, Jesus was given over to the Jews. When they sold Joseph, he did not say anything to his brothers, and Jesus did not speak or say anything to the judges who judged him. Joseph's master wrongfully delivered him to the prison, and the children of his people wrongfully condemned Jesus. Joseph gave up his two garments, one into the hands of his brothers, and one into the hands of the wife of his master; and Jesus gave up his garments, and the soldiers divided them among themselves. Joseph at the age (405) of thirty years arose before Pharaoh and was the lord of Egypt, and Jesus at about thirty years came to the Jordan, was baptised, received the spirit, and went forth to preach. Joseph sustained [957] the Egyptians with bread, and Jesus sustained the entire world with the bread of life. Joseph married the daughter of the evil and unclean priest, and Jesus drew near to himself the church from the unclean peoples. Joseph died and was buried in Egypt, and Jesus died and was buried in Jerusalem. Joseph's brothers brought forth his bones from Egypt, and Jesus' father brought him up from among the dead, and raised up his body with him to the heavens uncorrupted.

VI. JESUS THE ARCHETYPE OF THE PERSECUTED

XXI-10. Moses was persecuted, and Jesus was persecuted. When Moses was born, they concealed him so that he would not be killed by his persecutors. When Jesus was born, they fled with him to Egypt, so that Herod his persecutor would not kill him. In the days when Moses was born, they would drown children in the river, and at the nativity of Jesus the children of Bethlehem and its borders were killed. To Moses God said, "The men who are seeking your life have died" (Ex. 4:19); and to Joseph the angel said in Egypt, "Rise, take the child and go to the land of Israel, for those who seek to take the life of the child have died" (Matthew 2:20).

Moses brought forth his people from the bondage of Pharaoh, and Jesus redeemed all the peoples from the bondage of Satan. Moses [960] was raised in the house of Pharaoh, and Jesus was raised in Egypt when Joseph fled with him there. Miriam stood at the edge of the river when Moses floated in the water, (406) and Miriam bore Jesus after the angel Gabriel had informed her. When Moses sacrificed the lamb, the first-born of the Egyptians were killed, and when they crucified Jesus, the true lamb, in killing him the people who killed him died. Moses brought down manna for his people, and Jesus gave his body to the peoples. Moses sweetened the bitter waters by the wood, and Jesus sweetened our bitterness by his cross, with the wood of his crucifixion. Moses brought down the law to his people, and Jesus gave his testaments to the peoples. Moses conquered Amalek by spreading out his hand, and Jesus conquered Satan by the sign of his cross. Moses brought forth water from the rock for his people, and Jesus sent Simon the Rock to carry his doctrine among the peoples. Moses removed the veil from his face, and God spoke with him. Jesus removed the veil from the faces of the peoples, so that they might hear and receive his doctrine. Moses placed his hand upon his messengers, and they received the priesthood, and Jesus laid his hand upon his messengers, and they received the Holy Spirit. Moses went forth to the mountain [961] and died there, and Jesus went up to heaven and sits at the right hand of his father.

VII. JESUS, JOSHUA AND OTHER HEROES ALL PERSECUTED

XXI-10. Jesus [Yeshu'] the son of Nun was persecuted, and Jesus [Yeshu'] our redeemer was persecuted. Jesus the son of Nun was persecuted by the unclean peoples, and Jesus our redeemer was persecuted by the foolish people. Jesus the son of Nun took the inheritance from those who had persecuted him and gave it to his people, and Jesus our redeemer took the inheritance from those who had persecuted him and gave it to the alien peoples. Jesus the son of Nun caused the sun to stand [still] in the heaven and took vengeance on the peoples that had persecuted him, and Jesus our redeemer (407) caused the sun to set in the middle of the day so the people that had persecuted and crucified him might be ashamed. Jesus the son of Nun divided the inheritance for his people, and Jesus our redeemer promised to give to the peoples the land of the living. Jesus the son of Nun saved Rahab the prostitute, and Jesus our redeemer brought near and saved [lit.: resurrected] the church [which had been polluted by] prostitution [of idolatry]. Jesus the son of Nun on the seventh day overthrew and cast down the walls of Jericho, and Jesus our redeemer on the seventh day, on the Sabbath of the rest of God — this world will be dissolved and fall. Jesus the son of Nun stoned Achan who stole from the *ḥerem*, and Jesus our redeemer threw out Judah from among his disciple-companions [1] because he stole from the money of the poor. When Jesus the son of Nun [964] was dying, he set up a witness for his people, and when Jesus our redeemer was taken up, he set up a witness for his messengers.

XXI-12. Jephthah also was persecuted, and Jesus was persecuted. The brothers of Jephthah drove him out of his father's house, and the brothers of Jesus drove him out, raised him up, and crucified him. Jephthah who was persecuted arose as the head of his people, and Jesus who was persecuted rose and was the king of the peoples. Jephthah vowed a vow and offered up his first-born daughter as a sacrifice, and Jesus went up[= was offered]as a sacrifice to his father in behalf of all the peoples.

XXI-13. David also was persecuted, and Jesus was persecuted. David was anointed by Samuel to be king instead of Saul, who had sinned, and Jesus was anointed by John to be high priest instead of the priests, who had transgressed the law. David was persecuted after he was anointed, and Jesus was persecuted after he was anointed. David reigned first over one tribe only and afterward over all Israel; and Jesus reigned first over the few who believed (408) in him, but in the end he will reign over the entire world. Samuel anointed David when he was thirty years old, [965]

---

[1] *Tlmyd' ḥbrwhy*

and Jesus received from John the laying on of the hand when he was about thirty years old. David married two daughters of the king, and Jesus married two daughters of kings, the congregation of the people, and the congregation of the peoples. David repaid good to Saul his enemy, and Jesus taught, "Pray for your enemies" (Luke 6:28). David [was] the heart of God, and Jesus [was] the son of God, David received the kingdom of Saul who had persecuted him, and Jesus received the kingdom of Israel that had persecuted him. David wept in mourning for his enemy Saul when he died, and Jesus wept for Jerusalem which had persecuted him, because it was destined to be destroyed. David gave over the kingdom to Solomon and was gathered to his people, and Jesus gave over the keys to Simon and went up, going to the one who had sent him. For the sake of David the sins of his descendents are forgiven, and for the sake of Jesus the sins of the peoples are forgiven.

XXI-14. Elijah also was persecuted, and Jesus was persecuted. Jezebel the murderess persecuted Elijah, and the persecuting and murdering congregation persecuted Jesus. Elijah closed up the heavens from [giving] rain because of the sins of Israel, and Jesus in his coming withheld the spirit from the prophets because of the sins of the people. [968] Elijah destroyed the servants of Baal, and Jesus trampled Satan and his hosts. Elijah resurrected the son of the widow, and Jesus resurrected the son of the widow with Leazar and the daughter of the ruler of the synagogue. Elijah fed the widow with a little bread, and Jesus satisfied thousands (409) with a little bread. Elijah was taken up in a chariot to heaven, and our redeemer went up and [now] sits at the right hand of his father. Elisha received the spirit of Elijah, and Jesus blew [Parisot: inspiravit] in the faces of his messengers.

XXI-15. Elisha also was persecuted, and Jesus was persecuted. Elisha was persecuted by the son of Ahab, the son of the murderess, and Jesus was persecuted by the murdering people. Elisha prophesied, and there was abundance in Samaria, and Jesus said, "Whoever eats from my body and drinks from my blood will live forever" (John 6:55). Elisha satisfied one hundred men with a little bread, and Jesus satisfied four thousand, besides women and children, with five loaves. Elisha made oil out of water, and Jesus made wine out of water. Elisha redeemed the widow from her creditor, and Jesus redeemed peoples that were indebted. Elisha floated iron and sank wood, and Jesus [969] raised up that which was sunk in us and sank that which was light in us. One dead man recovered life upon the bones of Elisha, and all the nations who were dying in their sins were cast upon the bones of Jesus and lived.

XXI-16. Hezekiah also was persecuted, and Jesus was persecuted. Hezekiah was persecuted and shamed by Sennacherib his enemy, and Jesus was shamed by the foolish people. Hezekiah prayed and conquered his enemy, and our enemy was conquered by the crucifixion of Jesus. Hezekiah [was] the king of all Israel, and Jesus [was] the king of all the peoples. Because Hezekiah was sick, the sun turned backward, (410) and because Jesus suffered the sun was darkened of its light. The enemies of Hezekiah became dead bodies, and the enemies of Jesus shall be prostrate beneath his feet. Hezekiah [was] of the family of the house of David, and Jesus [was] the son of David in the flesh. Hezekiah said, "Peace and truth shall be in my days" (II Kings 20:19), and Jesus said to his disciples, "My peace I leave for you" (John 14:27). Hezekiah prayed and was healed of his ailment, and Jesus prayed and arose from the abode of the dead. After Hezekiah arose from his ailment, his years were prolonged, [972] and after Jesus' resurrection, he received great glory. After the prolonging of Hezekiah's life, death ruled over him, but after Jesus arose, death no longer rules over him forever.

XXI-17. Josiah also was persecuted, and Jesus was persecuted. Josiah was persecuted and Pharaoh the lame killed him, and Jesus was persecuted, and the people made lame by their sins killed him. Josiah purified the land of Israel from uncleanness, and Jesus purified and caused uncleanness to pass away from all the earth. Josiah honored and praised the name of his God, and Jesus said, "I have glorified and will glorify" (John 12:28). Because of the iniquity of Israel Josiah rent his garments (II Kings 22:11, 13), and because of the iniquity of the people Jesus rent the veil of the holy Temple. Josiah said, "Great is the wrath that is coming upon this people" (II Kings 22:13), and Jesus said, "Wrath will come upon this people, and they shall fall by the mouth of the sword" (Luke 21:23-24). Josiah removed uncleanness from (411) the holy Temple, and Jesus removed the unclean traders from the house of his father. For Josiah the daughters of Israel mourned and wailed, as Jeremiah said, "O daughters of Israel weep for Josiah" (II Chron. 35:25), and over Jesus the daughters of Israel cried and mourned, as Zechariah said, "The land will mourn, families for families" (Zech. 12:12).

[973] XXI-18. Daniel also was persecuted, and Jesus was persecuted. Daniel was persecuted by the Chaldeans, the congregation of evil men, and the Jews, the congregation of iniquitous men, persecuted Jesus. The Chaldeans accused Daniel, and the Jews accused Jesus before the governor. They cast Daniel into the pit of the lions, but he was saved and arose uninjured from its midst; and they sent Jesus down into the pit of

the abode of the dead, but he went up, and death did not rule over him. Concerning Daniel they hoped that, when he had fallen into the pit, he would not again come up, and concerning Jesus they said, "Now that he has fallen, he will no longer continue to rise" (Ps. 41:8). By Daniel the mouth of the ravenous and destructive lions was closed, and by Jesus the mouth of ravenous death, which destroys forms, was closed. They sealed the pit of Daniel and guarded it diligently, and they guarded the grave of Jesus diligently, as they said, "Set guards up to watch at the tomb" (Matthew 27:64). When Daniel went up, his accusers were confounded, and when Jesus arose, all of those who had crucified him were confounded. The king who judged Daniel was much grieved by the iniquity of the Chaldean accusers, and Pilate the judge of Jesus was greatly grieved, for he knew that in iniquity the Jews were accusing [976] him (Matthew 28:18).

Through the prayer of Daniel, the captivity (412) of his people went up from Babylonia, and Jesus prayed and restored the captivity of all the peoples. Daniel interpreted the visions and dreams of Nebuchadnezzar, and Jesus interpreted and explained the visions of revelation [2] and the prophets. When Daniel interpreted the vision of Belteshazzar, he received authority over a third of the kingdom, and when Jesus fulfilled visions and prophets, his father gave him all dominion which is in heaven and on earth. Daniel saw wonders and spoke secrets, and Jesus revealed secrets and fulfilled that which was written. Daniel was led away among the captives on behalf of his people, and the body of Jesus [was] a captive in behalf of all the peoples. On account of Daniel the wrath of the king was appeased from the Chaldeans so that they were not killed, and on account of Jesus the wrath of his father was appeased from all of the peoples, and they were not killed and did not die from their sins. Daniel asked of the king, and he gave his brothers authority over the affairs of the province of Babylonia (Dan. 2:49), and Jesus asked of God, and he gave his brothers, his disciples, authority over Satan and his host. Daniel said concerning Jerusalem that until the things which have been decided, it will remain in desolation, and Jesus said concerning Jerusalem, "There shall not remain in it [977] stone on stone, because she did not know the day of her greatness" (Luke 19:34). Daniel saw the weeks which should remain over his people, and Jesus came and fulfilled them.

XXI-19. Hananiah and his brothers also were persecuted, and Jesus was persecuted. Hananiah and his brothers were persecuted by

---

[2] 'wryt'

Nebuchadnezzar, and (413) the Jewish people persecuted Jesus. Hananiah and his brothers fell into the furnace of fire, and it became cold like dew upon the righteous; and Jesus descended into the place of darkness, broke its gates, and brought forth its prisoners. Hananiah and his brothers came forth from the furnace of fire, and flame burned those who had accused them; and Jesus lived and went up from the midst of the darkness, and the people who had accused and crucified him will be burned in the flame at the end. When Hananiah and his brothers went up from the furnace, Nebuchadnezzar the king trembled and was astonished, and when Jesus arose from the abode of the dead, the people that had crucified him trembled and were astonished. Hananiah and his brothers did not worship the image of the king of Babylonia, and Jesus restrained the peoples from the worship of dead idols. Because of Hananiah and his brothers peoples and languages praised God who had saved them from the fire, and because of Jesus the peoples and all languages praise the one who had delivered his son[980] so he did not see corruption. The fire did not hold sway over the clothing of Hananiah and his brothers, and over the bodies of all of the righteous who believed in Jesus the fire at the end will bear no sway.

XXI-20. Mordecai also was persecuted, and Jesus was persecuted. Mordecai was persecuted by the wicked Haman, and Jesus was persecuted by the rebellious people. By his prayer Mordecai saved his people from the hands of Haman, and by his prayer Jesus saved his people from the hands of Satan. Mordecai was rescued from the hands of the one who had persecuted him, and Jesus was saved from the hands of those who had persecuted him. Because Mordecai had sat and dressed in sack-cloth, he saved Esther and his people from destruction; and because (414) Jesus clothed himself in a body and was humiliated, he saved the church and her children from death. Because of Mordecai Esther pleased the king, went in, and sat in the place of Vashti, who did not do his will; and because of Jesus the church pleased God and has gone in to the king instead of the congregation which did not do his will. Mordecai commanded Esther and her maidens to fast, so that she and her people might be saved from the hands of Haman, and Jesus commanded the church and her children that she and her children might be saved from wrath. Mordecai received the honor of Haman who had persecuted him [981], and Jesus received great glory from his father in place of those who had persecuted him, who were of the foolish people. Mordecai trod on the neck of Haman who had persecuted him, and the enemies of Jesus will be placed under his feet. Before Mordecai Haman proclaimed, "Thus will be done to the man whom the king wishes to honor" (Esther 6:11), and as for Jesus, his preachers came out from the people that had persecuted him and said, "This is Jesus, the son of God" (Matthew 27:54). The blood of Mordecai was required at the hand of Haman and his sons, and his persecutors received the blood of Jesus upon themselves and upon their children (Matthew 27:25).

VIII. PERSECUTED CHRISTIANS LIKE CHRIST HIMSELF

XXI-21. I have written to you these memorials, my beloved, concerning Jesus who was persecuted and the righteous who were persecuted, so that those who are persecuted today may be comforted, those who are persecuted on account of Jesus who was persecuted. He himself wrote to us to encourage us saying, "If they persecute me, they will persecute you. And on this account they will persecute you, for you are not of this world, just as I am not of it" (John 15:20, 19; 17:14). For beforehand (415) he wrote to us, "Your fathers, brothers, and families will betray you, and every man will hate you because of my own name" (Luke 21:16-17). Again he taught us, "When [984] they will bring you before rulers and magistrates, before kings who possess the world, do not give thought in advance concerning what you will speak, or how you will reply, for I shall give you a mouth and wisdom, so that your enemies will not be able to vanquish you, for it is not you who are speaking, but the Holy Spirit of your father speaks in you" (Matthew 5:19, 20; Luke 11:11; 21:14, 15).

This is the spirit which spoke in the mouth of Jacob with Esau his persecutor; and the spirit of wisdom which spoke before Pharaoh in the mouth of Joseph who was persecuted; and the spirit which spoke in the mouth of Moses in all of the miracles which he did in the land of Egypt; and the spirit of knowledge which was given to Joshua the son of Nun when Moses placed his hand upon him, so that the peoples which had persecuted him completely perished from before him; and the spirit which sang in the mouth of David who was persecuted, by which he sang and soothed Saul his persecutor from the evil spirit; and the spirit which clothed Elijah and through him reproved Jezebel and Ahab who persecuted him; and the spirit which spoke in Elisha and prophesied and made known to the king who persecuted him the thing which was to take place afterward; and the spirit which burned in the mouth of Micaiah when he reproved Ahab, who persecuted him, and said to him, [985] "If you shall actually turn back, (416) the Lord has not spoken by me" (I

Kings 22:28); the spirit which strengthened Jeremiah so that he boldly stood and reproved Zedekiah by it; the spirit which guarded Daniel and his brothers in the land of Babylonia; and the spirit which saved Mordecai and Esther in the place of their captivity.

XXI-22. Hear, my beloved, these names of martyrs, of confessors, and of those who were persecuted. Abel was killed, and his blood groaned from the earth. Jacob was persecuted and fled and was an exile. Joseph was persecuted, was sold, and fell into the pit. Moses was persecuted and fled to Midian. Joshua the son of Nun was persecuted and made war. Jephthah, Samson, Gideon, Barak — these also were persecuted, these are the ones concerning whom the blessed apostle said, "Time is too little for me to relate their victories" (Heb. 11:32).

David also was persecuted by Saul and wandered in mountains, caves, and dens. Samuel also was persecuted and mourned over Saul. Hezekiah also was persecuted and bound up in affliction. Elijah was persecuted and wandered in the desert. Elisha was persecuted and was an exile. Micaiah was persecuted and was imprisoned. Jeremiah was persecuted, and they threw him into the pit of mud. [988] Daniel was persecuted and was cast into the pit of lions. Hananiah and his brothers also were persecuted and fell into the furnace of fire. Mordecai, Esther, and the children of their people (417) were persecuted by Haman. Judah Maccabee and his brothers also were persecuted and endured reproach. Seven brothers, the sons of the blessed woman, in bitter torments endured scourgings and were true confessors and martyrs. Eleazar, though old and advanced in years, set a good example, made his confession, and became a complete martyr.

XXI-23. Great and excellent is the testimony [= martyrdom] of Jesus. He outdid in affliction and confession all of those who came before and afterward. After him was the faithful witness, Stephen, whom the Jews stoned. Also Simon and Paul were complete witnesses. Jacob [James] and Yohannan [John] walked in the path of their master, the Messiah. Also some of the messengers [apostles] in various places confessed and went forth true witnesses. Also to our brothers in the west in the days of Diocletian came great trouble and persecution to the entire church of God which was in all of their regions. Churches were overthrown and uprooted, [989] and many made confession and were witnesses. He returned to them in mercy after they were persecuted. Also in our own days these things have taken place, even on account of our sins, but also so that what is written might be fulfilled, as our redeemer said, "These things are to be" (Matthew 24:6; Luke 21:9). The apostle also (418) said,

.

"Also over us is set this cloud of confession" (Heb. 11:1), which is our honor, in which many confess and are killed.

The demonstration on persecution is completed.

CHAPTER ELEVEN

DEMONSTRATION XXIII

ON THE GRAPECLUSTER
[Excerpts]

The theme of the rejection of Israel and its replacement by the gentiles recurs in Demonstration XXIII, in the figure of the blessed grapecluster (Is. 65:8): "Thus says the Lord: As the wine is found in the cluster, and they say, Do not destroy it, for there is a blessing in it, so I will do for my servants' sake and not destroy them all." The history of the blessing and of the curse of Adam is as old as humanity. Here Aphrahat rehearses that history and brings it to its conclusion in the Messiah.

I. History of the Blessing

[40, line 4](462) XXIII-13 . . . Thus we have heard the word which the prophet proclaimed, saying to the people, "Just as a grapecluster is found on a twig, and a man says to his fellow, Do not destroy the twig because the blessing is on it, [so] he says, Thus I shall do on account of my chosen ones, and I shall not destroy all of them, but I shall bring forth seed from Jacob and from Judah, the inheritor of my holy mountain" (Is. 65:8-9). The *branch* is the people of Israel, and the *blessing* which was in it is the king, the Messiah.

XXIII-14. From the beginning this grapecluster was preserved in Adam, the first-born. But when he also sinned, the seed of the righteous was taken from him (463), and the blessing was preserved in Seth and in all his generations. When all flesh corrupted its way on the earth, the blessing was preserved in the quiet man, in Noah, who was found righteous and innocent in the perverse generation. The blessing was preserved in the ark of wood, and all the evil-doers perished in the anger which was poured out, when the grapecluster was taken away and withdrawn from them.

Noah and his sons went out from the ark, and the blessing was preserved in Shem, the [41] father of righteous men. The spirit declared through the mouth of the quiet man when he blessed his sons after the flood, saying, "God will increase Japheth, and he will dwell in the tabernacle of Shem" (Gen. 9:27). He cursed Canaan, the seed of Ham, who had despoiled his father, and he was cut off from the blessing. This blessing descended in the ten generations from Noah until Abraham. He [Noah] lived after the flood three hundred and fifty years, and he fathered a multitude of sons and daughters in his days. And when they reached Babylonia, the land of the Chaldeans, there God confused the languages of all the earth. Noah remained in Ur of the Chaldees, as he dwelt and guarded the blessing of the righteous after the flood two hundred and ninety-two years.

XXIII-15. Abraham was born in Ur of the Chaldees, in the eight hundred and ninety-second year of Noah, long after languages were confused. (464) When Noah was nine hundred and fifty years old, he completed his time and died in good old age, in the fifty-eighth year of the life of Abraham. Noah died in Ur of the Chaldees. Then Abraham went forth from Ur of the Chaldees [44], and entered and dwelt in Haran a short time. From Haran God moved him to the land of Canaan, the son of Ham of the cursed seed, upon whom subjugation was decreed. When Abraham was one hundred years old, in the four hundred and ninety-second year of the life of Shem, father of righteous men, then Isaac was born. Shem lived after Isaac was born one hundred and twelve years. Isaac fathered Jacob and Esau at the age of sixty years. Shem lived after Jacob and Esau were born for sixty-two years. Abraham died at the age of one hundred and seventy-five years, and Shem lived after the death of Abraham for thirty-seven years. Isaac was one hundred and thirty-seven years old when he blessed Jacob, his son, in whom the blessing of the righteous was hidden.

Jacob was seventy-seven years old when he fled to Haran, and at the age of eight-four years he married Leah and Rachael. At the end of one hundred and twelve years of the life of Isaac, Shem died, in the fifty-second year of the life of Jacob. When Jacob was ninety-seven years old, God said to him, "Return to the land of your fathers, [45] and I shall do good to you, and I shall be with you." Jacob was ninety-seven years old when he returned from (465) Haran. Isaac his father was one hundred and fifty-seven years old, and Isaac lived after Jacob returned from Haran for twenty-three years. In the forty-third year of his blessing, the twenty-third year after he [Jacob] returned from Haran, he [Isaac] died, at the age of one hundred and eighty years.

Then Jacob went down into Egypt, twenty years after his father had died, twenty-two years after Joseph his son was sold into Egypt, sixty-eight years after the death of Shem. Jacob was in Egypt seventeen years, and he died at the age of one hundred and forty-seven years, fifty years after he came back from Haran, twenty-seven years after Isaac his father died.

When Jacob died Joseph was fifty-six years old, and the blessing was preserved in Judah, the son of Jacob, before he went to Egypt. Judah fathered Perez. When Jacob and Judah went down to Egypt, this blessing was hidden in the loin of Perez. And Perez fathered Hezron, and Hezron fathered Aram, and Aram fathered Aminadab, and Aminadab fathered Nachshon, the head of the children of Judah.

[48] XXIII-16. After Aminadab it [the blessing] resided in Eliezar the son of Aaron the priest, from whom was born Phineas. From Aminadab the blessing of the sovereignty and of the priesthood went forth. Leadership and kingship were from Nachshon, and priesthead was from the son of the sister of Nachshon, who gave birth to Phineas, who assuaged the wrath of God when he was angry. From Nachshon was born Sela. Sela gave birth to Boaz. (466) From Boaz went forth the leadership of kings through Boaz and Ruth the Moabite. On this account, Boaz married Ruth the Moabite, so that Lot might be a partner in the blessing of the righteous. And from the son of Ruth was born the family of the house of David. From their seed was born the king Messiah. God did not reject the hospitality of Lot, the son of Abraham's brother, who went forth with him from Haran, and because he hospitably received strangers like Abraham his uncle, God gave him a portion in the blessing of the righteous through Ruth the Moabite, whom Boaz married. God further remembered Lot by the hand of Naama the Ammonite, whom Solomon married, and who gave birth to Rehoboam the king. Solomon married many wives, seven hundred free women and three hundred concubines. It is not written that from one thousand wives he had seed, except Rehoboam from Naama the Ammonite, [49] whom he had married during the life of David his father; for when Solomon rose to the monarchy, Rehoboam was a year old. Solomon ruled forty years, and when Solomon died, Rehoboam ruled, at the age of forty-one.

XXIII-17. Lot took part in the blessing of the righteous through Ruth the Moabite and Naama the Ammonite, from the two tribes which were from him. Boaz fathered Obed, and Obed fathered Jesse, and Jesse fathered David. This blessing was preserved among all of the kings of the house of Judah (467) from David until Jehoiachin, among eighteen kings. David sinned, but through the blessing which was hidden in him, he was forgiven his iniquity. Solomon transgressed the law and abandoned his God, but because of the blessing which was hidden in him and in his seed God said, "I shall make him great all of his life" (I Kings 11:34). Rehoboam greatly multiplied foolishness, but because of the blessing which was in him God said, "I shall not tear away the entire kingdom from him, but I shall give to him a lamp in Jerusalem on account of David my servant" (I Kings 11:36). Abijah the son of Rehoboam sinned, but because of the blessing which was in him Jeroboam [52] and his entire army were given into his hand. In Asa the blessing of the righteous was fervent, and he did righteousness. God listened to his prayer, and his enemies were given into his hands.

The blessing was preserved in Jehoshaphat, and he did that which was right before the Lord. Jehoram multiplied in sinning, but because of the blessing, he was preserved. He sinned, but he was not blotted out like the house of Ahab, although he was a son-in-law of the house of Ahab. Athalia the daughter of Omri the king of Israel, missed him.

The grapecluster was preserved in Joash the son of Ahaziah, and he was not killed with his brothers when Athaliah wiped out the seed of the royal house, when she saw that Ahaziah her son was killed by Jehu the son of Nimshi [Parisot's text: Yamshi]. Jehoash sinned and shed innocent blood, and he ignored the blessing of Jehoiada the priest and wiped out his seed after him. Because of (468) the blessing his seed was preserved. Amaziah arose and governed the monarchy, and he sinned with idols, worshipping other, foreign gods. Because of the blessing his seed was preserved. Uzziah arose after him and rebelled against the priesthood and did not listen to it. The Holy One punished him with the plague of leprosy all of his days. Jotham arose in the monarchy and sinned very much, but [53] because of the blessing his seed was saved. Ahaz arose to the throne and greatly sinned, worshipping dead gods, saying, "You are my gods and lords, and to you I bow down." But because of the blessing his seed was preserved. Hezekiah, the righteous king, arose over all of Judah in Jerusalem. He prayed and supplicated before God. His prayer was hearkened, and he destroyed his enemies. The blessing of the righteous which was in him served splendidly. He was sick and prayed, and he was healed from his infirmity.

XXIII-18. Now there are people, my b 'loved, who bring calumny against Hezekiah. Why was he made infirm in his illness so that he died, although he had done great righteousness before his God? And what benefit came to him in this addition [to his life], for a blemish was placed on him in addition [-al years], for he took pride in his riches before the messengers of the king of Babylonia and did not praise the name of his God, who had healed him from his sickness? On this account Hezekiah the righteous king was given an infirmity: He did not yet have a son, and in his loins the blessing of the righteous was hidden. Thus he said (469) in his torment. "The blessing which has come down through all of the former generations [56] from Adam until me, through forty-six generations, [56] why does it not go forth from me and [why] is the grapecluster extinguished in me? Lo, is the branch now given over to destruction?"

When he had thought about these things and prayed most diligently, Isaiah the prophet came to him and said to him, "Thus says the Lord: Lo, I am adding on to your years. You will live fifteen more years" (II Kings 20:5-6). And he added on to his life fifteen years. Then, in the eighteenth year of his reign, in the third year of the additional [years], he fathered Manasseh. He ruled twenty-nine years, fourteen at first and fifteen afterwards, so the word of the Scripture was fulfilled: "The righteous add to their days, but the years of the wicked are diminished" (Prov. 10:27). The years of the generation of destruction that was in the time of Noah and of the sinning kingdom of the house of Ephraim were diminished, but he added to Hezekiah and also to Job. To Hezekiah he added fifteen years, and to Job he augmented years, possessions, and children. If a man will contend that Job did not receive increase in every thing, let him understand without dispute; for thus is it written, "God multiplied the last things of Job more than the first things" (Job 42:12-13). There were born to him seven sons and three daughters. [Aphrahat now proceeds to discuss the latter years of Job; col. 57, lines 1-16.]

[II, 57, line 17] (470, line 9). XXIII-19 Manassah, an evil son of a righteous man, was born and greatly sinned, more than all who had come before him. He came to the throne at the age of twelve and ruled fifty-five years. He greatly multiplied his sins and worshipped idols. Because of the blessing his seed was preserved, and he fathered Amon. Amon ruled and walked in the ways of Manassah, but because of the seed which was in him he governed the kingdom. From him was born [60] a righteous man, Josiah, of blessed memory. In the days of his rule he removed the pollution from the land of Israel. Because the sins of the people urged them on, he was gathered before the evil event, and it did not come upon the people in his days, as Hulda the prophetess prophesied, when he sent to her to ask the word, and she replied to him, "Thus says the Lord God of Israel: Because your heart was broken and you were sick on account of (471) the sins of the people when you heard the words of the law, lo, I am gathering you with your fathers, and you will not see the evil event which is coming on this people" (II Kings 22:18, 20). He was gathered in before the evil event, when Pharaoh the lame, the king of Egypt, killed him. Jehoahaz his son rose to the throne, but because the blessing was not in him, he was unworthy of the throne of the house of David. He ruled three months and afterward Pharaoh the lame, the king of Egypt, led him away. He died in Egypt, and his memory was blotted out. Jehoiakim ruled the kingdom, for in him the blessing of the righteous was hidden. In the third year of his reign Nebuchadnezzar conquered him as a tributary, and led away Daniel and his brethren into captivity [61]. He served Nebuchadnezzar for eight years, and when his sins multiplied and he rebelled, Nebuchadnezzar killed him. They threw him out and tossed him outside the gates of Jerusalem, and he was buried with the burial of an ass.

Jehoiachin his son ruled after him, and because the blessing of the righteous was hidden in him, he ruled three months. When he rebelled against the king of Babylonia, the army of the Chaldaeans came against him and exiled him, and he went to Babylonia. He was imprisoned for thirty-seven years in Babylonia, as the seed of the righteous was hidden in him.

The people in Jerusalem was abandoned on account of pollution. Zedekiah rose over the remnant of the people in the kingdom. Jehoiachin fathered Shealtiel in Babylonia.

(472) When the blessing was in Babylonia, the Babylonians ruled the kingdom in peace and serenity. When Shealtiel was born in the land of Babylonia, in him was hidden the blessing of the righteous. Shealtiel fathered Zerubbabel. Then, in the days of Zerubbabel, the exile returned from Babylonia through Ezra the scribe, during the reign of Cyrus the Persian. And Zerubbabel was the ruler of the people of the exile, as [64] the prophet said, "Zerubbabel the son of Shealtiel is the lord of Judah. And Joshua the son of Jehozadak was the high priest. . ." (Hag. 1:1).

XXIII-20. When the blessing returned from Babylonia to Jerusalem, the kingdom of the Babylonians came to the end, and Cyrus the Persian ruled. After sixty-three years the blessing returned from Babylonia to Jerusalem, from after the time Jehoiachin was exiled until the exile returned through Ezra.

Zerubbabel fathered Abiud. Abiud fathered Eliakim. Eliakim fathered Azor. Azor fathered Zadoq. Zadoq fathered Achim. Achim fathered Eliud. Eliud fathered Eleazar. Eleazar fathered Mathan. Mathan fathered Jacob. Jacob fathered Joseph. Joseph was called the father of Jesus the Messiah (Matthew 1:12-16).

Jesus the Messiah was born of Miriam, the virgin, of the seed of the house of David, from the Holy Spirit, as it is written, "Joseph and Miriam his bethrothed, the two of them were from the house of David" (Luke 2:4-5). The apostle testified, "Jesus (473) the Messiah was from Miriam, the seed of the house of David, by the Holy Spirit."

Joseph was called the father of Jesus, although he [Jesus] was not born of his [Joseph's] seed. But the name of fatherhood was handed down [65] from Adam to Joseph, for sixty-three generations. The name of fatherhood was taken from Joseph and placed upon the Messiah. From Joseph he received the name of fatherhood, from John, the name of priesthood, and from Miriam he acquired a body and received the name of one who was born. After sixty-two weeks the Messiah was born and was killed. The grape-cluster of the blessing was taken from the branch, and the entire branch was given over to destruction. The vineyard was so destroyed that it could no longer be worked, and brought forth thorns and bitter fruits. The twig was destroyed, and the leaf was eradicated.

[Parisot II, 40-65]

II. THE BLESSING AFTER JESUS

[92, line 17] (483, line 21). From Jesus the blessing descended to the house of the peoples. He said to the Jews, "The kingdom of God has been taken from you and has been given to the people that gives fruits" (Matthew 21:43). But to us he said, "I am with you until the completion of the world" (Matthew 28:20). Again he said, "You are in me, and I am in you" (John 14:20). The apostle testified, "If in any one of you the spirit is not present, then that one is not his" (Rom. 8:9). Again he said, "You are the temple [93] of God, and spirit of the Messiah dwells in you" (I Cor. 3:15). The prophet said, "I shall dwell among them, and I shall walk with them" (Lev. 26:12). And he himself encouraged us not to fear the trials which are coming upon us, for he said to us, "If they listen to my word and keep it, then also yours will they keep. If they persecute me, they will also persecute you" (John 15:20). He said to us, "You are not of the world, just as I am not of it" (John 15:19). He said, "If you were of the world, then the world would love its own" (John 15:19). Since we have received these commandments from Jesus our lifegiver, we are not able to walk outside of the ways in which he walked. If the Messiah was persecuted, also us; if the Messiah they hated, also us; if the Messiah they imprisoned, also us; if the Messiah they smote on his cheek, also us; if the Messiah suffered, also [will] we [93 line 17].

[Parisot II, 92 line 17 — 93 line 17]

II

STUDIES

CHAPTER TWELVE

APHRAHAT ON JUDAISM

I. INTRODUCTION

The Demonstrations pertinent to Judaism are divided into two groups, first, those in which Aphrahat provides the simple Christians with an apology against the critique of Christianity coming from Jews, second, Aphrahat's critique of Judaism. The unifying theme of both groups is that God has rejected the Jews and called in their place the "people which is of the peoples," the Christian church. Everything else derives from this basic principle.

The Jews' critique as represented by Aphrahat is composed of some rather superficial, limited observations of everyday Christian realities. What did Aphrahat's Jews know about Christianity? They held against Christians the facts that they worshipped Christ, that many were monks and nuns, and that Christians were persecuted, the three worldly aspects of Christian life. The Jewish critique does not reveal very profound knowledge of Christian biblical interpretation, liturgy, theology, or piety. The whole Jewish argument amounts to some rather invidious remarks about the most obvious aspects of Mesopotamian Christianity.

The Christian critique of Judaism, though better represented, was not much more profound. The things in which Jews took pride—circumcision, Sabbath, dietary laws— and the Jews' vivid expectation of being restored to the land of Israel by the Messiah in time to come would have been known to all Christians who had any contact at all with Jews, and to some who knew only antecedent patristic writings on Judaism. Circumcision was a dominant issue in first-century theology, hence would have intruded in any Christian discussion of, or with, Judaism. The Sabbath came weekly and radically altered the Jews' pattern of life for that day. The dietary laws, like circumcision, were brought to the Christians' attention in earlier theology, but also, like the Sabbath, were to be observed in everyday life. These "Jewish mysteries" were repeatedly mentioned in earlier anti-Judaic literature.

Still, the *sorts* of dietary laws Aphrahat noticed are strikingly limited: prohibition as "unclean" of some foods, particularly meat, and permission of others, that is, biblical, not rabbinic kashrut. The complex rabbinical interpretations and traditions of these laws, involving ritual slaughter, separation of meat from milk, and similar central observances, and the rabbinic vocabulary made no impact whatever on Aphrahat's consciousness. He would have been quick to refer to them, for example in his list of the "commandments which were not good," but that whole list (XV-8) consists of items anyone could have compiled from Scripture: sacrifice, purification rites, taboos against corpses, and the like. Indeed if one had read Scriptures but never known a Jew, he would have been able to list identical items.

The further reference to the difficulty of carrying out these "harsh" laws cannot have derived from everyday observation of Jewish life. The joy Jews took in the Sabbath, their optimistic messianic hope, and the rite of circumcision must have been known to Aphrahat, for he repeatedly remarked that Jews do take pride in them "but to no avail." On the other hand, he must have recognized that from the destruction of the Temple most of the items on the list of "bad commandments" no longer applied to the workaday world of ordinary Jews. Now it is possible, to be sure, that Jews in northern Mesopotamia (even those who were not kohanim) continued to observe taboos concerning corpses. But Aphrahat could not have known a Jew who had ever sacrificed in the cult, purified lepers, discharges, menstrual and childbirth impurity through Temple rites, or who had brought a sacrifice on account of sin. True, rabbinical Jews and perhaps others as well washed themselves on account of uncleannesses mentioned in Scripture and in Aphrahat's list. If Aphrahat had known such Jews, he would have had to observe that they did so contrary to the law: "The law required that these purifications be done in the Temple cult, not in a land which was unclean to begin with." He must have compared such Jews to the Pharisees of the New Testament who whitewashed the sepulchre while holding dead bones. His argument about the celebration of the Passover outside of Jerusalem certainly applied with equal, if not greater, force in this context. But he gave not the slightest hint that Jews he knew practiced these rites. I therefore conclude he knew none. His criticism of Judaism thus derived primarily from Scriptures, rather than from actual knowledge of Jewish neighbors. Earlier Christian writers on Judaism likewise debated chiefly with Scriptures and with Jews they imagined represented by them. Aphrahat did much the same.

Aphrahat indeed was provoked to present a critique of Judaism not by much, if anything, he observed in the Judaism of everyday life, but rather by the circumstance that numbers of Christians, both of Jewish origin and otherwise, were disturbed by the Judaic critique of Christianity, troubled by the Jews' assertion that they were the people of God, the heirs of the promises of Scripture and bearers of the grapecluster, and upset by the Jews' own immense joy and pride in their religious tradition. For this purpose it best served *not* to look too carefully at the ordinary life of Jews, but rather to direct the argument to Scriptures in order to prove on Scriptural foundations that by the Jews' *own* holy books Christianity is vindicated.

It is striking that while Aphrahat sometimes referred to Christian heresies and occasionally to other cults and religions, he devoted most of his remarks about outsiders to the Jewish problem. In this respect he resembles Justin more than any earlier Church Father. In my studies of rabbinical sayings pertinent to other religions and cults of various periods,[1] I found that rabbis had no interest in, and slight knowledge of, other religions besides Christianity. Mazdaeism, the religion of the state, elicited only a limited polemic.[2] On the other hand Babylonian rabbis paid considerable attention to the Christian problem and gave evidence of their concern about the conversion of Jews to Christianity. Likewise, from Aphrahat, the religion of the state, the cults of the Semitic peoples among whom the Christians lived and from whom they in considerable measure were drawn and the religious traditions of Mesopotamia and Babylonia drew passing attention at best. Judaism, by contrast, was an obsession. The relationship between the two Scriptural religions was unique, utterly different from the relationship of either one of them to any other contemporary religious tradition. Since the Iranian state then persecuted Christianity, it is striking that Aphrahat did not find it necessary to provide Christians with arguments to arm them for the disputations to which they were forcibly called by Mobads. He rarely offered proofs against the propositions of Mazdaeism, never explained to ordinary Christians why they should not be persuaded by the arguments of the Magi, why they should stand firm with Christ against Zoroaster. While Jews were merely another minority, Aphrahat had to strengthen the wavering faith of the flock against the attraction of Judaism and the destructive influence of the Jews' critique.

---

[1] Vol. I, second printing revised, pp. 94-103, 156-177; Vol. II, pp. 35-9, 52-64, 72-91; Vol. III, pp. 29-37; Vol. IV, pp. 56-66; Vol. V, pp. 19-29.

[2] I imagine XIII-10, God was not wearied by creating the world, was addressed chiefly to Mazdeans, not to Jews, who did not maintain the contrary. In Škand Gumanik Vičar (Vol. IV, pp. 403-423) that the Jews' (and Christians') God was weak and insufficient to creation is a crucial element in the Zoroastrian critique of Judaism. This is the only argument in the Demonstrations under study which was clearly addressed to Mazdaeism, so far as I can see.

Aphrahat thus gave evidence that Judaism engaged Christians more than did any cult or religion, even the one backed by the full power and prestige of the state. Its appeal to Jews in the church is obvious. Jewish converts would have been troubled by the continued Jewish expectation of a future messiah, by the Jews' confidence that they were chosen by God and would be redeemed by him, and by the appeal of those religious rites and habitual practices given up on adherence to the new faith. Such rites not only must have been earlier rooted in their own personal lives, but also were practiced everywhere around them. The new convert from the Jewish community could not have forgotten and was not able to ignore the Sabbath, festivals, dietary rules, and the like, and as soon as his wife produced a male child, he would have to face the crisis of conscience of whether to circumcise or baptise (or, more likely, do both). Above all, the Christian-Jew of Mesopotamia must have asked himself whether he had given up redemption in the future in exchange for a rather dubious salvation, for Christians were persecuted, while Jewry was not. Where indeed was their God? Perhaps the other Jews were right in maintaining the salvation had not yet come.

But the Christian drawn from the non-Jewish community — and I imagine Christians of gentile origin by now constituted the majority of the Mesopotamian and Babylonian church — would have had moments of doubt as well. In becoming a Christian, he entered not merely a personal salvific cult but a new community, a social entity with its own view of sacred history. This view of salvific history incorporated Scriptures shared with Jews, yet differently interpreted by them. Since Christianity not only taught the gentile to worship Christ and one God, but also introduced him to the Scriptures of the Jews, as Aphrahat said even of himself, it paradoxically served to prepare the gentile for Judaism. What, after all, did the Scriptures maintain? They spoke of the salvation of Israel, the covenant of circumcision, dietary laws, the sanctification of the Sabbath, the paschal sacrifice, and Israel's redemption. True, Christians understood these passages in their own way. But when he read Scriptures, what was to prevent the new Christian, familiar with Jews' views because he lived in close association with them, from accepting the interpretation not of the church but of the synagogue? Hence the primary difference between the Christian drawn from the synagogue and the one drawn from the fire-temple or the cult of the local gods was psychological: The ex-Jew had experienced the old being and known the vivid expectations of salvation inhering in it, and the ex-gentile had not. But, not burdened by a sense of guilt for having left the old covenant, the gentile Christian may have found it easy to continue his search for salvation on that very road that Christian baptism had opened to him — to Judaism. To be sure, external evidence of large-scale conversion of Christians to Judaism is lacking, but Aphrahat himself, born a gentile, and the thrust of his arguments against Judaism constitute for us the most striking evidence that the possibility of such conversion was ever-present.

Aphrahat therefore had to confront the Judaic challenge for three reasons. First, he wrote for a relatively new church-community, many of whose members could not have come from families Christian for more than three generations, and some of whom came from Judaism. Christianity in Babylonia, a church to which he addressed himself, was even more recent. The first catholicos was still alive when he wrote. Second, the Christians were living in close contact with Jews loyal to the old covenant in pretty much the formulation everyone knew from the Hebrew Scriptures. Third, to be Christian was a dangerous thing and would remain so for many centuries. That confrontation, as I said, did not demand detailed knowledge of current Judaic beliefs and practices. Since the argument was to begin with provoked by Scriptures held in common, the content of Scriptures, not everyday realities, defined both the structure of the argument and the way in which it would be carried on. The Christians' adherence to the "Old Testament" along with the New laid the foundations for the argument between Judaism and Christianity. If the "Old Testament" was regarded as "preparation for the Gospel," it was also true that the New Testament equally served as preparation for Judaism. Historical and social circumstances were propitious, for the two communities were more or less equal in size and prestige. Both were small and unimportant. Persecution was the lot of the one, peace of the other. It therefore is hardly surprising that the Christians had squarely to face the appeal of the Hebrew Scriptures as Jews understood them. Otherwise, Christianity would have fulfilled its mission not as the fulfillment of, but as the preparation for adherence to, Judaism.

II. APOLOGY AGAINST THE JUDAIC CRITIQUE

Aphrahat left little doubt that the Jewish critique of Christianity was not artificial or theoretical, but came from believing Jews in everyday contact with faithful Christians. His occasional animadversions to the "debater of the people", however, may well have been literary artifices, as in Justin and Celsus-Origen. The "debater of the people" need not have been a single individual and sometimes may have served as imaginary foil for the apologist. But I do not doubt that some stories of Jews Aphrahat met or heard about and of their critique of Christianity were founded on actual events and served no solely literary purpose. When Aphrahat said Christians doubted the value of celibacy and were upset about the Jews' assertion that they are to be saved in time to come and that they, not the Christians, are the people of God, we need not deny that these were facts of Christian life, not merely excuses to present contrary arguments. The weight of Aphrahat's demonstrations leads to the conclusion that vital dialogue, not merely theoretical, theological issues, elicited much of his concern, as it had for Paul, probably also Tertullian.

The "debater of the people" occurred, specifically, in XII-3, where Aphrahat used Deut. 32:21 to prove the Jews indeed have been outraged by the "people which is not a people" and said, "If I, a gentile, anger you, then you fulfill that very Scripture." This is a neat argument, and the "debater of the people" here served so conveniently as to raise doubt that a real encounter necessarily lay behind the reference. Further, in XV-5, the "wise debater of the people" was asked why Samson took honey from an unclean beast; the "lying scribe of the law" (XV-8) was challenged to prove that the commandments which were not good were not those concerning impurity. Aphrahat occasionally referred to the possibility of Jews' composing a reply, "And if they say . . . we reply . . ." (e.g. XVI-5). He thus did not have to address himself to a mythical character for the purposes of dialogue. Hence we have no reason to impute all such references to literary artifice. "Wise man, teacher of Israel" (XVII-9) was further asked to interpret Is. 9:6-7. His answer was not recorded, but a hypothetical argument was immediately thereafter introduced (XVII-9, "If you should say that the Messiah has not yet come . . ."). Then the "fool" of XVII-10 is certainly hypothetical: "But, O fool, the prophets have not permitted you to say that the Messiah has not yet come . . ."

The "debater of Israel" appeared in the argument about the blessing of procreation (XVIII-2), again (XVIII-4) about the celibacy of Moses, and (XVIII-7) about that of Joshua, Elijah, Elisha, and others. Immediately preceding, Aphrahat turned to "men who lack intelligence and hold this opinion," without imputing that opinion to anyone in particular. In the same demonstration (XVIII-12) Aphrahat referred to hearing from a Jew the accusation that Christians are unclean but Jews are holy, because Christians practice celibacy and Jews participate in the settlement of the world. The repeated references to Jewish opponents in the demonstration on celibacy indicate that this was a favorite theme for Jewish critics of Christianity, hence in Aphrahat's mind was closely tied with Jewish debaters. The most important references to the Jewish sage come in the demonstration on persecution. The occasion for the demonstration, like that for the one on celibacy, was hearing a Jew's "blaspheming." Aphrahat reported he himself took up the argument, proving, first (XXI-2), that the Christian concept of faith is not so gross as the Jews suggest; second (XXI-3, 4, 5), that the Jews' understanding of Ez. 16:55 is false. Sodom and Jerusalem are comparable because, just as the one was destroyed and never again rebuilt, so the other was destroyed and never again would be rebuilt.

We therefore see that the "debater of the people" was only occasionally mentioned; some, though not all, of the appearances suggest a real-life encounter. If so, we may reconstruct the occasion for argument(s) with little difficulty, for all the passages that seem to have been based upon actual events concerned a concrete and considerable Jewish criticism: celibacy first, persecution as well. Here the Jewish sage made telling points. The other references may or may not have come from a living opponent; but since these led Aphrahat to offer long and heated responses, I imagine they were based on real-life encounters.

That the Jewish sage (XXI-1) referred to the New Testament is not surprising. If he was engaged in disputation with Christians he would likely have learned something about Christian belief. What is astonishing is that he quoted accurately. Rabbinical references to Christian beliefs rarely, if ever, actually cited Christian Scriptures, but rather constituted a collection of nasty stories about what Christians do and about their master's magic, lasciviousness, and other bad traits. This sort of direct citation of Scripture for the purposes of disputation was characteristic not of the rabbinic, but of the Christian, party to the argument. Either the Jewish sage mentioned here derived from non-rabbinical circles, like the Jews described by Justin, Celsus, and Tertullian, or he was a figment of Aphrahat's imagination. In this instance, I presume the latter. Christians, not Jews, must have wondered why their faith, which should be able to move mountains, cannot move Mobads. But it was wise to attribute the doubt to a Jewish critic, rather than to publicize trouble at home.

The Jewish critique of Christianity consisted of four main elements. The first is that the Christians worship a man, not God; second, the Christians practice celibacy, which is contrary to nature and to divine law; third, the Christians are persecuted and their God does nothing to save them; finally, the Christians have not been called by God.

Christ

Jesus was foretold by the prophets and in every detail fulfilled their predictions. It was they who called him the son of God, "hence Jews have no grounds to criticize us in that regard" (I, 804-5).[3] Jews say the Messiah has not yet come, yet in every respect prophetic predictions have been realized. Indeed, "The peoples will hope for him" (Gen. 49:10) has been fulfilled through Aphrahat, "for before he came, I believed in him, and when he will come, he will not censure me on that account." Aphrahat thus interpreted some of the messianic passages in the future, at the time of the second coming. But in general he argued the prophets' promises of redemption were already carried out in the life and passion of Jesus.

The Jews accused the Christians of worshipping a man as son of God, although God has no son. But they knew that righteous men have been called God — Moses and Solomon, for instance. Furthermore, they themselves were called the sons of God. Hence there was nothing strange in regarding Jesus as the son of God. Furthermore the title of divinity was given to great men. Though God possessed all sovereignty, he likewise did not withhold the title "sovereign" from men. Even evil pagan kings were called sovereign, such as Nebuchadnezzar. Though God is father of all, he did not withhold the title "father" from men. Since God made man, it was not strange that Christians called a man "son of God." Indeed, Jews themselves paid respect to idolators, kings and other authorities, and were not censured on that account. They did not worship them as their Maker, but merely as authorities. But if so, how much more ought Christians to worship Jesus "through whom we know God"! Daniel paid worship to Nebuchadnezzar, Joseph to Pharaoh, "and we to God." Furthermore, Jesus was foretold by the prophets, and the story of his passion was adumbrated in Scriptures. None of these Scriptures was fulfilled in the ancient heroes of Israel, but only in Christ.

Aphrahat's arguments can only be called disingenuous. Christology in all its variety rarely, if ever, understood that Jesus was son of God in precisely the same way that other men were sons of God.[4] Ample Scriptural testimonies were available to prove much more than this, but Aphrahat ignored them. Christianity in every form began with the

---

[3] References are to volume and column in Parisot, *Patrologia Syriaca*.

[4] Compare, for example, Justin, *Dialogue with Trypho*, Chapter 100, (*Ante-Nicene Fathers* I, pp. 248-9).

assertion that Jesus was much more than merely a man. Why then did Aphrahat resort to such a curious argument? I imagine that in part the exigencies of real-life debate with Jews necessitated it. He could scarcely expect to persuade Jews that Jesus was called "son of God" in a sense other than the ordinary one. Had he done so, he at the outset would have conceded the correctness of their criticism that Christians worship a man as son of God and would have been left to argue what in the first place the Jews denied: Jesus really *was* Christ. Still, it is puzzling that it seemed to Aphrahat both legitimate and important to present such an argument to his Christian brethren. Is it possible that the Christology of Mesopotamian Christianity is here accurately represented? I doubt it. If not, then what we have is the Christology presented to new converts, particularly those from Judaism. Thus we find stress that there is nothing *alien* to scriptural Judaism in "our reverence for Jesus." Just as Israel was the son and first-born of God, so too was Jesus. Just as the Jews respect pagan kings, whom they do not worship as their maker, "so do we worship Jesus." Would Aphrahat have proceeded, "whom we do not worship as our maker"? Hardly. Rather, it is the consequent *qal veḥomer* that is important: How much the *more* so ought we to revere Jesus! Still, in the end Aphrahat reverts to the classical arguments drawn from prophetic Scriptures tested against the passion stories. Jesus was the Christ, not merely man, the son of God in a way in which no other was his son. The Jewish critique seems never to have alluded to the doctrine of the Trinity, the Virgin Birth, and similar matters. Aphrahat was not constrained to defend these beliefs. The reason must be sought in the theology of his church (see Ortiz de Urbina, *Die Gottheit Christi bei Afrahat*).

Celibacy

The Jews accused the Christians of unnatural living and violating the laws of God by preserving virginity and sanctity. But procreation by itself was no blessing. The generations after Adam were numerous, but were wiped out. Noah, on the other hand, did not marry, and since he feared lest his seed participate in the curse of Cain, he was accounted innocent and upright in his generation. Numbers alone meant nothing. God wanted not multitudes of men, but obedient men, however few. Indeed, the greatest heroes of ancient Israel were solitaries and celibates, just like the Christians today, their true heirs. Moses remained celibate from the time that God first spoke with him. Before then he had two sons. Afterward he had none. Israel was unable to receive the revelation of the

Torah until the people had sanctified themselves, refraining from sexual relations for three days. Even then they were unable to bear the theophany. "How much the more beloved and worthy of revelation are those who remain chaste and celibate all their days!"

Virginity was better than marriage. Priests were allowed to marry only virgins, not widows or divorcees. This proved that virginity is better than marriage. There were some, moreover, who would have been better left unborn, indeed whose parents would have done better had they not procreated: Zimri, Achan, Eli, and Samuel. Not only Moses, but many of the prophets were celibate. Joshua, Elijah, Elisha, Jeremiah, Ezekiel (by God's own doing) — none of them married.

"It is not that we reject marriage. Rather, we regard celibacy as superior to marriage. Some things are better than others, though God made all: sun than moon, light than darkness, Adam than Eve, and celibacy than marriage. The condition of virginity is better than the condition of marriage." After rain fell, the virgin earth brought forth thorns. Adam, Seth, Samson, David, Amnon, and Solomon were all better off when they were virgins; concupiscence was their ruination.

The meaning of Scripture confirms this. Scripture said that a man should leave his father and mother, and the truth is, before marriage a man loves his parents with a whole heart, but afterward he loves his wife. God is the father, the Holy Spirit the mother of whom Scripture speaks. The solitary is one in spirit with God the father.

The Scriptural argument is central, serving two important purposes. First, Aphrahat did have a considerable Scriptural case to make. Second, the Jews asserted that the Christians behave contrary to nature and the will of God, who explicitly told men to procreate. Christianity as Aphrahat interpreted it demanded that Christians live a celibate life. Like the demands of the rabbis upon ordinary Jews, this was expected not merely of a few religious virtuosi, but of as many Christians as could do it. Indeed, it represents the Christian equivalent of the rabbis' hope that all Jews would become students of Torah as they taught it and emulate the rabbinical way of life.

Aphrahat's argument thus was in three parts. First, he showed that numbers alone are of no great consequence. Second, and of preponderant interest, he demonstrated that Scripture itself approved of, indeed recommended, celibacy. Revelation could only be received by (temporary) celibates. The greatest heroes of ancient Israel were monks "just like ourselves." Third, in any case "we do not reject marriage, but merely regard celibacy as the better way of living." These arguments, unlike those on Christology, do not depend upon beliefs peculiar to Christians. They rather pointedly appeal to beliefs held by Jews and Christians alike. The Scriptural citations and interpretations all refer to the Hebrew Scriptures. Aphrahat made no effort to link passages in the Hebrew Scriptures to their fulfillment in Christ and his passion. That Jesus did not marry is not even mentioned in this context. On the contrary, Aphrahat's argument was from the plain meaning of Scriptures. Only one Scripture posed a practically insuperable problem: *Therefore a man should leave his parents and cleave to his woman.* Here alone was it necessary for Aphrahat to resort to the *midrash* taken from Ephes. 5:13. For the rest, the most potent Judaic critique was met with the least particular, singularly *Christian* arguments. Clearly, the argument was with Jews in the synagogue, not with converts in the church. The "debater of the people" presented living arguments; Aphrahat appropriately responded to the necessities of the dialogue.

Persecution

Both pagans and Jews regarded the persecution of Christians as evidence that they had no God, for if they did, he would assuredly have avenged their present plight. A Jewish sage quoted Matt. 17:19 about the puissance of faith. If faith supposedly can move mountains, why cannot Christian faith halt the persecutions? But Christian faith was no different from that expressed by Isaiah, who said that if you pass through the sea, "I am with you." If an Israelite today walked through the sea, he would be drowned. Further, Israel hoped to be redeemed, but the prophet compared her to Sodom; just as Sodom was destroyed and never again would be resettled, so has Jerusalem been destroyed and never again will it be resettled. Israel permanently and finally has been rejected.

But, more to the point, there was nothing shameful in being persecuted. In times past Israel was persecuted. The greatest heroes of Israel were persecuted, and their persecution prefigured that of Jesus. "We are persecuted because we follow him, and in our persecution we are no different from heroes of times past: Jacob, Joseph, Moses, Joshua, Jephthah, David, Elijah, Elisha, Hezekiah, Josiah, Daniel, Hananiah and his brothers, Mordecai, the Maccabees." The roster of the persecuted saints of olden times included Abel, Samuel, Micaiah, Jeremiah, the seven sons of Hannah in Maccabean times, and Eleazar. "Nor should we ignore the persecution of Our Lord, as well as of Simon Peter, Paul, Jacob [James] brother of the Lord, John, the suffering in the time of Diocletian.

Persecution comes on account of our sins, but in being persecuted, we are able to emulate Our Redeemer himself."

Aphrahat's defense was in three parts. First, he took the offensive by arguing that the Jews both will never be redeemed and also were persecuted. These assertions cannot have made much difference to Jews. They were to begin with directed to the Christian audience. Christians should not be impressed by the Jews' present prosperity. They too had faced persecution. What is worse, while Christians were redeemed and now look forward to the second coming, the Jews rejected true salvation and will have no other. The apology thus testified to the Christians' own doubts, more than to the Jews' arguments.

The second part of the apology would have carried more weight with a Jewish opponent. Persecution is nothing to be ashamed of. On the contrary no great hero of Israel's own past escaped persecution. To be sure, some of the things Aphrahat called "persecution" are not so represented in Scripture, but that does not matter. What is important is that facing a time of troubles is hardly proof of anything other than that "we have sinned." This argument would have been especially important to Christian Jews, who thereby could identify their current situation with the history of ancient Israel.

The third part was the moving comparison of current trials with those of Christ himself. To be persecuted is to participate in the life of Christ. The brief, possibly conventional admission that Christians are persecuted for their sins was not emphasized, let alone developed, for the argument that persecution is not shameful was hardly well-served by the admission that persecution comes on account of sin. Sin, after all, *is* something to be ashamed about. I imagine that Aphrahat included the reference only because elsewhere, not in the contest with Judaism, he made much of the sins of the church. In his long pastoral letter to Seleucia-Ctesiphon (Demonstration XIV) he accounted for current difficulties chiefly on the basis of the church's own failings. But here, as I said, such an argument was out of place, hence subordinated.

Vocation of Gentiles

Before Israel, gentiles were called through Abraham. But of old the gentiles worshipped idols. Israel, however, was rejected on account of its disobedience (I, 760ff.). When God saw that Israel would not listen to him, he turned to the gentiles, and this also was the pattern for the prophets, who spoke first to Israel, then to the gentiles. The rejection of Israel was symbolized by the rejection of its cult. The prophets repeatedly referred to the uselessness of Israelite cult. Therefore its destruction in 70 A.D. merely sealed the rejection of the people long before that date. Indeed, even from of old a good gentile such as Jethro was better than an Israelite. "A true Israelite is one who obeys God, not one who merely is born Israel-after-the-flesh."

The vocation of the gentiles played an important role in Aphrahat's critique of Judaism, for it was bound up with his allegation that Israel had been rejected. But for the purposes of the apology it remained necessary to register the claim that the Christians have *replaced* the Jews as the true Israel. That claim further depended upon the assertion that the gentiles also were called by God. Aphrahat indeed held that the gentiles were called before Israel, but because of idolatry did not listen. Hence Israel was chosen for a time. But the prophets reversed the pattern. They called to Israel, and, finding themselves rejected, consistently turned to the gentiles. For this argument Aphrahat found numerous proof-texts. Indeed practically every useful Scriptural reference to "nations" or "peoples" for Aphrahat became a reference to "the people which is of the peoples," namely the church which would come into being in the messianic time. These prooftexts were cited, but rarely, if ever, actually expounded in detail. They formed an elaborate, if shallow, line of defense.

Aphrahat's apology against the Judaic critique thus served the purpose not of disputation with Jews but rather of the defense of the faith of ordinary Christians. Several demonstrations "against the Jews" began with a reference to Christian concern for the Jewish critique. As I said, the two most telling criticisms were of celibacy and the Christians' current difficulties with the state. The replies normally depended upon Scripture, which suggests that the troubled Christians would be comforted to know that the Hebrew Scriptures supported the Christian argument. I imagine that in this setting, it was Christian Jews who would have been especially glad of that fact, though the Christian gentiles could not have been indifferent. For the purposes of defense, as we have already noted, Aphrahat's best device was offense. Hence the whole apology is brief and specific. The critique of Judaism is extensive, detailed, but generalized, as we shall now see.

III. Critique of Judaism

The two basic elements in Aphrahat's critique of Judaism were, first, that in general, the Jews have been rejected and are no longer the people of God; second, that in particular, the religious practices of Judaism do not now and never did lead to salvation. The rejection of Israel was time and again underlined in two ways. First, Israel had no hope in the future, for all the prophetic promises either have already been fulfilled for them in times past, or, if unfulfilled, pertained to the New Israel or to the (Christian) Messiah. Thus, for instance, Aphrahat argued that Israel has not received, and cannot receive, the heavenly kingdom (I, 224-5), and this he proved by the usual references to Jer. 6:30, Is. 52:11, and other recurring texts referring to the rejection of Israel.

In accord with antecedent conventions beginning in the New Testament, Aphrahat persistently spiritualized the concrete practices and assertions of Judaism. A true child of Abraham is one who obeys God, not one who is born of Israel. True circumcision is obedience to God, not a mark on the flesh. But Aphrahat went.much further. The vigor with which he argued against the salvific value of circumcision, the Sabbath, and the dietary laws strongly suggests that Jews whom he knew believed that God wanted them to do these very things, and that in doing them Israel attained merit and would achieve salvation. Aphrahat did not argue that good works as such are of no value. Indeed, his discussion of Christianity included references to many sorts of Christian good works. He argued, rather, that these *particular* works were and are of merely worldly, and not supernatural, value. This was the core of his argument: Jews cannot find, and never could have found, salvation through circumcision, the Sabbath and the dietary laws. They played no role whatever in the salvific drama. Jews who became Christians should not be concerned at leaving behind these particular religious rites, for in them no one, Jew or gentile, was ever saved. The opposite is the case. Either contingent, this-worldly necessity or the sin of Israel had called forth the particular rituals, circumcision to distinguish Israel from the peoples of the land of Canaan, the Sabbath to provide rest for the weary, and the dietary laws to remove Israel from the worship of Egyptian idols. These historical arguments are utterly without precedent in antecedent patristic writings against Judaism.

The Rejection of Israel

The foundation-stone of Aphrahat's argument was that Israel was rejected for rejecting the Messiah, and that the nations therefore were called in their place. This theme recurred throughout, and no argument was ever complete without reference to it. Indeed, proof-texts for many propositions more often than not reverted to the rejection of Israel. The first appearance of the argument was in the first demonstration, on faith (I, 16) where Ps. 118:22 was applied to the Christian messiah, then illustrated by Luke 19:13-14, further buttressed with Ez. 13:10-11. Aphrahat's quite original history of the grapecluster (II, 40-65, 92), moreover, was the story of the rejection of Israel and the vocation of the nations. The story of the grapecluster came to its climax with Jesus, after whose time the blessing was taken from the branch, and the branch brought forth no more blessing. The actual rejection of Israel took place when the lamp was raised up, that is, at the crucifixion (I, 28). The Jews have been rejected by God, who sent them prophets to call to them. They refused to listen to these prophets, as Jeremiah testified (Jer. 6:16-17)(I, 512-13). The Jews furthermore said that in the future God would make a new covenant with them. But the one who called them rulers of Sodom and people of Gomorrah was not likely to do so. It was he who called Abraham and made him the father of the peoples, and not just of Israel (I, 533).

The comparison of Israel and Sodom was important to Aphrahat for several reasons. First, he found in Is. 1:10 an excellent text to prove that Israel indeed has been called Sodom by the prophets. This permitted him to attribute to Israel the evil of the Sodomites, further to allege that like Sodom Israel had been rejected and would not be rebuilt. The themes came first in I, 469, where Aphrahat demonstrated that since Isaiah called to the Sodomite rulers, and since Sodom was long ago destroyed, he must actually have referred to the Israelites of his own time. The reason was that since the Israelites of Isaiah's day did the deeds of Sodom, they were properly called Sodomites and people of Gomorrah.

No Future Redemption for Israel

The first corollary to this proposition was that the Jews could have no hope for future redemption. They to the contrary asserted that the messianic references to future redemption in prophetic literature have yet to be fulfilled. But this was demonstrably not the case, for one such reference was misunderstood by them — that in Ez. 16:55 — and other references were to the redemption that had already taken place in the time of Haggai and Zechariah. On the contrary, Daniel prophesied concerning the actual future of Israel, and his prophecy was fulfilled: "Israel would be restored, then the Messiah would be killed, Jerusalem would be destroyed, and the city would never again be rebuilt. So it has come to pass." The argument was fundamentally a historical one. History proved the propositions of faith, which were not matters of belief but rather of correct understanding of facts. Christians were right because they knew those facts. Jews were wrong because they refused to take seriously what had happened.

The Jews hoped that they would be redeemed and brought back to their land. They relied on the promises of the prophets. But these promises have already been fulfilled. No redemption lay before Israel. It was all in the past. The prayer of Daniel was central to the case, for the claim of Israel was that redemption would come in the future. Daniel's prayer had already been answered long ago. Daniel himself had prophesied that no redemption would follow after the Messiah would be killed and Jerusalem destroyed a second time. Hence it was important carefully to analyze just what Daniel said and was told. Just as Daniel's prayer was actually fulfilled, so was his vision of the Messiah realized.

Even in the time of Cyrus, the Jews did not want to leave Babylonia, but many of them remained behind. This was a sign that they rejected divine providence, as in the time of the Egyptians they rejected redemption, but were forced by the Egyptians themselves to leave the country. So too the continued residence of Jews in Babylonia even now demonstrated their rejection of the redemption, just as in the time of Cyrus.

True, God promised Israel redemption, but God can, for good reason, change his mind. The prophets one after another testified to God's rejection of Israel: Moses, David, Jeremiah, Hosea, Amos, Micah, Malachi, Nahum, all provided evidence of the final and complete rejection. In fact God saved Israel twice, just as he had promised, once from Egypt, the second time from Babylonia. All the prophetic promises pertained to the past, none to the future. So the Christian argued, "You hope that when the Messiah comes Jerusalem will be rebuilt, but in fact the Messiah came and Jerusalem was destroyed, as Daniel foretold" (I, 805).

The Jew's messianic hope indeed can never be fulfilled, for the prophet Ezekiel said that Israel would be restored "just like Sodom." But Sodom was destroyed long before Israel, and never rebuilt. The meaning of Ezekiel is this: Just as Sodom was destroyed and never rebuilt, so Jerusalem was destroyed and never will be rebuilt (I, 944-5). Sodom's sin was less than Israel's. How can any one suppose other than that Jerusalem's destruction is forever? Indeed, Amos (5: 2) clearly stated that the virgin-daughter of Israel would never again be restored (I, 945, 948-9).

Vocation of the Peoples Instead of Israel

The second corollary to the proposition that Israel has been rejected was that Israel would no longer be the people of God, but that the gentiles' church had taken their place as God's people. The theme of the vocation of the peoples in place of the people of Israel first appeared in the fifth Demonstration, where the complete argument came in just a few lines (I, 232, lines 3-19). First, the church was chosen instead of Israel. The proof-text, Deut. 32:21, was important because it refers to the "people which is no people." Aphrahat understood that Scripture to refer to "the new people which formerly did not exist, but was scattered elsewhere." This new people was set free (it is clear that the freedom is from Satan), while the Jews remained in bondage. This bondage was worldly, yet of supernatural significance. If the saints were to inherit sovereignty, how then could the Jews be saints, for they were not sovereign but slaves? The next step, which we have already seen, was the most important: The Jews cannot claim that their redemption still lies in the future, for in fact it is over and done with. It has passed from Jacob to Esau, now understood by both Jews and Christians to mean Rome, and, so far as the Jews are concerned, that was the end of the story.

"It is true that Israel is the child of Abraham, but Abraham was the father of a multitude of peoples, not of Israel alone." Furthermore, Israel was a faithless child of Abraham, for the Jews turned away from the good deeds of the patriarchs and behaved like Sodomites and Gomorrans. The proof-texts showed that Israel itself rejected the heritage of the fathers, so others received it. This is underlined: When any one of the peoples did righteousness, he was then a child of Abraham. But when the Israelites did the deeds of the alien peoples, then they became Sodomites. The criterion for the true heirs of Abraham was doing righteousness. By this criterion Israel was rejected according to the testimony of the prophets (I, 468-9).

Particular Religious Practices of Judaism

From the generalized critique Aphrahat turned to the specific criticism of Israel's religious practices, "in which Jews take great pride and through which they expect to be saved." Not only have they been rejected, but they never *could* have attained salvation through the commandments. Apart from the ten commandments, which were all God revealed to Moses at Sinai, the specific rites and practices of Judaism were the result either of Israel's provoking God by its sin, on the one hand, or of God's concern for the welfare of all his creatures in general, not of Israel in particular, on the other. The Sabbath illustrated the latter argument, circumcision and the dietary laws the former one.

The theme of the rejection of Israel rarely, if ever, appeared in the demonstrations on specific religious practices, particularly Passover and the Sabbath. When it occurred in connection with dietary laws, it was meant to show that the sacrifices were never pleasing to God; and in regard to circumcision, it proved that circumcision was of temporary and limited value, but with the disobedience of Israel was replaced. It did not serve Aphrahat's purpose to emphasize the theme of Israel's rejection elsewhere, for his point was that the particular practices had never had salvific import, not that they had served but then were rejected along with Israel (a position he occasionally held, to be sure). This accounts for the small part played in these demonstrations by Israel's rejection.

Israel's actual observances even transgressed the law as it was given. This proposition was illustrated by Passover. Israel unlawfully observed the Passover, for in biblical times it was lawful to sacrifice the paschal lamb only in Jerusalem. Yet today Jews celebrated Passover among the unclean peoples (I, 508-9). The Jews observed Passover not as commanded (I, 532). "The Jewish Passover is limited and incomplete. Then they eat bitter herbs and recall their sins, but our redeemer removed bitterness from the nations, and forgave our sins through his sacrifice" (I, 521).

Sabbath

Jews took pride in the Sabbath, holding that in virtue of keeping it, they would be saved and find life (I, 541). But the Sabbath was merely a day of rest and did not distinguish between righteousness and sin. If it pertained not only to man but to cattle, then how was righteousness at issue? The cattle did not participate in the resurrection of the dead. They moreover sinned especially on the Sabbath. In ancient times righteous men did not keep the Sabbath. Adam was not given the opportunity to acquire merit through keeping the Sabbath. Noah was righteous because he did not marry in the generation of destruction, not because he kept the Sabbath. Joshua made war on the Sabbath, as did the Maccabees. Even the priests in the Temple violated the Sabbath. In none of these instances was Sabbath-violation accounted as sin. The Sabbath was a kindness to creatures, allowing them to rest from their labor. It had nothing to do with salvation.

Dietary Laws

Jews took pride in dietary laws. But food could not defile a man. It was not a matter of salvation to eat, or to refrain from eating, various sorts of food. The Jews were careful in no way to partake of food prepared by gentiles, nor would they drink gentile wine (I, 732-3). But the real reason God gave the dietary laws was to restrain the Israelites from the worship of the gods of the Egyptians (I, 733ff), for in Egypt they had worshipped the Egyptian gods, and even in the wilderness continued to do so. Hence after the incident of the golden calf God recognized their impulse and restrained it by denying them the right to eat what they had eaten in Egypt, and requiring them to eat the gods of the Egyptians and to sacrifice them to him. The dietary laws hence served a merely occasional, temporary, this-worldly purpose. By no means did they contain the power to achieve salvation. The heroes of Israel did not keep the dietary laws. Samson ate honey from the skeleton of the lion. Elijah and Elisha were fed by ravens, which are unclean (I, 744-5). Adam was permitted to eat any food, only not to consume the blood. Noah likewise ate as he liked. If sin or righteousness were involved, he would have commanded those early generations to observe dietary laws (I. 736).

Nor did God need sacrifices. They in fact constituted the divine response to Israel's sin, — a discipline to overcome Israel's evil impulse. God himself had no use for Israel's sacrifices. They were provoked, just as were the dietary laws, by disobedience.

Circumcision

Circumcision without faith was useless. Faith preceded circumcision. Furthermore, circumcision was merely one among several signs of the covenant. Each served its time and then was replaced by another, and so it was with circumcision, useful in the past but now replaced by baptism (I, 472-3). Circumcision was not given as an eternal covenant, but only so long as it pleased God did it have supernatural value. It was merely one of the commandments of the law, but when the law was not kept, circumcision likewise ceased to have value.

Other signs of the covenant and other commandments were given for a time, then revoked. (Commandment and covenant in Aphrahat's mind were one and the same.) Because Adam did not keep the commandment-covenant not to eat from the tree of the knowledge of good and evil, he was condemned, and the covenant of Adam was annulled, replaced by another. The faith of Enoch and the innocence of Noah, not circumcision, accounted for their having pleased God. The covenant of Noah was to be fruitful and multiply, signified by the rainbow (I, 473).

The vocation of Abraham came before he was circumcised and had nothing to do with circumcision. It was on account of his faith, not his circumcision (I,476). After believing, he was told to circumcise. But if it were through circumcision that men find life, he should have circumcised, then believed. The true purpose of circumcision was to distinguish Israel from the nations among whom they would dwell, so that if a Jew sinned, he could not claim to be exempt because he was not subject to the law; circumcision would prove otherwise.

The Egyptians themselves practiced circumcision. They learned the rite from Joseph, who circumcised his sons, and continued to do so. Hence when Pharaoh's daughter found Moses, it was not from the mark of circumcision that she knew he was a Hebrew, for everyone was circumcised. Rather, she understood from the fact that he was found floating in the Nile that he was a Hebrew, since the Egyptians were not commanded to expose their children or to drown them. Further, had the Egyptians not been circumcised, Moses could not have grown up in Pharaoh's palace, for at any time he would have been found out.

If Israel found life through circumcision, so also ought the other peoples of antiquity who practiced the same rite to have been saved (I, 497). Yet they were idolators, so salvation through circumcision was manifestly impossible.

Aphrahat did not explain how the fact that other peoples practiced circumcision squared with his argument about its purpose for Israel. If circumcision was meant to distinguish Israel from the other peoples, then its purpose would have been vitiated by neighboring peoples' practice of circumcision. I imagine he would argue that the Canaanites were not circumcised, but only the peoples on the frontiers. Hence for the purpose of distinguishing Israelites from Canaanites circumcision would suffice.

I do not understand why Aphrahat was so anxious to prove the relationship of the various ancient peoples to one another. The long argument seems to me to play no part in the argument on circumcision.

Circumcision did not avail those who perished in the wilderness. They sinned through lack of faith. Had they believed, they would have entered the promised land. The children of the wilderness believed, and this was regarded as circumcision. Hence the circumcision at the Jordan was seen as a second one. Israel did not circumcise in the wilderness, since there then was no practical need. They were dwelling by themselves. Only when they entered Canaan was it necessary to do so. So, Aphrahat held, circumcision was merely temporary. In all things the law and covenant have been changed, from Adam, to Noah, Abraham, and Moses. To each God gave a covenant together with its signification. Only the final covenant, with Jesus, would never be changed (I, 497), Adam's was not to eat from the tree. Noah's was the rain-bow. Abraham first believed, then was told to circumcise. The true and eternal circumcision (I, 500-1) was the one Jeremiah had demanded: Circumcise the foreskin of the heart, and this circumcision would be eternal. The former covenants together with their observances were not kept, therefore annulled. Although the One who gave the old and new covenants was one and the same (contrary to the Marcionite view), he spoke of the new not as of the old. In the new covenant there was no fleshly circumcision. The true circumcision was baptism for the forgiveness of sins, and a child of Abraham was one who circumcised the foreskin of his heart and believed (I, 497).

Summary

The structure of Aphrahat's critique of Judaism is as follows:

I. *Israel is rejected because Israel rejected the Messiah.*
    Therefore:
    1. Israel has no hope for future redemption,
        a. Proved by Isaiah's comparison of Israel's restoration to that of Sodom. The latter did not take place, and neither will the former. What they have in common is that both Jerusalem and Sodom will remain in devastation.
    2. The gentiles have been called to take Israel's place,
        a. Proved by Moses' reference to a "people which is no people" to anger Israel. That no-people is the church of the gentiles, which angers Israel by shaming them into desisting from idolatry and by taking Israel's blessings.

II. *Judaism's particular religious practices do not have, and never did have, salvific value.*
    1. Jews do not legally observe the law: *Passover*
    2. Jews do not understand the purpose of the law: *Sabbath*
        a. It is merely a day of rest and does not serve to distinguish sinners from the righteous or bring life.
    3. Jews' own sin provoked the imposition of the law: *Dietary Laws and Circumcision.*

    a. Dietary laws were necessitated by Israel's continued adherence to Egyptian idolatry; therefore Israel was told to eat the Egyptian gods, not to eat the food they formerly ate;

        i. and to sacrifice Egyptian gods to God, though God had no need of sacrifice.

    b. Circumcision was a temporary sign of a transient covenant. Without faith circumcision cannot save. But faith obviates the need, for baptism is the true circumcision. Faith leads to the circumcision of the heart.

        i. Circumcision was not unique to Israel. Others did it, were not saved.

        ii. Circumcision merely distinguished Israelites from gentiles, was necessitated by Jews' assimilation among pagans.

The argument is not a complex one, and, as we have repeatedly noticed, it is built mainly from historical facts, not from theological propositions. One kind of argumentation predominates nearly to the exclusion of all else, and that is, the case built upon common sense interpretation of universally accepted historical texts.

iv. Aphrahat's Jews

What characterized Mesopotamian Jews and their religious life? Aphrahat stressed the importance to Jewry of Sabbath and festival observance (Parisot I, 44), indeed made *not* keeping the Sabbath and other temporal distinctions one of the chief "works" of faith. This strongly suggests Jewish converts continued to practice the old faith in the matrix of the new, and for sound theological reasons Aphrahat warned them to desist. The other elements in the same list do not necessarily apply to Jews or Jewish converts. "Empty doctrines" surely referred to heresies within the church, for example. False witness, blasphemy, and adultery were never held to be sins committed by Jews but not by Christians. Hence I suppose that only the first part of the list of works of faith pertained to Jews in the Church.

The single most powerful element in the Jew's faith was the hope to be redeemed and restored to the land. This must account for the vehemence of Aphrahat's argument. Time and again Babylonian Jews showed how vividly they expected the coming of the Messiah. The Dura synagogue paintings portrayed their messianic expectations. Less than two decades after Aphrahat wrote, in 363, some Babylonian Jews believed that the Messiah had come to bring them back to the land of Israel. They marched out of Mahoza, only to be slaughtered by Shapur's troops. The government was well aware of the danger of Jewish messianism. In 468, expecting the imminent coming of the messiah four hundred years after the destruction of Jerusalem, Jews took aggressive action against Magi in Isfahan and were therefore slaughtered. The exilarch and rabbis probably shared this expectation, the former assuming he or one of his relatives was actually the messiah. When in 614 the Persians took Jerusalem, Palestinian Jews momentarily expected the messiah. On the eve of the Moslem conquest Babylonian Jews again followed a messianic leader. And these merely are the events known to us. Rabbinical literature is notoriously silent about things the rabbis did not like. They above all feared political messianism, remembering the lessons of 'Aqiva and Bar Kokhba. We can therefore only imagine what other messianic excitements stirred up Babylonian and Mesopotamian Jewry but went unrecorded by the rabbis.

The Jews were careful not to eat food prepared by gentiles or to drink wine of gentiles (I, 732-3). The gentiles bless these things in the name of their gods, and the Jews on that account will not touch their food. The taboo against gentile wine and food is well attested in the Babylonian Talmud. The Babylonian rabbis certainly enforced those taboos in their courts. Aphrahat did not hint that the taboos were unique to a particular group within Jewry; on the contrary he rightly portrayed it as a singular and well-known Jewish trait.

Further, Jews believed that they are the people of God and the children of Abraham (I, 781, 185), and that procreation and family life are divinely ordained. These two traits are well attested elsewhere.

It is striking that Aphrahat did not argue merely that the old laws have been replaced by the new covenant or that salvation is not by works. He was forced to argue that even when the old covenant was in force, laws Israel kept were of temporary, practical, and merely this-worldly consequence. God did not give commandments for justification. The Sabbath was for worldly rest. Circumcision was intended as a merely practical distinction between Israel and the nations. The dietary laws were supposed to insure that Israel would cease from worshipping the gods of Egypt. Why is it that the salvific value of these practices is denied not only in theological, but also in historical terms? I imagine that the context of the argument provides part of the reason. Jews continued to practice these laws, Jewish converts to worry about not keeping them.

Hence generalized arguments about salvation through faith in this context would have proved insufficient, for the faith people had actually held included these very works. Nor was it enough to suggest that the laws once, but no longer, applied, on account of the new covenant. Jews clearly held they did. It was necessary to confront the works of the law both in all their specificity and in their attractive contemporary setting. This confrontation required the denial that those particular laws *ever* had had the kind of salvific value Jews even now maintained they still do have. Only by proving the works of circumcision, Sabbath, and *kashrut* were, at the outset, of practical and worldly consequence could Aphrahat hope to persuade the ordinary Christian Jew not to concern himself for them. The shape of Aphrahat's argument, as well as his specific remarks, therefore testified to the powerful hold of the commandments over the life of Jewry. But, it should be stressed, the "mysteries" of circumcision, dietary prohibitions, and the Sabbath were referred to in nearly every Christian critique of Judaism from the first century onward. What is unique in Aphrahat is his insistence that these practical commandments had never served to bring salvation, even in the age in which they were part of the divine covenant or commandment. No earlier Church Father made such an assertion. Hence we had best account for Aphrahat's insistence on that point by reference to the unusual circumstances of Iranian Christianity.

The influence of Jewry on the neighboring Christians also is reflected in the Christians' concern for the proper date of Passover and its meaning. Aphrahat had to remind the troubled simple folk (I, 516ff.) that the true sacrifice is the Messiah. The date of his crucifixion and resurrection was to be observed not on the 14th of Nisan, which can have no meaning for Christians at all, but on the 15th. In this way he sought to separate Christians from Jewry on the festival that dominated the liturgical year of both communities.

Aphrahat referred to Jews' now making the paschal celebration among the unclean peoples, although in biblical times it was lawful to do so only in Jerusalem. Did he then know of Jews who actually slew the paschal lamb (I, 508-9)? On the one hand all the laws he cited refer specifically to the paschal sacrifice. This would lead to the conclusion that Jews now unlawfully carried out just such a sacrifice. On the other hand, he may have meant that the observance of the *festival* of Passover, described in particulars in the laws on the paschal sacrifice, could only take place in Jerusalem. If that is his meaning, then he did not mean to say Jews now sacrificed the lamb in Mesopotamia. But then it is a difficult argument on Aphrahat's part, for the Christians celebrated the paschal sacrifice of Jesus wherever they were. Aphrahat in no place argued that it is legal for them to do so outside of Jerusalem. Yet he carefully explained how Jesus is the new paschal sacrifice. Hence he was left to hold that it was illegal for Jews to celebrate Passover outside of Jerusalem (and sacrifice is no issue), but it was of course proper for Christians to celebrate Passover anywhere, though the Christ whose sacrifice they offer fulfilled the very laws one can keep only in Jerusalem. I imagine he would have said that in doing so, Christ had fulfilled those laws *once for all*. Hence they no longer pertained to the church. But since Israel did not celebrate the Passion, the law continued, by their own interpretation, to apply to them. I therefore do not suppose he referred to actual Jewish animal sacrifices in Mesopotamia.

We find no hint that Aphrahat knew about, or argued against, an Oral Tradition. He never referred to a concrete and specific rabbinic tradition. Aphrahat never openly mentioned Jewish doctrines other than those he found in the Written Scriptures, particularly in the Pentateuch. The dietary laws he criticized all are biblical. Not a word was said about ritual slaughter of animals and separation of milk and meat, the characteristically *rabbinical* interpretations or applications of Scriptural dietary laws. The "debater of the people" was not called rabbi, did not allude to traditions other than written Scripture, and hardly came up to the rabbinical standard of Scriptural exegesis. I doubt that Aphrahat ever heard of a Jewish rabbinical assertion that along with the written Scriptures God revealed to Moses an oral tradition as well, preserved by the rabbis-Pharisees alone. It is simply unthinkable that had he known about such a Jewish conviction, he would have failed to refer to it as an example of the Jews' wrongheadedness, their falsification of divine revelation.

If rabbinical schools or circles existed in Mesopotamia in his day, the best evidence of their limited impact on Mesopotamian Jewry is Aphrahat's failure to take issue with them and their teachings. We have seen that the realities of the day time and again shaped his arguments for him. Is it possible that widespread rabbinical influence would not have provoked him to powerful invective, I imagine, against, first, belief in a dual revelation (to be disproved by countless Scriptures), second, rabbinical perversion of the law? Since Aphrahat showed himself sensitive to the realities of Jewry and gave no testimony to the presence of rabbinical leadership or influence within the Jewish community, I conclude that Mesopotamian Jews known to him had little or no contact with Babylonian rabbis or with others of their estate in Mesopotamia.

To summarize: Aphrahat's Jews based their Judaism on the Hebrew Scriptures and took literally both the theology and the practical commandments they found in them. It is difficult to point to a single belief or practice referred to by Aphrahat which did not derive directly and simply from Scripture. It is not merely that Aphrahat did not allude to an oral tradition, to rabbis, or to other marks of the presence of Pharisaic-Rabbinic Judaism. Everything he did say points to a single phenomenon, and that is, a Judaism based upon canonical Scriptures and little else.

We know of two centers of Judaism in the Iranian empire, Babylonia and Mesopotamia. The former is well documented in the pages of the Babylonian Talmud. For the latter we have little literary and archaeological evidence, certainly nothing to permit us to describe the whole phenomenon. But what we do know about Mesopotamia is congruent to Aphrahat's picture of the Jews. We know that in the first century A.D. the royal family of Adiabene converted to Judaism, and the Judaism to which they converted probably consisted of worship of Yahweh, reverence for the Jerusalem Temple, and belief in the Hebrew Scriptures. It is true that, for reasons of their own, Adiabenian nobles made every effort to cultivate the friendship of Palestinians, including the Pharisees, who preserved a good memory of the family of Monobazes. But we have no reason to imagine the Adiabenians at home had adopted the Pharisaic form of Judaism. Of their later history we have no record. It seems to me likely that the royal family fled eastward during Trajan's invasion, and afterward settled in Armenia. But if the conversion affected more than a few nobles, then some Jews must have been left behind.

These were, moreover, not the only Jews in Mesopotamia, for the remnants of the ten tribes exiled seven centuries earlier continued to survive, it is thought, in the territories they had settled long before. Further, in Nisibis a rabbinical academy flourished from the first century into the second half of the second century, and during the Bar Kokhba war and subsequent repression, the disciples of R. 'Aqiva fled from Palestine and for a time took refuge there. Their influence could not have been considerable, and while a rabbinical settlement may have continued in Nisibis, it never achieved much importance so far as we can tell. Of the three groups of Jews in Mesopotamia, Adiabenians, Nisibins, and descendants of the ten tribes, for historical and geographical reasons it seems to me likeliest that Aphrahat knew about the Adiabenians. The Jews referred to and represented in Aphrahat's demonstrations probably were the descendants of the first century converts to Judaism.

CHAPTER THIRTEEN

APHRAHAT AND THE RABBIS

i. Introduction

Aphrahat's Jews thus persisted in the worship of Yahweh, reverence for Scripture and the Temple, practice of the commandments contained in Scriptures, and (after 70) expectation that the people of God in time to come would be saved by the Messiah. To the south of Mesopotamia, in the Babylonian Jewish communities of Pumbedita, Sura, Maḥoza, and elsewhere, rabbinical Judaism, characterized by belief in the Oral Torah of the rabbis, had meanwhile taken root through the establishment of rabbinical schools. The schools not only taught doctrines but also effected them through the small-claims court system of Jewry, committed into their hands by the Babylonian exilarch approximately two centuries before Aphrahat.

As I said, we have no reason to suppose Aphrahat ever met a rabbi or a Jew under rabbinical discipline and authority. It of course is possible that he did, but the demonstrations contain not the slightest overt hint of such an encounter. The "debater of the people" was anything but a rabbi. He would typify another sort of local authority, a master of Scripture and whatever indigenous local traditions had gathered around it, rather than the rabbi who possessed a considerable independent corpus of exegetical and legal traditions. On the other hand the relationship between Aphrahat's scriptural interpretation and that of the rabbis calls for study, for the content of Aphrahat's critique ought not to have escaped the attention of the Babylonian masters, whether they heard about it from Aphrahat (unlikely), or from Jews bothered by the sorts of things Aphrahat and other Christians were saying (more likely).

Louis Ginzberg (*JE* I, pp. 663b-665b) stated, ". . . it may be confidently asserted that no church father was ever so strongly influenced by rabbinical Judaism as this defender of Christianity against the Jews." He noted that Wellhausen regarded Aphrahat as evidence of "how completely the Syriac Church was bound to Jewish tradition, even in the fourth century." "Funk and Ginzberg both show many parallel passages from Rabbinical literature with which the Scriptural explanations of Aphraates coincide. In certain very important questions concerning the soul, God, retribution, etc., he shows himself a docile pupil of the Jews." Ginzberg pointed to the doctrine of the two attributes of God, justice and mercy, as decidedly Jewish; "Aphraates, in agreement with the rabbis, declares that God's mercy is for men living; while His justice is administered after their death." Several similar "agreements" are listed. Ginzberg stated, "His frequent vigorous attacks on Jewish sages and disputants also show that, in spite of the great influence that the rabbinical teachings exercised over him, he entered the lists against his teachers more than once." Both Funk and Gavin have likewise made much of parallels between materials drawn from various rabbinical traditions of both Palestine and Babylonia, on the one hand, and Aphrahat's Scriptural exegesis on the other.

Gavin: For Gavin, the affinities of Aphrahat and Judaism were numerous and important. Gavin's concrete instances of Aphrahat's alleged "dependence upon Jewish thought and affiliation with it" began with Aphrahat's doctrine of creation, man, and soul. That man pre-existed in God's mind has its parallel, he said, in the rabbinical distinction between six things which preceded the creation of the creatures (p. 38). The preparation-of-the-world parable ("like a man who provides everything his son may need. . .") is parallel to a story in the medieval *Alphabet Midrash of R. ʿAqiva*; "like a king who built a palace and when he has finished it, then spreads a feast and afterwards invites the guests." Gavin concluded, "We may see from these examples how Aphrahat combines several Jewish elements in the piecing together of his first creation story in the seventeenth homily. Even a superficial examination shows that its tenor and method are obviously quite in the style of the Rabbis." The midrash of course is late. The parable in Aphrahat is used for a very different purpose. It is to show that God made everything ready, then created man. For the Jewish midrash the parable shows why God created man before the Sabbath. The point in common is simply the commonplace image of the father/king who prepares a meal, surely not uniquely rabbinical. For that parable Aphrahat did not have to turn to rabbinic materials. The pre-existence of man is not on the list of the six (elsewhere, ten) things created before creation. The only point in common is the belief in creation before creation. Gavin's conclusion that Aphrahat "combines. . . in piecing together" seems to me unsupported. His language furthermore imputes to Aphrahat a kind of rabbinical education manifestly lacking. Aphrahat did not "piece together" rabbinical materials. The data Gavin here cited are different from Aphrahat's. His assertion that the tenor and method are in the style of the rabbis is quite true, but that does not prove Aphrahat actually knew or studied with rabbis, rather that Christian and Jewish exegesis had much in common, starting with Scriptures. Indeed they did, but the points in common cited here are insufficient to demonstrate concrete rabbinical influence on Christian exegesis. Common style seems to me to point toward common traditions and cultural setting, nothing more.

Gavin further referred to the fall, death, and the curse (pp. 40-53). Aphrahat's interpretation of the confrontation of Adam and God, that God called him to repentence, is "almost word for word" given in Midrash Rabbah to Numbers, in the name of R. Tanḥuma b. Abba, "When Adam had transgressed, the Holy One looked for him to make an act of repentence, but he did not." That is quite so, but neither comment ventures far from the biblical account to begin with. Further, what would such an alleged word for word correspondence actually mean? Is Aphrahat supposed directly to have cited a Palestinian rabbi whose teaching appears in a late compilation? If not a citation, than all we have is an unanalyzed parallel. Of a similar order is Gavin's comparison between Aphrahat's view that the serpent was Satan and the opinion of Simeon b. Laqish, that all evil is traceable to a single source, for "Satan, the evil impulse, and the angel of Death are all one." But Simeon b. Laqish said nothing about the *serpent* in Genesis! It is Gavin who drew that inference.

Gavin more persuasively demonstrated that for Aphrahat and the rabbis the *evil impulse* meant pretty much the same thing. But he further commented that Aphrahat's eschatology was closer to Josephus and Philo than to the rabbis. Again (p. 57), the "doctrine of the Spirit in Aphraates shows Jewish [meaning rabbinic] affiliations, but yet is not entirely under Jewish influence, inasmuch as the basis of his doctrine is Pauline." These observations show that Gavin's mind was not on Aphrahat's dependency, proved by quotations or citations, but rather on the comparison of several bodies of thought to one another. Such a quite legitimate comparison, however, does not demand extensive emphasis, such as Gavin gaves, upon the roots of one in another, in this case of Christianity in Mesopotamian rabbinic Judaism.

Gavin paid slight attention to Mazdean elements in both Aphrahat's and rabbinical thought. He thus called Aphrahat's chiliasm "strikingly Jewish" (p. 57), for the rabbis believed the world would last six thousand years, two thousand of emptiness, two thousand of Torah, and two thousand of the messianic era. This doctrine has a parallel in Zoroastrian thought. It is by no means necessary to conclude that "this rabbinic speculation came into the church." Rather, this *Zoroastrian* speculation long ago entered sources drawn upon by both church and synagogue.

Gavin's conclusion is as follows (p. 58): "In innumerable concrete instances of exact parallels in thought as well as in his general envisagement of theological problems, we find that Aphraates is a 'docile pupil of the Jews'. In his account of Creation . . . Aphraates is peculiarly at one, in the idiom of his thought and the perspective of his field, with contemporary Rabbinic Judaism. Where he diverged, he only recombined elements taken from the rabbis to reassemble them into the contour of a mosaic of a Christian character."

On the one hand it is quite true that Aphrahat interpreted Scripture much as did rabbis. For instance the method of contrasting supposedly conflicting verses and then harmonizing their contradiction, as in I, 796, the comparison of Ps. 90:1-2 and Lev. 26:11-12, is characteristic of Babylonian rabbinical midrash, which would "throw verses at one another" in precisely the same rhetorical manner. Likewise, as Gavin points out, we notice any number of arguments *a forteriori* (*qal vehomer*), e.g. I, 788, I, 565, "If God rested, how much the more should man rest," and so forth. But the *qal vehomer* is not the invention of the rabbis. Its presence by itself does not connote rabbinical influence or prove dependence on rabbinical instruction. If from no other source, Aphrahat could have learned it from Scriptures. It is therefore not the sort of datum to demonstrate rabbinical influence, even an affinity between rabbis and Aphrahat. Gavin did not notice the appearance of a rabbinical epithet for God, "He who spoke and the world came into being," which occurs in I, 565 and 797. Nor did he see that Aphrahat referred to Jesus' circle as his *talmidé haverim*; that he called the Torah *'uraita*, as did the rabbis; or that Aphrahat's interpretation of Ex. 12 in terms of the life of the Church is to be compared to the Passover *Haggadah's* interpretation of Ex. 12 in terms of the life of Israel (see I, 525ff). One could go on. No reader of Aphrahat familiar with rabbinic literature can fail to compile a long list of parallel concepts, words, expressions, rhetorical devices, interpretations of men, events, and doctrines.

But what do these parallels and commonalities prove? As we saw, Gavin on the one hand spoke of "affiliations" or affinities; on the other, he was prepared to point to exact parallels and to claim precise, word-for-word correspondences. He even conjured the strange portrait of a Christian theologian's designing a mosaic of rabbinical stones, merely recombining elements taken from the rabbis to reassemble for the Christian picture. This is exaggerated and false on the face of it. In the end he called Aphrahat a "docile pupil of the Jews"! I cannot think of a less docile pupil, if Aphrahat directly learned anything at all from Jews, rabbinical or otherwise.

Did Aphrahat, like Paul, actually study in a rabbinical school? Unlikely. Then what do correspondences or parallels mean or prove? Clearly, the comparison of one body of thought with another for philosophical purposes is instructive. But the results are not necessarily historically consequential. They do not show that one side learned from the other, only that the both came to the same conclusion, for never articulated reasons. To say more than this, one must show not only that both parties said the same thing, but also both that one had the opportunity to learn from the other, and that one side was more likely to have learned from the other. Normally a correspondence between a rabbinical sentiment of any period and a Christian opinion of any period is cited as evidence of Christian dependence on (rabbinic) Judaism; no one has made a serious effort to ask about rabbinical dependence on Christianity. Furthermore, if we find neutral, non-polemical stories pertinent to Scriptural heroes in Aphrahat with no rabbinical parallel whatever, are we safe in concluding rabbis never knew such stories or told them? It seems to me probable that the limited range of extant rabbinical literature simply has not encompassed each and every significant exegetical and midrashic tradition in all rabbinical schools or all periods. If that is the case, even the *absence* of particular parallels is of no *prima facie* probative value.

The real problem for the historian is how to envisage and reconstruct the historical situation underlying literary facts. True, parallels constitute facts, but are the facts serviceable for historical inquiry? If, as I said, both parties say much the same thing in much the same language, we may offer several hypotheses. First, one party may actually have studied with the other. Second, both parties may have learned from a third party (as in the case of the chiliastic saying). Third, neither party may have known the other's view, but each may have come to the same conclusion independently. This is especially likely where both parties possessed sacred Scriptures in common, not to mention various sorts of traditions that had taken shape long before the formation of either group. Further, since the early church was shaped by men familiar with Pharisaism, points in common later on may well be accounted for in terms of earlier history. So Aphrahat can tell us little, if anything, about his own affinities with rabbinical Judaism. He may well show only that Semitic Christianity preserved some elements of the Pharisaic heritage. But even that is questionable, for reasons stated earlier.

If we could select among these alternatives, historical inquiry would benefit. But in the present stage of research, parallels are drawn from every period of rabbinical literature, a literature not yet carefully and thoroughly divided according to its places and times of origin, strata, schools, and the like. If to a Palestinian rabbi of the second century a saying which first occurs in an eighth or ninth century compilation is attributed, how would Aphrahat have heard it? How many assumptions must we make to suppose it is a consequential parallel at all?

Common cultural and linguistic characteristics surely do not necessitate the conclusion that one party borrowed from another. They do not allow the allegation that Aphrahat was a pupil, docile or otherwise, of any sort of Jews. As I said, they show merely that both the rabbis and Aphrahat drew upon the same cultural, conceptual, and linguistic heritage, a heritage only partially available to us. Unless we assume that all rabbinical opinions on Scriptures are unique to, and singularly characteristic of, rabbis, the undeniable existence of common traits and even common opinions on the same Scriptures and theological issues tells us only that the rabbis and Aphrahat lived in a single cultural continuum. Since the Mesopotamian Church was, as Gavin stressed, the creation of Christian Jews, we may at least hypothetically account for the phenomena Gavin points out. The Palestinian heritage brought by the Christian Jewish missionaries probably included many of the concepts and cultural traits revealed to us for the first time by Aphrahat. No one would have seen anything peculiarly rabbinic in many such traits, e.g. the idea of the evil impulse.

The broader issue facing those who seek roots for Christian beliefs and practices of various places and times in Jewish beliefs and practices of various places and times is this: What is meant by Judaism? Gavin, not alone, sees "Judaism" and "rabbinic Judaism" as pretty much identical, and to him rabbinic Judaism is a monolith, unchanged and unchanging from some remote time in antiquity until the completion of the Babylonian Talmud and even later, medieval midrashic compilations. These conceptions obviously are false. If so, we have to ask, What are the particular traits we should regard as *characteristically* rabbinical, among the larger corpus of literature recognized as Judaic or Jewish? And once a trait is seen to be "rabbinical," to which period, school, or country are we to assign its provenance? It will simply not suffice to postulate that everything in rabbinical literature was everywhere known, moreover that we now know pretty much everything rabbis ever said, thought, or did.

Funk nonetheless cited a number of specific instances in which Aphrahat and a Jewish source such as Targum Onqelos said much the same thing. In *Die haggadischen Elemente in den Homilien des Aphraates, des persischen Weisen* (Vienna, 1891), which was his doctoral dissertation, Funk made his conception clear: "What traditions did he borrow from [*entnommen*] Jewish haggadic literature?" In Funk's mind, therefore, was a picture of a docile pupil of the Jews, who borrowed Jewish (rabbinical) traditions and then formed his "mosaic" for Christian purposes. Again he referred (p. 9) to Aphrahat's building "his biblical understanding in complete dependency [*in völliger Abhängigkeit*] on Jewish [rabbinical] exegesis." Funk's conception therefore was that a parallel demonstrated nothing less than complete dependency of Aphrahat on Jewish tradition.

What evidences did Funk bring to show this "complete dependency"? One parallel concerns the interpretation of "Seven times Cain will be avenged" (Gen. 4:15), which Aphrahat understands to mean that Cain will be punished in the seventh generation, just as does Targum Onqelos (p. 23-4). The discussion of the obvious etymology of the name of Noah is similar for both Aphrahat and the Midrash (p. 25). Noah waited until his five hundredth year to marry so as not to be implicated in the earlier curse. R. Judah (Gen. R. 26:2) says that God made Noah sterile. Aphrahat, Funk asserted, was polemicizing *against* this rabbinic view when he emphasized that Noah would have been potent had he wanted children. The former parallel is no parallel at all. God's making Noah sterile and Noah's refraining from marriage are not the same thing. The latter assertion is plausible, but Aphrahat did not have to know the rabbis' view to raise for himself the question of why Noah had no children before his five hundredth year. Aphrahat's reply derives from his apologetic intent, not necessarily from a desire to respond to a rabbinical assertion. Aphrahat wanted to show that Noah was intentionally celibate, not accidentally or providentially childless. No anti-rabbinical polemic needs to be postulated here. Aphrahat and Onqelos say somewhat the same thing about Gen. 6:3 (p. 27). Aphrahat holds that Abraham circumcised himself when he was told Isaac would be born. Gen. R. 46:2 says Abraham circumcised himself so that Isaac would be born of holy seed. Funk states, (p. 29), "Dies betont auch Aphraates durch die Worte, 'nachdem er sich beschnitten hatte, wurde Isak empfangen und geboren.'" Perhaps so, but Aphrahat gives no hint that he regards circumcision as the *condition* of producing 'holy seed.' I think it unlikely that he held such an opinion. In any event he did not say so. The identity of Moriah with Jerusalem (p. 30) derives from Jewish tradition, and of course occurs in rabbinical literature as well. That St. Jerome learned the tradition from Jews is indicated by his saying that "the Hebrews say so." But Aphrahat could by now have acquired the tradition within the Church. In any event finding the same thought in Aphrahat and in a *targum* may indicate only that *targumic* traditions and church traditions drew on the same antecedent materials. Nor is it to be taken for granted that the *targumim* are quintessentially Pharisaic-rabbinic.

These examples of Funk's results should indicate that comparative study of exegesis is interesting and fruitful, but in no way justifies the conclusion that Aphrahat completely depended on Jewish exegesis. Complete dependence hardly is demonstrated by a few — less than two dozen — parallels, and, more to the point, the parallels drawn by Gavin and Funk upon close examination do not always seem really parallel at all. But even granting that a rabbi and Aphrahat might actually be found to have said the same thing in much the same words — which is rarely, if ever, the case — we then, as I said, have to test a number of hypotheses to account for that fact. One of these hypotheses would be that Aphrahat had actually studied with that rabbi, or his teacher or disciple, and so stated. If such could be shown probable, then in that instance Aphrahat's complete dependence would be proved. There are no such instances. Affinities, similarities, relationships of other sorts prove nothing of the kind.

Rather than contribute additions to long lists of parallels, I shall examine another aspect of the relationship between Aphrahat and rabbinical literature: How do Babylonian rabbis and their Tannaitic predecessors deal with the sorts of Scriptures and issues Aphrahat raised in his apology for Christianity and critique of Judaism. The purpose is not to prove dependencies. One can hardly maintain that rabbis knew what Aphrahat said. But, as I said at the outset, Jews in fact were bothered by the sorts of things Aphrahat and other Christians said. Those who did convert to Christianity therefore were probably persuaded by the Christian perspective on Scriptures. Can we now reconstruct a Babylonian rabbinical demonstration "against the Christians"? Clearly, appropriate materials for such a reconstruction must derive from Babylonian rabbis only,[1] along with Tannaitic Palestinian sayings found

---

[1] But I have cited a few Palestinians as well, where their sayings seemed important and no equivalent Babylonian sayings are to be found. These are in any event drawn mainly

in the Babylonian Talmud and therefore presumably known to
Babylonian masters in the third and fourth centuries. Of special interest
therefore will be materials deriving from Tannaitic collections and from
the third and fourth century masters contemporary with
Aphrahat,particularly Rava and Abbaye (d. ca. 337, 352 respectively).
This is a limited inquiry, but I believe its foundation is more secure than
earlier ones.

II. REJECTION OF ISRAEL

Our interest in comparing the exegesis of talmudic rabbis and
Aphrahat is to discover points of contact, Scriptures on which the Jewish
exegetes and Aphrahat make comments revealing a possible awareness
of contrary, hostile interpretations. It is of no uncontingent consequence
here that both parties occasionally say the same thing about the same
verse. What is significant is evidence of a common interest that produces
conflicting, or otherwise reciprocally pertinent, interpretations. For this
purpose it is unnecessary to review everything every rabbi said about
every Scripture and biblical hero referred to in Aphrahat. Such a study
would be of interest, particularly when undertaken in the broader, more
appropriate context of a wide-ranging comparison of rabbinical and
patristic exegesis. My framework is narrower, and my intention is merely
to lay down the main outlines of the comparative exegetical study that
lies before us. In so narrow a framework, finding mere parallels leads to
no firm conclusions about anything. We cannot fruitfully speculate
about the elements of a common exegetical heritage upon the basis of
some supposed parallels in a single Church father and a few third and
fourth century rabbis.

I follow the references given in A. Hyman, *Sefer Torah HaKetuvah
veHaMesurah* (Tel Aviv, ¹937, I-III) to the Tannaitic Midrashim,
Babylonian and Palestinian Talmuds. I have not consulted late Midrashic

---

from the Babylonian Talmud, evidence that they were, at the very least, known to later
Babylonian masters.

² Except as cited by Louis Ginzberg, *Legends of the Jews*. I have shown reason to doubt
that the data in late midrashic collections pertaining to Yoḥanan ben Zakkai are part of a
living tradition or may in some form be attributed to Yoḥanan or his early disciples. In
general Yoḥanan-traditions in the late midrashic collections are either word-for-word
replications of stories found in earlier collections, or completely new and unrelated to
anything found earlier. A story first occurring in a ninth-century collection, with no
perceptible roots in any tradition occurring earlier, is more apt to be pseudepigraphic than
to be a tradition which circulated orally and only now has been written down. This is
especially so because the stories appearing for the first time in late collections are highly
literary and fully developed, in marked contrast to the primitive forms in which materials

collections or medieval compilations.[2] Materials cited are those attributed to third and fourth-century Babylonian masters or to first and second-century Palestinians, along with some later Palestinian masters.

We shall begin by reviewing Scriptures on which Aphrahat provides exegeses he says he has heard from Jews.

Scripture	Aphrahat	Rabbinical References
Ex. 34:14	I, 785 God has no son.	b. Git. 57b: Rav Judah cites Ex. 34:14 in the story of "a woman and her seven sons," to prove one must not worship other gods. No reference to use of the Scripture to prove God has no son.
Lev. 26:44	I, 933 Proves that God is with us here and always.	b. Meg. 11a: Samuel: *I did not reject them* — in days of Greeks; *abhor* — in days of Nebuchadnezzar; *to destroy* — in days of Haman; *to break my covenant* — in days of Persians; *for I am the Lord their God* — in the days of Gog and Magog. Beraita: *for I am the Lord* — in time to come, when no nation or people will be able to rule over them. This is congruent to Aphrahat's Jewish exegesis, but Aphrahat does not parse the verse.
Deut. 32:39	I, 785 God has no son.	b. Pes. 68a: Rava/Rabbah proves God raises dead. [Also b. Sanh. 91b]. Mekh. Shirata IV.29: Disproves allegation that there are two powers, proves there is only one God. [Also Baḥodesh V. 291] No reference to use of the Scripture to prove God has no son.
Ez. 39:28	I, 849-52 Jews hope for third redemption.	No reference.

appear in earliest collections. All this is spelled out in my *Development of a Legend: Studies on the Traditions concerning Yoḥanan ben Zakkai* (Leiden, 1970).

The results of these studies call into question the certainty that later materials attributed to earlier masters actually derived from those masters or their disciples, and they to the contrary suggest that later materials are pseudepigraphic. Hence it serves no meaningful purpose to cite what later collectors or editors attributed to masters who lived eight, nine, or ten centuries earlier. In the absence of evidence that such attributions are based upon verifiable chains of tradition, and in the face of contrary form-critical results, it is wisest to rely on materials collected merely two or three centuries after they were supposedly said. And, I may add, even this serves merely as a working hypothesis.

We see that three of the four passages are interpreted by rabbis, while one elicited no rabbinical comment whatever. Among the four, only one Scripture provoked a rabbinical exegesis that contains something like what Aphrahat said Jews say. The comments attributed to Samuel and to a tannaitic master on Lev. 26:44 do indeed indicate Jews held the Scripture proves God is with the Jews in times of crisis. But the rabbinical exegetes applied the Scripture's elements to specific crises and derive no general principle from it, though the inference drawn by the rabbis is approximately what Aphrahat claimed. Still, the plain sense of the Scripture is that God would not abandon the Jews but would always be with them. The specific applications of that principle to the several crises are not spelled out in Aphrahat's citation. One did not have to be a rabbi to say about Lev. 26:44 what Aphrahat attributed to Jews. On the basis of the materials before us we cannot suppose Aphrahat actually cited rabbinical exegetes. The weight of evidence points to the opposite conclusion. Aphrahat knew Jews who quoted Scripture, pretty much following its plain meaning. He did not seem to know Jews who interpreted Scripture in characteristically rabbinical modes. But the evidence is too limited to come to a definitive conclusion. To these instances we may add the following:

Scripture	Aphrahat	Rabbinical References
Is. 32:2-3	I, 933 Why cannot Jews walk unharmed through fire, etc.	No comment.

Clearly the difficulty raised by Aphrahat was not recognized by talmudic masters. They did not feel the need to comment on why Jews cannot walk unharmed through fire, nor did the facts of nature raise doubts in their mind as to divine providence.

Israel was rejected because they did not obey God or the prophets (I, 845-8). The symbol of their rejection is the rejection of sacrifices (I, 768). The Jews were, to be sure, saved from Babylonia, but they were not better than before (I, 848). The repertoire of Scriptures proving these propositions follows.

Scripture	Aphrahat	Rabbinical References
1. Ex. 12:33	I, 849 Jews rejected redemption.	No pertinent comment.

Scripture	Aphrahat	Rabbinical References
2. Deut. 9:24	I, 468, 852-3 Israel always rebellious.	No comment.
3. Deut. 31:29	I, 748, 852, 874 Moses predicted Israel's future sin.	No pertinent comment.
4. Deut. 32:21	I, 469, 511, 760, 782, 854 Provoke with people which is no people.	b. Yev. 63b: R. Hannan b. Rava in the name of Rav: This is a bad wife with an expensive marriage-settlement. There is no hint of awareness of the Christian interpretation, and nothing directed as a polemic against more concrete historical interpretations of the Scripture.
5. Deut. 32:32	I, 468, 511, 765, 782, 852, 860 God never accepted Israel's repentence.	No pertinent comment.
6. I Sam. 3:14	I, 748-9 Sin of Eli not expiated through sacrifice	b. R.H. 18a *Beraita*: Rava: with sacrifice their sin will not be atoned for, but it will be forgiven through Torah and acts of compassion [= b. Yev. 105a]. y.R.H. 2:5: R. Kahana & R. Ḥiyya b. Ba, Not through sacrifice but through prayer [= y. Sanh. 1:2]. Here is a clearcut conflict of interpretation. Aphrahat takes the passage to mean sacrifice is of no value, and the contemporary Babylonian rabbinic interpretation agrees — but posits study of Torah and acts of compassion as the substitute for sacrifice. The difference of course is that for Aphrahat Israel's convenanted relationship with God has ended, while for the rabbis God had always preferred Torah to sacrifice, as the curse of Eli and his house made clear so long before.
7. I. Sam. 15:14	I, 748-9 No use for sacrifice.	No comment.

	Scripture	Aphrahat	Rabbinical References
8.	Is. 1:2	I, 773, 790 Jews were heirs.	No pertinent comment.
9.	Is. 1:10	I, 468, 469, 472, 533, 765, 963 Israel = Sodom	b. Ber. 19a: A man should not give Satan an opening. R. Joseph: What Scriptures proves it? Is. 1:9-10.[= b. Ket. 8b]
10.	Is. 2:5-6	I, 765 House of Jacob = gentiles.	No comment.
11.	Is. 5:1-6	I, 469, 861 Wild grapes produced by vineyard.	b. Suk. 49a: R. Yosi interprets the song of the vineyard in terms of the Temple in Jerusalem, altar.
12.	Is. 11:11	I, 868 Redemption a second time, no third time.	No comment.
13.	Is. 29:13	I, 768, 888 Israel rejected.	No comment.
14.	Is. 30:1	I, 468, 766 Rebellious Israel	No comment.
15.	Is. 33:1	I, 849 Prophetic promises can be annulled.	No comment.
16.	Is. 33:13	I, 514, 773 Called gentiles	No comment.
17.	Is. 34:4	I, 949ff. Israel never gave up idolatry.	No comment.
18.	Is. 43:24	I, 565 Israel burdened God.	No comment.
19.	Is. 50:1	I, 564 Israel burdened God.	b. Sanh. 105a: Samuel said, Ten men came and sat before the prophet. He said to them, Return and repent. They answered, If a master sells his slave or a man divorces his wife, has one a further claim on the other? [That is, God has no further claim on us, having sold us to Nebuchadnezzar, so we have no reason to repent.] He replied Is. 50:1, meaning that you were sold for your *own* iniquities and the premises of their argument were false. Hence they should repent.

Scripture	Aphrahat	Rabbinical References
20. Is. 52:11	I, 864 Rejection of Israel.	No comment.
21. Is. 54:9	I, 949 God no longer angry because Jerusalem desolated *forever*.	b. Sanh. 99a: R. Judah in name of Samuel: The days of the Messiah will last as long as from creation to now. R. Naḥman b. Isaac: As long as from Noah's days until now, Is. 54:9. For an equal period he will not be angry with Israel. b. Soṭ. 11a: Ḥama b. Ḥanina interprets passage to prove there will never again be a flood over the whole earth. [Cf. y. Ta. 3:9.]
22. Is. 55:5	I, 773ff. Called gentiles.	No comment.
23. Is. 59:2	I, 773ff. Rejected Israel.	b. Sanh. 65b: Rava said, If the righteous desired it, they could be creators, Is. 59:2. That is, but for sin, men would have power equal to God's creative power.
24. Is. 66:3	I, 748-9 Sacrifices no good.	No comment.
25. Jer. 2:10-13	I, 952 Israel worshipped heavens.	No pertinent comment.
26. Jer. 2:21	I, 469, 765, 860 Alien vine, bad wine.	No comment.
27. Jer. 3:8	I, 860, 886, 953 Rejection.	No comment.
28. Jer. 3:16	I, 509, 532 Rejection: illegal for Jews to make ark of covenant.	No comment.
29. Jer. 6:30	I, 468, 753, 765, 768, 853, 939 Rejected silver.	No comment.
30. Jer. 9:10	I, 533 Jews annulled covenant.	No comment.
31. Jer. 12:1	I, 953 Israel rejected.	No pertinent comment.

Scripture	Aphrahat	Rabbinical References
32. Jer. 12:7	I, 766, 860 Israel rejected.	No pertinent comment.
33. Jer. 15:1-2	I, 753 Rejected Israel and its sacrifices.	No pertinent comment.
34. Jer. 18:7-10	I, 852 God can change mind.	No comment.
35. Jer. 31:31-2	I, 499, 533 Jews say God will make new covenant, but they are rejected.	No comment.
36. Jer. 31:34	I, 499, 773ff. God called gentiles.	No comment.
37. Jer. 44:16-17	I, 761-4, 888 Rejection of Israel.	No comment.
38. Ez. 8:10	I, 768-9 Rejection of Israel.	b. Sanh. 92b: Isaac Nappaḥa: These are men who covered the Temple with abominations.
39. Ez. 8:10-12	I, 768, 773ff. Rejection of Israel.	No pertinent comment.
40. Ez. 15:4	I, 469, 766, 769, 861, 886 Fire burned bough.	No pertinent comment.
41. Ez. 16:45	I, 468, 765 Israel descends from Amorites and Hittites.	No comment.
42. Ez. 16:48-9, 52-55	I, 472, 936ff. Israel is like Sodom, therefore will never be rebuilt.	b. Sanh. 104b: Inquity of Israel greater than Sodom. Rabbah in name of R. Yoḥanan: There was an extra measure of punishment in Jerusalem, which Sodom was spared, Ez. 16:49 and Lam. 4:10.
43. Ez. 23:4	I, 769 Both Israel and Judah rejected.	No comment.
44. Hos. 2:2, 3, 15	I, 768-9 Both Judah and Israel rejected.	b. Pes. 88a: R. Yoḥanan said, The ingathering of the exiles is greater than the day of the creation of the world.

Scripture	Aphrahat	Rabbinical References
45. Hos. 2:11	I, 509 Rejection of sacrifices	Ber. 35b: R. Ḥanina b. Papa compared Hos. 2:11 and Deut. 11:14. One refers to the time that Israel does God's will, the other when they do not do God's will.
46. Hos. 3:4	I, 509 Rejection of sacrifices	No pertinent comment.
47. Hos. 5:7	I, 768-9 Israel rejected.	b. Yev. 17a: Samuel said the Scripture was basis to declare the ten tribes perfect heathens. b. Qid. 70a: Rav said Hos. 5:7 refers to one who marries for money.
48. Hos. 6:4-5, 8	I, 853-6, 949-952 Israel rejected.	b. Ber. 59a: R. Samuel b. Isaac derives information on morning clouds. b. Ta. 6b: R. Papa to Abbaye, If it rains in the morning . . . Re Hos. 6:8, b. Mak. 10a: Abbaye said murderers are commonplace in Gilead.
49. Hos. 7:13	I, 853-6 Israel rejected.	b. A.Z. 4a: R. Abba says, Hos. 7:13 means that God planned to redeem them through their property in this world so they should merit the world to come, but they declined the punishment, as R. Papi said in Rava's name they rejected the this-worldly punishment. The comments all assume the referent is the ten northern tribes.
50. Hos. 9:10, 11, 12, 15, 17	I, 853-6 Israel rejected.	b. Ber. 56b: Recite this Scripture if you dream of clouds.
51. Hos. 10:1, 6	I, 853-6 Israel rejected.	No comment.
52. Hos. 11:12	I, 768-9, 853-6 Israel rejected.	No comment.
53. Hos. 13:9, 11	I, 853-6 Israel rejected.	No comment.
54. Amos 4:9	I, 857-60 Israel rejected.	b. Shab. 32b-33a: Rava said refers to the women of Maḥoza.

	Scripture	Aphrahat	Rabbinical References
55.	Amos 4:11	I, 857-60 Israel rejected.	No reference.
56.	Amos 5:2, 16, 21, 22-25	I, 748-9, 857-60, 948 No further hope	b. Ḥag. 6b: ʿAqiva said Levites offered sacrifice in wilderness, since *they* had not worshipped the calf.
57.	Amos 8:11-12	I, 773ff. Israel rejected.	b. Shab. 138b, *beraita*: The Torah is destined to be forgotten in Israel.
58.	Amos 9:7-8	I, 857-60	b. M.Q. 16b: Refers to Israel, whose deeds are different from those of all the nations as the skin of the Ethiopian is different.
59.	Micah 2:3, 2:10, 3:17	I, 856 Rejection of Israel	No reference.
60.	Micah 7:4, 14, 17	I, 864 Rejection of Israel	b. ʿEruv. 101a: Joshua b. Ḥananiah said *re* 7:4, the good men among us defend us. b. Pes. 68a: Rav said *re* 7:14 Bashan is Elisha; righteous will resurrect the dead.
61.	Nahum 2:13	I, 864 Rejection of Israel	No pertinent comment.
62.	Nahum 3:1	I, 864 Rejection of Israel	No reference.
63.	Haggai 1:8, 2:5-8, 10	I, 865 Redemption in the past	b. Sanh. 97b, re. Ḥag. 2:6, R. ʿAqiva expounded, the first monarchy is seventy years, the second, fifty-two, and that of Ben Koziva two and one half years.
64.	*Zech. 1:14-15,* *17*	I, 865, 868-9 Redemption in the past.	No reference.
65.	*Zech. 2:4-5,* *6-7, 12*	I, 868-9 Redemption in the past.	b. B.B. 75b: Resh Laqish: God will expand Jerusalem in the future.
66.	*Zech. 4:9*	I, 868-9 Redemption in the past.	No reference.

	Scripture	Aphrahat	Rabbinical References
67.	Zech. 7:6	I, 748-9 Sacrifice no good.	No reference.
68.	Mal. 2:8	I, 863 Rejection of Israel.	b. Bekh. 26b, beraita: Applies to misdeeds of priests, Levites, and poor who are paid in sacred tithes.
69.	Mal. 2:9	I, 863 Rejection of Israel.	b. Ta. 20a: Rav Judah said this was stated as a blessing.
70.	Mal. 2:11	I, 863 Rejection of Israel.	b. Sanh. 82a: R. Kahana heard this vs. in a dream. Rav explained to him it referred to idolatry, etc.
71.	Mal. 2:17	I, 863 Rejection of Israel.	No reference.
72.	Mal. 3:6-7.	I, 863 Rejection of Israel.	No pertinent comment.
73.	Ps. 49:13-15	I, 748-9 Sacrifice no good.	No pertinent comment.
74.	Ps. 69:28	I, 769 God rejected Israel	No reference.
75.	Ps. 80:8, 9, 13	I, 861 God rejected Israel.	b. Hul. 92a: R. Jeremiah b. Abba, The vine is Israel.
76.	Daniel's Vision Chapter 9	I, 869ff. Vision of the future, no redemption after destruction.	b. Sanh. 97b: R. Samuel b. Naḥmani said in name of R. Jonathan, Blasted be the bones of those who calculate the end, for they would say, Since the predetermined time has arrived and he has not yet come, he will never come. Rav said, All predestined dates [for redemption] have passed, and the matter now depends on repentence and good deeds. Louis Ginzberg, Legends of the Jews (Phila., 1946) VI, p. 436, n. 19, comments, "If Daniel himself failed in fixing the time accurately, it would be futile for any other mortal to attempt this task." The rabbinical response (if any) to Aphrahat's chronology would simply be, Daniel was wrong.

On the basis of the materials we have just reviewed, one can hardly locate either a rabbinic dialogue with Christianity or a Christian dialogue with rabbis known to us. In the main neither side could have confronted the other's Scriptural testimonies. The rabbis scarcely paid attention to the Scriptures Aphrahat was certain proved one or another Christian belief. The most striking result of our survey indeed is to discover that the rabbis simply did not interest themselves in the Scriptures that most interested Aphrahat. It is a puzzling phenomenon, for if, as we have until now supposed, any sort of dialogue or encounter took place between Jews of rabbinical persuasion and Christians, then we should have expected the echoes of that conversation to be heard in biblical exegesis. Nor do I imagine that the rabbis deliberately ignored Scriptures important to Christian critics of Judaism. On the contrary, we have every reason to think that while specific reference to what Christians said may not have been made, general comments orienting the interpretation of pertinent Scriptures away from the Christian reading of them ought certainly to have been provoked. The rabbis, after all, did not live divorced from the everyday life of ordinary Jews, nor were they indifferent to Christianity and its appeal to Jewry. Their way of dealing with the Christian threat did not include confrontation with the substance of the Christian argument. It was rather to speak in hints, by indirection, e.g. about Balaam meaning Jesus, or about Hezekiah in Ps. 110. We found scarcely anything that suggested an anti-Christian polemic of any sort.

Fundamentally, rabbis (and probably other Jews as well) simply could not take seriously the most basic convictions of Christianity. They expected the Messiah, but did not think Jesus was the Christ. They hardly entertained doubts about the continuing election of Israel. It never entered their mind that the sacrifices were not going to be restored in the future. They therefore assumed, within the qualifications laid down by prophecy, that past sacrifice was of value. They took for granted the fact that ancient Israel had sinned — indeed, the burden of their contemporary politics was that Israel should overcome the consequences of sin through obedience to Torah. But they also were confident that through suffering and exile Israel would expiate the sins of old and achieve reconciliation with God.

Each party to the argument remained wholly within his own doctrinal presuppositions. This accounts for the absence of any genuine encounter at all. Aphrahat's concern was for ordinary Christians. The force of his argument, as we saw earlier, was to strengthen their wavering convictions. The rabbis exerted influence and power over ordinary Jews. Their intent was to teach every Jew to conform to the rabbinical way and so to render all Israel a replication of the ideals of the Torah, hence of Heaven itself. With whom, then, did Aphrahat argue? The "debater of the people" seems to me to have been a marginal figure. He was sufficiently interested in Christianity to engage in debates with its exponent. Such an interest was not characteristic of rabbis of the age, so far as we can tell. Still, it is curious that among the few items more or less pertinent to Aphrahat's interpretation, several were attributed to his contemporaries and near-contemporaries, e.g. Rava (Nos. 6, 23, 49, 54), R. Joseph (No. 8), and Rabbah (No. 42). For Aphrahat's part, it may well be that the condition of the church provoked his argument with the synagogue. Had Christianity stood firm from within, his debates with outsiders paradoxically would have occupied much less attention than otherwise. The fact, therefore, that the bulk of his critique of Judaism in the end was addressed to men of little faith within the church must shape our understanding of the Scriptural elements of the argument.

Aphrahat took at face value every reference to the rejection of Israel. Each proved for him the same proposition, that Israel was rejected of old. Concomitantly, all allusions to "the peoples" or "the nations," or indeed to anyone who was not part of ancient Israel, e.g. Jethro and Rahab, concerned the "people which is of the peoples." How might a rabbi have confronted such arguments? As to the former, he would have said, True, Israel was rejected of old, but her punishment was the consequence of that rejection, and through suffering she has been and again will be reconciled with God. The peoples of course will be called by God when the Messiah will come at the end of time. Aphrahat further maintained that the prophetic promises were all fulfilled. Those pertinent to Israel's redemption were carried out in Egypt and Babylonia. Those concerning the Messiah were completed in Jesus Christ. To this the rabbis would have responded, if at all, by simple denials. The promise yet endures. The Messiah has not yet come. There was little more to be said.

To be sure, some rabbinical comments on Scriptures important to Aphrahat tended to turn aside the force of his arguments. The provocation with the "people which is no people" of Deut. 32:21 (No. 4, also No. 47) becomes "a bad wife with an expensive marriage-settlement." I cannot imagine that Rav, in so interpreting the Scripture, intended to respond in some way to the Christian understanding. Similarly, that the sin of Eli would not be expiated through sacrifice (No. 6) was seen by Aphrahat as evidence that sacrifice never availed. The rabbis by contrast said that sacrifice did not avail, but study of Torah and deeds of compassion would serve to expiate sin. In saying so, they to be sure entered a polemic — but it was not against Christianity. They rather continued to address themselves to the Temple cult in terms of ancient Pharisaism. Pharisaism had held that even though the Temple was destroyed, Israel retained a means of atonement, which was the Pharisaic program of study of Torah, practice of the commandments, and doing deeds of compassion.

The comparison of Israel to Sodom made its impression on the rabbis (No. 9), but only to lead them to draw the inference that one should not give Satan a chance to open his mouth. No one could take seriously the proposition that Israel was like Sodom, that Israel now, like Sodom of old, would never be restored to its ancient greatness. The conception was so alien to the rabbinical imagination that no refutation could possibly have been needed. Had rabbis heard the exegesis of Is. 11:11 (No. 12), it is unthinkable that they could not have formulated an appropriate reply. The treatment of Is. 54:9 (No. 21) is a good example of what the rabbinical exegetes could have achieved had they wanted to. Condemnation of ancient Israel served for the rabbis as the source for their plea to contemporary Jewry. The ancients were separated from God by their sins — "but we can become like God through true penitence" (No. 23). Since rabbis did not imagine Israel to have been permanently and utterly rejected, it was unnecessary for them to argue the contrary. What interested them was the lessons to be learned from ancient times, and these they spelled out. It follows that epithets directed against Israel of old, e.g. Jer. 6:30 (No. 29) required no comment whatsoever. If, to be sure, Israel was worse than Sodom, as in Ez. 16:48-9, 52-55, then it was not damaging to observe that Israel was punished more than Sodom (No. 42). In any event Hosea had addressed himself to the northern tribes, and the rabbis regarded themselves as heirs of Judah. If Aphrahat's special interest in Hosea and other northern prophets was aroused by the probability that the Israelites of northern Mesopotamia were believed to be descendents of northern Israelites, he never gave an indication of that fact. The argument is with *all* Israel, and no distinction is drawn between those punished in 621, 586, and 70.

The rabbis were quite well prepared to condemn Jewry in their own day. They indeed were far more severe critics than was Aphrahat. Hence they could apply the Scriptures in Amos to the women of Maḥoza (No. 54) and to the generation then alive. The famine of Amos 8:11-12 (No. 57) was a famine of Torah. Where the rabbis differed from Aphrahat was in their love for Israel, old and contemporary. He criticized only *en passent*, for his intent was to prove Israel had been rejected. They criticized pointedly and often, for their intent was to improve the condition of Israel. Naturally, for his purpose Aphrahat could readily interpret all promises of redemption as in the past, e.g. in No. 65, while the rabbis would just as naturally embellish those promises as they applied them to the future condition of Israel.

The single most striking difference between Aphrahat and rabbis was on Daniel 9. Here Aphrahat offered a concrete timetable of redemption, proving that Daniel had foretold both the redemption of Israel and its ultimate rejection. Obviously Aphrahat came at the end of a series of those who attempted to interpret in concrete historical events the meaning of Daniel's vision. The Palestinian rabbis had long since rejected all such efforts to calculate the end of time, vigorously opposing anyone who claimed to know when the Messiah would come. But they did so not in response to Christianity. They were concerned with the recurrence of the tragedy of Bar Kokhba's time, when many Jews including important rabbis believed Bar Kokhba was a Messiah and followed him to a terribly destructive war. The comment attributed to 'Aqiva (No. 63, which is certainly pseudepigraphic), reflects the rabbinical judgment on that particular episode — the whole thing lasted a mere two-and-a-half years. If Aphrahat had argued with a rabbi about the meaning of Daniel, he probably would not have found an equivalent contrary view, for we have no rabbinical calculation of the coming of the Messiah or the meaning of the weeks of Daniel similar to Aphrahat's. The rabbis would have said that Daniel as read by Aphrahat was simply wrong, for obvious reasons, and that the true meaning of Daniel's vision would only be known when it was fulfilled.

III. The Peoples in Place of the People

Aphrahat cited numerous Scriptures to demonstrate the vocation of the gentiles, apart from the entire Demonstration (XVI) devoted to this belief. The rabbis rarely refer to these same Scriptures. Of nineteen items, we find comments on only eight. None of these eight comments is shaped by a concern to refute Christian doctrine. All could have been made had no one ever asserted that Scriptural references to "the peoples" meant the church. I imagine such an allegation was either unknown to the Babylonian rabbis, or, if known, viewed as ridiculous, utterly unworthy of comment.

Scripture	Aphrahat	Rabbinical References
77. Gen. 17:5	I, 468, 498, 534, 760 Gentiles called before Israel	No pertinent source contains this interpretation or its opposite. y. Bik. 1:4, R. Judah: In the past you were the father of Aram, now you are father of all the nations.
78. Gen. 49:10	I, 760, 806, 886 Jacob spoke of gentiles	b. Sanh. 5a, Beraita: refers to Babylonian exilarchs and Palestinian patriarchs. [= b. Hor. 11b]. b. Sanh. 98b: School of R. Shila says name of Messiah is Shilo.
79. Ex. 32:10	I, 772-3 Vocation of peoples	b. Ber. 32a: R. Abbahu says Moses insisted God forgive Israel, which he did. R. Eleazar says, Moses compared Israel to three-legged stool (Abraham, Isaac, Jacob), and said *his* people would be like a one-legged stool, hence it could not stand, so God had better not reject Israel. The rabbis do not see the Scripture as pertaining to the formation of a new people but rather as testifying to the forgiveness of the old one.
80. Num. 24:21	I, 598, 777-780 Jethro better than Israelite	b. Sanh. 106a: R. Jonathan says, Balaam said to Jethro, Kenite, you were not with us in that conspiracy. Who set you among the strong men of the world? And this is what R. Ḥiyya b. Abba said in the name of R. Simai, Three were in that conspiracy, and these are they, Balaam, Job, and Jethro. Denigrating Jethro is certainly a useful way of replying to the argument that he was a righteous gentile, and superior to Israel. It is of interest that Palestinians shaped this tradition.
81. Deut. 32:21	I, 509, 513 Fulfilled in gentiles' church.	See No. 4

Scripture	Aphrahat	Rabbinical References
82. Is. 2:2	I, 513, 760-1, 861-4 Addressed to church.	No pertinent comment.
83. Is. 33:13 (See Deut. 32: 21)	I, 513, 775 Addressed to church.	No comment.
84. Is. 42:6 (See Deut. 32: 21)	I, 781-2 Israel prevented from idolatry by shame before gentiles who worship God.	No comment.
85. Is. 49:6, 51:4	I, 772-3 Vocation of peoples.	No comment.
86. Jer. 6:8-9	I, 761-4 Vocation of peoples.	No comment.
87. Jer. 6:16-18	I, 512-3, 763 When Jews would not listen, Jeremiah turned to gentiles and rejected Israel.	No comment.
88. Jer. 12:7-9	I, 512, 754, 764-5, 859 Painted bird = church.	b. Zev. 119a: R. Judah said the inheritance of God spoken of in Jer. 12:9 is Jerusalem. R. Simeon said it refers to Shiloh.
89. Jer. 16:19	I, 761 Conversion of gentiles.	No comment.
90. Mal. 1:11	I, 768 Gentiles chosen.	b. Men. 110a: R. Judah in the name of Rav interpreted the Scripture to mean God is everywhere worshipped. R. Samuel b. Naḥmani said it refers to disciples of the sages who everywhere study the Torah.
91. Ps. 18:44-5	I, 772-3, 813 Christians are sons.	No reference.
92. Ps. 22:28	I, 773ff. Vocation of gentiles.	No. reference.
93. Ps. 47:1	I, 773ff. Gentiles called.	No reference.

	Scripture	Aphrahat	Rabbinical References
94.	Ps. 69:28-9	I, 769 Rejection of Israel and vocation of gentiles.	No pertinent comment. b. R.H. 17b: refers to righteous and wicked.
95.	Ps. 74:2	I, 513, 773 Refers to church.	No reference.
96.	Ps. 87:6	I, 769 God counts gentiles.	No reference.

To the rabbis it was unthinkable that gentiles had taken, or could take, the place of Israel in the divine plan. Israel was chosen of old, and the mark of her chosenness was providential punishment for her sins, as Yoḥanan ben Zakkai had said at the time of the destruction of Jerusalem in 70 A.D. Just as God was sufficiently concerned with Israel to punish sin, so he could be relied on to reward her repentence and in the end of days to restore her fortunes. Scriptures central to Aphrahat's argument, e.g. Gen. 49:10 (No. 78), were not interpreted in response to Christian assertions, but quite apart from them. Gen. 49:10 referred to the patriarchs and exilarchs; but even if, as in the school of R. Shila, one understood the Scripture to refer to the coming Messiah, it could not be turned to the Christians' advantage. That Abraham was the father of many nations moreover posed no problem to the rabbinical exegetes. The many gentile nations were just that — gentiles — and they were not the "people which is of the peoples." God did not reject Israel and form a new people, but he forgave the old and would in time call all peoples. Within that paradigm, all Scriptures employed by Aphrahat could be satisfactorily interpreted by the rabbis.

We again note the parallel tendency of Aphrahat and the rabbis to see things pretty much in their own terms. Just as Mal. 1:11 (No. 90) means to Aphrahat that the gentiles were chosen in place of Israel, so it means to R. Samuel b. Naḥmani that the Torah is everywhere studied. The respective interpretations do not merely differ; they are completely unrelated, just as the systems of values they reflect have nothing to do with one another.

Still, I cannot argue that Samuel b. Naḥmani's interpretation was completely unrelated to the Christian assertion that Mal. 1:10-11 referred to the spread of Christianity. A careful study of the sayings of R. Jonathan and R. Samuel b. Naḥmani might show a consistent pattern by which they responded to Scriptural interpretations important in the Church with contrary, rabbinical readings. As we shall see, most Church

Fathers engaged in debates with Judaism referred to that very Scripture and others on which Aphrahat and the rabbis in question also commented. But since both rabbis were Palestinians, we have no grounds to imagine that they stood in some sort of relationship to Aphrahat in particular, and the greater likelihood is that he never heard of them (nor, for obvious, chronological reasons, they of him).

IV. THE PASSION FORETOLD

From the beginnings of Christianity the "Old Testament" served as a treasury of proof-texts for the proposition that Jesus was the Christ foretold by prophecy. Aphrahat's repertoire contains little that is new. His citations of the New Testament indicate the extent to which its application of Hebrew Scriptures to the passion had shaped his hermeneutical imagination. We need hardly be surprised to find few pertinent rabbinical remarks.

Scripture	Aphrahat	Rabbinical References
97. Gen. 49:10	I, 804, 885 Fulfilled in Christ, proved by me, Aphrahat.	See No. 78.
98. Ex. 4:22-3	I, 774, 788-9, 846 Israel called sons of God.	b. Shab. 31a: Gentile convert in Hillel's time noted that Israel was called children of the Omnipresent. Mekh. Shir. II. 2: God exalted Israel as Israel exalted God. The rabbinical comments understand the verse just as did Aphrahat, probably because they both read it in its plain sense.
99. Ex. 7:1-2	I, 788 Moses called God.	Mekh. Pisḥa I. 11: From this I would know only that Moses was a judge. The rabbis understood 'elohim to mean judge, not God. Aphrahat understood the word to mean God, as we noticed. But the rabbinic usage long antedated the polemical context and cannot be thought a response to Christian arguments about Jesus.

Scripture	Aphrahat	Rabbinical References
100. Ex. 12:5 (see also Ex. 12:4, 9, 11)	I, 505, 525 Interpreted in terms of passion.	Rabbinic comments, e.g. b. Zev. 25b, Bekh. 12a, etc. make no allusion whatever to the Christian interpretation. That is to say, they do not bother to emphasize it is a *real* lamb referred to. Either the rabbis did not know the Christian interpretation, or, if they did, they did not think it necessary to refute it.
101. II Sam. 7:14	I, 788 Solomon called son of God.	No comment.
102. Is. 7:14	I, 804 Christ foretold.	No comment.
103. Is. 9:6-7	I, 804ff. Christ foretold.	b. Shab. 55a: R. Yohanan, When was the merit of the patriarchs used up? b. Sanh. 94a: Bar Qappara: The Holy One wanted to make Hezekiah the messiah and Sennacherib Gog and Magog, but he did not praise God for miracles as had David, so was unworthy. y. Sanh. 10:1, R. Yudan said merit of patriarchs was used up in days of Hezekiah.
104. Is. 52:13-15, 53:2, 5, 10	I, 808ff., 812 Apply to Christ.	b. Ber. 5a: R. Huna, Whoever the Holy One desires is humbled with suffering; but he must accept the suffering with love. His reward will be to have children and live a long time and his learning will remain with him. [All *re* Is. 53:10.]
105. Is. 53 & Ex. 12	I, 516 Apply to passion.	No pertinent reference.
106. Zech. 9:10	I, 761 Applies to Christ.	No reference.
107. Zech. 14:6-7	I, 812 Foretold passion.	No pertinent reference.

	Scripture	Aphrahat	Rabbinical References
108.	Ps. 2:6	I, 804 Applies to Christ.	No reference.
109.	Ps. 16:10	I, 808ff. Applies to Christ.	No pertinent comment.
110.	Ps. 22:17-18, 23	I, 808ff. Applies to Christ.	No reference.
111.	Ps. 69:21, 26	I, 812 Applies to Christ.	No reference.
112.	Ps. 110:3	I, 804ff. Applies to Christ.	y. Ber. 5:3, Resh Laqish refers to Abraham.
113.	Ps. 118:22 (With Ez. 13: 10-11, Luke 19: 13-14)	I, 16 Jesus is stoned, rejected.	b. Pes. 119a: R. Samuel b. Naḥ mani in name of R. Jonathan. This was said by Jesse and others in that time.
114.	Dan. 9:26-7	I, 805, 882, 939, 943 Daniel foresaw Jesus.	b. Ta. 28b: Mishnah: Five misfortunes befell our fathers on the 17th of Tammuz. Rava interprets the passage in Dan. 9:27 to prove there were two idols in Daniel's time.

Aphrahat's touching remark on Gen. 49:10 (No. 97), that he himself had hoped for the coming of Christ before he knew about him, could not have elicited a rabbinical response. It is striking, on the other hand, that Nos. 98-100 all did provoke comment on the part of rabbis. Clearly, the rabbis understood Ex. 4:22-3 just as did Aphrahat. But the reason is equally clear: both parties interpreted the plain sense of the Scripture, which called the Israelites children of God. On the other hand, Moses was "God," meaning merely a judge to the rabbis, a view that probably antedated any sort of Jewish-Christian argument. The rabbis did not follow the typological or allegorical interpretations of Christianity and so did not respond by emphasizing the worldly reality of the lamb. The this-worldly sense of Is. 52 and 53 is noteworthy. The rabbi drew a moral lesson: God humbles the one he loves. The Scriptures did not in the rabbi's mind refer to the coming Messiah (or, for that matter, to the Jewish people), but rather to *anyone* whom God loved. The reward for God's love would be long life and children. The Scriptures were not understood in an eschatological dimension. Strikingly, the Palestinian Samuel b. Naḥmani in the name of R. Jonathan did understand Ps.

118:22 (No. 113) to refer to the Messianic household — but to Jesse. This comes as close as one can to an actual response to Christian exegesis. It was not Babylonian, though to be sure it was known in Babylonia. While we cannot suppose it was shaped in response to Aphrahat, we may imagine that it would have served in a debate with him, had such taken place. Clearly, debates on the Christ must have elicited rabbinical response in terms of the Scriptures Christians cited for the purposes of their argument. I should suppose that in Palestine such arguments may have been carried on. But we have no evidence that Babylonian rabbis participated in them.

v. Celibacy

Much Aphrahat said about licentiousness was acceptable to rabbis. They would have agreed Samson, David, Amnon, Solomon, and the rest were ruined by women (I, 836ff). But they did not draw from that fact the conclusion that marriage is not so good as celibacy. They to be sure had an ambivalent view of women. Women had no place in their schools. While Christian monasteries and the life of holiness provided a role for women, the same was not the case in the rabbinical movement. Moreover, when the sessions were held, husbands and wives remained apart for long periods of time, so we may say that the rabbis practiced a temporary celibacy for much of their lives. But the rabbinical tradition could never reconcile itself to the life of celibacy and regarded marriage as the normal condition of man. Virginity was called for only before marriage or outside of it.

	Scripture	Aphrahat	Rabbinical References
115.	Gen. 2:24	I, 840 Means you should be celibate, love Father and Holy Spirit.	No pertinent comment. y. Qid. 1:1 contains exegeses in which the Scripture proves one may not have 'unnatural intercourse' etc. No one interprets the verse to prove one must marry, or that marriage is a good thing, probably because that is the plain sense of the Scripture and it entered no one's mind to suppose otherwise.
116.	Ex. 19:15	I, 825 No revelation until people celibate.	b. Yev. 62b [Beraita]: Moses decided of his own accord not to have sexual relations and God agreed with him.

Scripture	Aphrahat	Rabbinical References
		The rabbis thus came to precisely the same conclusion as Aphrahat, namely that Moses remained celibate because he was constantly receiving revelations. But they did not draw the same conclusion, that celibacy was better or more conducive to the holy life than marriage. They furthermore do not refer to the temporary celibacy of the whole people. Nonetheless, the *qal veḥomer* drawn by Aphrahat is likewise drawn by the *beraita* regarding Moses' continuing celibacy. The interpretation is therefore the same on both parts, but the conclusion is different. This is an example of a parallel leading to contradictory conclusions. It would not prove that the rabbis responded to Aphrahat or to arguments similar to his. Indeed, it would suggest just the opposite, that they did not find it necessary to respond at all. Otherwise they could not have come to the same interpretation of the Scripture.
117.	Jer. 16:2, 17:16	I, 833 Why Jeremiah did not marry.	No comment.

It was unnecessary to argue that marriage is a commandment of God and that those who interpret Gen. 2:24 in a "spiritual" sense are in error. Such a "spiritual" interpretation was simply unthinkable. Contrary argument therefore was not called for. Aphrahat's interpretation of Ex. 19:15 is another matter. Here he had clear proof that revelation was withheld from those who engaged in sexual relations. The rabbis furthermore agreed that Moses did not have sexual relations after Sinai. As I noted (No. 116), we have here a genuine parallel. It neatly demonstrates that parallels do not meet. Since it obviously never entered the mind of a rabbi that one should, like Moses "our rabbi", remain celibate, we must conclude no one put such a thought there. Once again we are left with the impression of slight, if any, contact between rabbis and Christians. Had rabbis known what Christians said about Ex. 19:15, they could hardly have said much the same thing without also adding that those who draw such-and-so-conclusions are wrong. Rabbis could not have known what Christians said about the Scripture and remained free to say the same thing without any sort of additional comment. The parallel therefore leads to the conclusion that the rabbis knew nothing of the quite parallel Christian exegesis of the verse.

vi. The Practical Commandments

Aphrahat's chief argument was that practice of the commandments did not lead to salvation. He did not invent this argument, for from the time of Paul onward, Christian polemic was directed against circumcision, dietary, laws, the Sabbath, and similar practical commandments. We need hardly be surprised, therefore, to find Palestinian rabbinical sayings in praise of circumcision and the like. But we do not have to suppose the rabbis made such statements only in direct, self-conscious response to Christian polemic. The structure of rabbinical faith, not the necessities of disputation, led to a high evaluation of the commandments. The rabbis and other Jews certainly did believe God wanted Israel to keep the Sabbath, to circumcise, and to keep all the laws of the Torah. They would have said so even if no one had maintained the contrary. The Jewish community believed, along with the rabbis, in the continued validity of the biblical commandments and in their salvific value. When, furthermore, we find that rabbis and Aphrahat said much the same thing about the commandments, we need hardly postulate influence of the one upon the other, for both read Scriptures, and the plain sense of Scriptures readily produced both common understanding of biblical heroes and precepts, and differing interpretations of their significance.

It is noteworthy that rabbis said much the same thing about some of the practical commandments as Aphrahat. The rite of circumcision served to distinguish Israel from the nations (Ginzberg, *Legends*, III, pp. 86, 375). Obviously the Sabbath was a day of rest for man and beast. No one needed to prove that proposition. On the other hand, the institution of sacrifices was understood as an act of divine grace, "that the people might see that God did not mean to be angry with them forever" (Ginzberg, III, p. 285). The sacrifices served to reconcile Israel with God

(Ginzberg, III, p. 458). The dietary laws were intended to restrict the enjoyment of meat "in order to grant them [Israel] reward for the observance thereof" (Ginzberg, V, p. 190, n. 56 end). The important difference between Aphrahat and the rabbis lay, therefore, not in the historical explanation for the practical commandments, for it did not disturb the rabbis to discover practical purposes for the commandments. It was rather the value to be assigned to the practical commandments. Here the rabbis and Aphrahat part company, for while the latter insisted the commandments had no salvific value, as we have seen time and again, the rabbis held the commandments now served to reconcile Israel to God and to increase the merit of Israel, and in time to come would help Israel to merit salvation.

Scripture	Aphrahat	Rabbinical References
118. Gen. 1:29	I, 736 Any food all right but not blood.	b. Sanh. 59b: Rav Judah-Rav; Adam was not allowed to eat meat. Meat was first permitted to the children of Noah. Here is a clear conflict, for Aphrahat states that both Adam and Noah were permitted to eat meat.
119. Gen. 7:1ff.	I, 549-51, 555 Noah did not keep Sabbath.	No reference to what constituted the excellence of Noah. Noah did not marry until he was 498 years old, lest his children perish, so Ginzberg, Legends Vol. I, p. 159; the late source is not pertinent to our study, however.
120. Gen. 15:6	I, 476, 558 Faith, not circumcision.	Mekh. Beshallaḥ IV. 59: Shemayah says, The faith with which their father Abraham believed in me is deserving that I should divide the sea for them. IV. 141: Abraham inherited this world and world to come because of his faith. No reference to faith's excluding the salvific value of commandments.
121. Gen. 17:10	I, 476 Circumcision valid for limited time.	No pertinent comments.

Scripture	Aphrahat	Rabbinical References
122. Gen. 39:9	1, 557 Joseph did not keep Sabbath.	No pertinent comment.
123. Gen. 43:32	I, 736 Egyptians worshipped oxen.	No pertinent comment.
124. Num. 33:4	I, 740 Egyptians worshipped cows and sheep.	Mekh. Pisḥa VII. 53: The gods referred to here are of stone and wood. There is no reference to the smiting of cattle as part of the gods of Egypt.
125. Deut. 10:16	I, 481, 485 Circumcise heart, flesh without heart no value.	No comment.
126. Josh. 5:2, 5, 6	I, 486 Israelites not circumcised before; 2nd time —first time was of the heart.	No pertinent comment.
127. Josh. 6:4 (Hebrews 4:8-9)	I, 568 Joshua violated Sabbath at Jericho.	y. Shab. 1.8: In an obligatory war, even on the Sabbath one may lay siege, as in the case of Jericho. The Palestinian tradition thus regarded the action of Joshua as paradigmatic. Aphrahat's interpretation that this proved the Sabbath has no salvific value is not pertinent to the rabbinical view. Rather, one commandment set aside another, in this case the conquest of the land set aside the observance of the Sabbath. Both nonetheless were *mitzvot*.
128. Josh. 24:15-22	I, 740-1, 963 Israelites worshipped gods of Egyptians.	No pertinent comment.
129. Judges 15:18	I, 744 Samson ate food from lion, unclean animal.	No pertinent comment.

	Scripture	Aphrahat	Rabbinical References
130.	Is. 28:12	I, 569-72 Sabbath of God.	No comment.
131.	Is. 56:4	I, 569-72 Sabbath of God.	b. Shab. 118b: Ḥiyya b. Abba in name of R. Yoḥanan: whoever keeps the Sabbath in accord with its law is forgiven even the sin of idolatry; R. Yoḥanan in name of Simeon b. Yoḥai: If Israel keep two Sabbaths properly, they will be immediately redeemed.
132.	Is. 65:5	I, 569-72 Sabbath of God.	No comment.
133.	Jer. 4:4	I, 500 Circumcise heart.	No comment.
134.	Jer. 9:25-6	I, 480 Circumcision without faith of no value.	b. Ned. 31b [Mishnah]: Circumcision of gentiles is regarded as uncircumcision. Mekh. Amalek III. 105ff., Great is circumcision because 1. R. Ishmael, thirteen covenants made over it; 2. Yosi Galilean, it sets aside Sabbath; 3. Joshua b. Qorḥa, no merit of Moses could suspend punishment for its neglect; 4. R. Nehemiah, it sets aside laws concerning plagues, etc.
135.	Ez. 4:13-14	I, 508-9 Jews will eat among unclean peoples.	No pertinent comment.
136.	Ez. 20:11, 25-6	I, 753 Evil commandments are purity laws, etc.	b. Ber. 24b: R. Miasha grandson of R. Joshua b. Levi: This refers to one who recites Shema' in unclean place. b. Meg. 32a: R. Yoḥanan, This refers to one who studies without singing.

Sabbath: Violations of the Sabbath at Jericho did not prove the Sabbath had no salvific value. On the contrary, rabbis recognized that various commandments sometimes came into conflict. They did not infer on that account that commandments were of diminished value. Conquest of the land was a commandment that set aside keeping the Sabbath, just as the Temple cult had to be maintained on the Sabbath day. Aphrahat's conclusions from the siege of Jericho and the Temple cult were correct. His interpretation of them was false, so far as rabbis were concerned (No. 127). But no Babylonians were involved in the dispute. Keeping the Sabbath properly would lead to redemption, a view held in Tannaitic times (No. 131). Here the two traditions met head on. But Aphrahat did not introduce the issue, and the Babylonian rabbis did not refer to it.

Dietary Laws: Aphrahat's tradition on Adam's eating meat is not shared by the rabbiṣ. Rav (No. 118) supposed Adam was a vegetarian. But I do not suppose Rav's assertion necessarily was intended to counter a Christian argument that Adam did not keep dietary laws (apart from the one about the tree). In the same context a rabbi could have maintained that the restriction against eating from the tree was a kind of dietary law, which would have proved that "making distinctions among foods" *was* of salvific consequence. But no one joined the argument. The matter was not raised.

The rabbis consistently interpreted Scripture in concrete, specific terms. Scripture (e.g. No. 124) proved the Egyptians worshipped gods of stone and wood. But the matter is dealt with so tangentially that a polemical point seems hardly at issue. Elsewhere rabbis came to the same conclusion as Aphrahat (Ginzberg, II, pp. 96,120ff.) Many of the instances in which heroes of ancient Israel did not keep the dietary laws according to Aphrahat's understanding of them are simply ignored (e.g. No. 129). I suppose the rabbis did not regard such behavior as a noteworthy violation of the law. As to the characterization of the dietary laws and purity rites as "bad commandments," this of course was unthinkable. The rabbis understood Ezekiel to mean that one could *make* commandments into bad things, by failing to derive pleasure from them (studying without song) or by carrying them out improperly (saying the *Shemaʿ* in an unclean place).

Circumcision; Rabbis did not imagine that "spiritual circumcision" could take the place of the actual circumcision of the flesh. They did not suppose that believing in God obviated circumcision, but rather held that believing in God leading to conversion to Judaism would necessitate circumcision. As in Gen. 15:6 (No. 120), the act of believing on Abraham's part produced considerable merit for his descendants. No one denigrated faith. But faith led to, not away from, the commandments. Hence the assertion that doing the commandments without faith is of no value was meaningless. So far as rabbis were concerned, Jewish circumcision *was* an act of faith. The problems Aphrahat raised about circumcision's not being performed in the wilderness were never noticed by rabbis. They apparently did not learn about them from Aphrahat or anyone else. Circumcision produced merit, but rabbis were not troubled that the generation of the wilderness, though circumcised, perished in the wilderness, or that the various evil kings of Israel and Judah "availed nought in their circumcision." This sort of argument would have been incomprehensible to them. In any event they did not recognize the issue.

Circumcision of the heart obviously was also required, for circumcision of gentiles was regarded as of no value. Hence circumcision practiced outside of the framework of Israelite law and faith was of no consequence. In this regard Aphrahat came very near the rabbinical view of circumcision. What separated them was the object of faith, not the necessity of believing. Idolators who circumcised were as though they were not circumcised—in this respect, the rabbis met Aphrahat's argument head on. But, as before, the rabbis who met that argument lived long before Aphrahat. Babylonian rabbis may well have cited such teachings in the context of disputes with Christians, but we have no evidence that they did so. We have no reason to believe the Tannaitic teachings regarding circumcision were especially important to the fourth-century Babylonian schools.

Aphrahat's assertions that Abraham, Isaac, and Jacob did not keep the Sabbath and that Abraham kept the law before the law was given (I, 557) probably were not contradictory. He meant that Abraham kept the moral laws, perhaps the Ten Commandments, but not the ritual laws, and not the Sabbath laws as Israel kept them. In any event rabbis asserted that Adam, Enoch, Shem, and Abraham observed the entire Torah (Ginzberg, *Legends*, V, p. 187, n. 51). Though these assertions came late (Ginzberg, V, P. 235, n. 140), the Book of Jubilees "sees its main task in furnishing the proof' that the patriarchs—from Adam to Jacob—observed the laws that were subsequently revealed to Moses" (Ginzberg, V, p. 259, n. 275). But, Ginzberg notes, this view has nothing to do with the Pauline doctrine in Romans 4:15. Ginzberg notes that authoritative Tannaim and Amoraim held Abraham observed only the seven commandments given to the children of Noah, as well as circumcision. Many rabbinic commentators would agree that Abraham kept only the ethical and moral laws of the Torah, Ginzberg says. In any event these issues were raised long before the time of Aphrahat. Still, the following passage is striking:

> Rav said, Our father Abraham kept the whole Torah, as it is said, *Because Abraham hearkened to my voice. . .* (Gen. 26:5).
> R. Shimi b. Hiyya said to Rav, Perhaps this refers to the seven laws [of the children of Noah]?
> Surely there was also circumcision. Then say it refers to the seven laws and circumcision.
> If that were so, why does Scripture say, *My commandments and my laws?*
> Rava or R. Ashi said, Abraham our father kept even the law concerning the *'eruv* of the dishes, [that is, the Oral Torah as well as the Written one].
>
> (b. Yoma 28b)

In this instance, Aphrahat's failure to comment on Gen. 26:5 is as striking as the rabbis' failure to remark on many Scriptures important to Aphrahat. The assertion of Rava that Abraham kept even the whole Oral Torah is one of the few instances in which a contemporary Babylonian rabbi referred to a point at issue in the Jewish-Christian argument. Standing by itself, it proves only that such materials *might* have made an appearance. Considering the breadth and variety of Scriptures introduced by Aphrahat and the large number of biblical heroes cited by him to prove his case, we can only be astonished at the paucity of such clearcut encounters.

Abraham's keeping the whole Torah is one point at which Aphrahat might well have showed himself a pupil of the rabbis, for he did refer to that belief. Strikingly, Aphrahat failed either to draw from it the conclusions rabbis drew—that Abraham did keep the Sabbath, dietary laws, and the like—or to draw from it a polemical conclusion—that Abraham kept the Torah's moral laws, which matter, but not the ritual ones, which do not. He referred to the matter quite tangentially. It was not important to his argument. More important, it did not seem to him to count heavily *against* his polemic. The latter fact seems to me of great significance. A pupil of the rabbis would certainly have recognized the force of rabbinical exegesis had he known it, and would have been quick to counter that exegesis with some other, more favorable interpretation of pertinent Scriptures. Just as the rabbis ignored Scriptures central to Aphrahat's argument, so we note in this instance that Aphrahat paid no attention to Scriptures both potentially dangerous to his case and important to that of the Babylonian rabbis.

VII. CONCLUSION

We earlier found reason to doubt the accuracy of characterizing Aphrahat as a "docile pupil of the Jews." We have now examined abundant evidence to show that Babylonian rabbis knew little, if anything, of Aphrahat's critique of Judaism, either in general or in any detail. Had rabbis been familiar with the sort of arguments he raised, whether coming from him or from others, it is unlikely that they would not have formulated appropriate replies. That Babylonian masters rarely, if ever, commented on Scripture in terms of the Christian view, opposing what Christians said and substituting a more acceptable interpretation, strongly suggests they had little, if any, contact with contemporary Christian exegesis. That does not mean rabbis were not concerned with Christianity's appeal to Jews. They did what they could to oppose the conversion of Jews to Christianity. But their efforts did not include the articulate refutation of Christian Scriptural arguments, perhaps the single most effective instrument available to Christians for the conversion of the Jews.

If Aphrahat ever was a docile Jewish pupil, rabbis did not know it. They heard nothing of the supposed alumnus of their schools when he went on to greater distinction. The corollary of our earlier observations on Aphrahat's lack of dependence upon the rabbis is the rabbis' complete independence of Aphrahat. Just as Aphrahat was not a docile pupil of rabbis, so rabbis were utterly unfamiliar with Aphrahat and the views of others like him.

When we find instances in which Aphrahat and rabbis held in common certain views of religion and ethics, we had best look for common exegetical traditions, on the one hand, or a common cultural and conceptual framework of reference, on the other. Since both parties spoke much the same language, read the same Scriptures, and lived in much the same sort of world, it is hardly surprising to discover that in substantial ways they saw reality in much the same terms. But parallel "envisagements of religion" (as Gavin put it) cannot mean much more than that. Parallels standing by themselves prove little. Many of the parallels drawn between Aphrahat and rabbinical literature prove not to be parallel at all. Some are so commonplace as to mean nothing to begin with, being little more than citations of the same Scripture in the same way. Indeed, if we compare the parallel comments on Scriptures with the substantially larger numbers of comments which are not parallel at all, and which stand in no polemical or exegetical relationship, and if we furthermore add to these the even larger number of Scriptures cited by Aphrahat on which rabbinical tradition preserves no comment at all, we can conclude only one thing. Aphrahat and the rabbis had practically nothing in common, other than that they lived in a single cultural continuum and believed in the same revelation. But since that obviously was the case, it is consequential that they exhibited not so many parallels, but so few.

This judgment is, nonetheless, extreme, for the decisive consideration is not whether we find significant numbers of parallels. Ginzberg, Funk, and Gavin did, after all, locate a few exegeses and other characteristics exhibited in common by Aphrahat and rabbis. We cannot ignore the impression made on them by what they found. We differ, however, in interpreting the meaning of such parallels as do exist. In this respect, we may best be guided by Nahum A. Sarna, who says (in his Prolegomenon to Moses Buttenwieser, *The Psalms* [N.Y., reprinted, 1969], p. xxx):

> Not every parallel needs to be traced to direct borrowing, nor indeed to any borrowing at all. As has been already suggested, the similarities may often be reflexes of well-established liturgical or literary patterns common to the entire Near East. Sometimes one may even be dealing simply with the independent development of analogical cultural features. Furthermore, the evaluation of parallels is an uncertain business, for they might have been mediated through a third culture and have lost much of their significance in the process. They might also, even where directly borrowed, have played a major role in the parent culture, but an inconsequential one in that of the recipient. . .

These are the sorts of considerations absent in the judgments of Ginzberg, Funk, and Gavin.

In the light of these findings, we must ask ourselves, How was it possible for Wellhausen, Funk, Ginzberg, and Gavin to portray Aphrahat as a "docile pupil of the Jews," to imagine that he picked and chose among rabbinical materials, and to conclude that he demonstrated "how completely the Syriac Church was bound to Jewish tradition, even in the fourth century" [Ginzberg, *JE* I, p. 663 col. a, quoting Wellhausen].

First of all, earlier students were more impressed by what they thought to be parallels between Aphrahat and "Jewish" (meaning, generally, rabbinic) materials, and were surer of what such parallels, precise and real or only approximate, implied, than am I. If one looks only for parallels, that is all he will see, find, and be impressed by. If, as we have done, one compares the bulk of Aphrahat's Scriptural references with rabbinical comments on those same Scriptures, he gains a different perspective. The handful of exegetical parallels seems considerably smaller against the measure of the mass of Scriptures on which we could find no consequential parallels, indeed no common hermeneutical or polemical referent at all. That difference of perspective was unavailable to anyone who did not do what we have now done.

A second, more important difference lies in the prevailing scholarly climate.[3] I am much impressed by two studies (among many) of parallels and what they mean. The first is Samuel Sandmel, "Parallelomania," *JBL* 81, 1, 1962, pp. 1-13. Sandmel characterizes "parallelomania" as follows:

> One, that some passages are allegedly parallel; two, that a direct organic literary connection is assumed to have provided the parallels; and three, that the conclusion is drawn that the flow is in a particular direction.

Sandmel defines the phenomenon as follows:

> that extravagance among scholars which first overdoes the supposed similarity in passages and then proceeds to describe source and derivation as if implying literary connection flowing in an inevitable or predetermined direction.

---

[3] To be sure, I do not maintain that the old style has disappeared completely. An example of the curious results of parallelomania is Willis A. Shotwell, *The Biblical Exegesis of Justin Martyr* (London, 1965), pp. 71-93. Shotwell cites numerous "parallels" between Justin and rabbinical materials, drawn from A. H. Goldfahn, "Justinus Martyr und die Agada", *MGWJ* 23, 1873, pp. 49-60, 104-115, 145-53, 194-202, and 257-269, and other early works. In these citations the dates of collections in which supposed parallels appear generally are ignored. Hence Justin, a second-century father, knows materials attributed to much later masters, or, more serious, appearing in much later documents. Shotwell is not unaware of this fact. He notes, for instance, "As it now stands this seems to be from about the ninth century A.D." But he draws no conclusions from the problem posed by the first appearance of materials so late—seven centuries after Justin!

He further includes materials from non-rabbinical documents alongside those from rabbinical ones, e.g. (p. 73), Enoch, II Esdras, and the Babylonian Talmud. In his eagerness to find parallels, Shotwell follows Goldfahn, "There is no direct confirmation of Justin's statement, but it seems to underlie a phrase in Babylonian Talmud . . ." Just what this is supposed to imply or prove I cannot say.

Shotwell has relied so wholly on Goldfahn and others that I doubt he has directly consulted a single rabbinical document. Yet he tells us, "It is obvious that Justin uses exactly the same methods of interpreting the Scriptures which he attributes to the Jews and their teachers." This may well be so, but the way to find out is not to rely on studies prepared according to entirely different conceptions of scholarly inquiry from those Shotwell undoubtedly takes for granted in other areas. I do not imagine, for instance, that he would be prepared to admit that a saying attributed to Jesus in a ninth-century European collection of Jesus-stories could be readily used in the historical study of the life and teachings of Jesus.

Our brief review of earlier findings suggests the appearance of these characteristics. Our examination of a few of the alleged parallels raised the question of whether everything Funk and Gavin called a parallel actually was more than a modest resemblance at best. It was furthermore clear that parallels were automatically assumed to indicate dependence. The issue of who was dependent upon whom was settled before it was investigated.

What is the historical setting in which such alleged parallels would have had to have been produced to yield the picture drawn by Funk and Gavin? Aphrahat would in fact have had to have known and studied, or at least talked, with rabbis. But if he had, we should have every reason to find substantially more evidence of that fact than lies before us. I indeed could find practically none. No interest in exploring alternate sources for alleged parallels characterized the earlier generation. Wherever Aphrahat approximated a Jewish sentiment — and nearly everything not essentially Christian was seen as Jewish and rabbinical — it is immediately concluded that he quoted or cited a Jew known to us in rabbinical literature. The possibility that traditions common to church and synagogue, beginning with the Hebrew Scriptures and *Targumim* may account for many similarities was never seriously entertained. Further, it hardly mattered where a parallel first occurred. From the earliest pre-Christian *Targumim* to the latest medieval compilations of midrashim, everything was an equally valuable testimony to the (necessarily rabbinical) Judaism of fourth-century Mesopotamia. The absence of rabbinical schools in Mesopotamia made no difference. The varieties of Judaism never seemed important. The distinctiveness of Aphrahat's own thought was always subordinated. How and where did Aphrahat become a rabbinical disciple? How and when did he repudiate his rabbinical education? We are never told. Nor is the significance of those parallels which actually are parallel carefully and systematically explicated. As we noticed, some of the true parallels suggest the very opposite of an actual encounter.

Sandmel phrases the underlying assumption with reference to Philo and the Palestinian rabbis:

> I am not prepared to suppose that Philo of Alexandria had to go to his mailbox at regular intervals, learn by letter what the rabbis in Palestine were saying, and then be in a position to transmute the newly received data into philosophical ideals.

As I have suggested here, so Sandmel states,

Where the literatures present us with acknowledged parallels, I am often more inclined to ascribe these to the common Jewish content of all these Jewish movements than to believe in advance that some item common to the scrolls and the gospels or to Paul implies that the gospels or Paul got that item specifically from the scrolls.

Similarly, acknowledged parallels may testify, in my view, to the cultural and conceptual universe common to all sorts of Jews and Christians (among others) in Mesopotamia and Babylonia. Sandmel concludes:

It would seem to me to follow that, in dealing with similarities we can sometimes discover exact parallels, some with and some devoid of significance; seeming parallels which are so only imperfectly; and statements which can be called parallels only by taking them out of context.

Curiously ignored by Sandmel, the second, and the most important commentary on the meaning of parallels is the work of my teacher Morton Smith, *Tannaitic Parallels to the Gospels*. Discussing the use of similarities and parallels in "The Present State of OT Studies," *JBL* 88, 1, 1969, pp. 19-35, Smith states:

A favorite means of revealing "essential" truth is to show that the patriarchal legends are "confirmed" by archeological evidence. This evidence turns out to consist of similarities in various details between the biblical stories and documents from the second millennium B.C. Which part or period of the second millennium B.C. makes no difference; debris in Sinai from the nineteenth century and treaties in Turkey from the thirteenth, agricultural settlements on the upper Euphrates from the eighteenth century and customs beyond the Tigris from the fifteenth—everything similar is confirmation. But, as de Vaux pointed out in his fine article on *Method in the Study of Early Hebrew History* with reference to the customs of Nuzi, "If they are limited to this region and to this period they cannot be used to enlighten the history of the patriarchs who were never east of the Tigris; if they are not limited to this region and this period they cannot be used to date the patriarchs."

The same failure to consider the possible survival of cultural elements is frequent in the misuse of literary parallels to date biblical material. The historicity of the Sinai covenant was argued from its similarity to Hittite treaties, but the same essential structure appears in the treaties of Esarhaddon of Assyria where the parallels are so close to Deuteronomy as to argue its literary dependence; so one has to ask, When did the Israelites become familiar with this enduring Mesopotamian diplomatic convention? And the answer is surely not while they were slaves in Egypt or nomads along the desert, but after they became a kingdom, and perhaps, indeed, only after the revival of Assyria. Thus the "ancient near eastern archeological evidence" is actually evidence for a rather late date. Any number of psalms have been dated early because of their Ugaritic parallels. But we know from

Philo of Byblos that traditions like the Ugaritic lived on in Phoenician cities down to Roman times, and Phoenician contacts with the Israelites were particularly close towards the end of the Persian period, when the Phoenicians seem to have controlled all the coastal plain of Palestine, had a trading colony in Jerusalem (Neh. 13:16), and were probably allied with Jerusalem in a revolt against the Persians. Relations continued close in the hellenistic age, as we know from remains of the "Sidonians" at Marisa; and there is nothing unlikely in the notion that the Jerusalem priesthood of these period, which was in close and friendly contact with the neighboring peoples, may have been responsible for the introduction of Phoenician elements into the temple psalms. So here, too, the "ancient near eastern parallels," like the other characteristics of these psalms, point to a very late date.

Whether or not future generations will observe different sorts of phenomena and come to different interpretations of their significance, it is clear that the prevailing scholarly climate of the latter part of the nineteenth century and the first of the twentieth led to a different understanding of what a parallel is and means. It simply did not occur to earlier students of Aphrahat to do what we have done, but the reason is not the superiority of the current generation, surely not of the current writer. It is rather the different interests and expectations of earlier times.[4]

The way forward has been shown by Smith in *Tannaitic Parallels to the Gospels* (Philadelphia, 1951: *Journal of Biblical Literature*, Monograph Series, Vol. VI). There Smith provides a repertoire of definitions for various sorts of parallels and explains what they mean. In my view it is the

---

[4] Nor should we suppose the change in climate is entirely for the better. The study of rabbinical parallels to the *aggadah* in patristic literature, by one well-qualified Talmudist after another from the last third of the nineteenth century to the end of the first quarter of the twentieth—that is, from Graetz and Goldfahn, through Krauss, Ginzberg, Funk, Lucas, and M. Freimann (cited below)—has practically ceased. That is a pity, since much remains to be done, even following the older methods. New issues and conceptions in the history of religions furthermore require the whole task to be done all over again.

I imagine the decline of classical education among scholars qualified to study talmudic literature accounts for the cessation of this interesting inquiry. When young men came from traditional Yeshivot to study in Western universities, they not infrequently pursued a classical course and then combined the two by comparing patristic to rabbinic literature. Some were fortunate enough to acquire a sound European gymnasium-training to begin with, alongside their Talmudic studies. This seems to have been the pattern in Hungary and Austria, for example, accounting for Bacher, Krauss, Funk, and so many others. For young American students of the Talmud it is a sufficient task to study the Talmud. The decline of Judaic studies in Europe needs no comment. In consequence, Talmudists rarely acquire a thorough mastery of Greek and Latin, and often when they do, their attention is drawn to Hellenic and Hellenistic materials in rabbinic literature; not infrequently, Classical Studies today in any event exclude attention to the Church Fathers. Undergraduate Classicists in America are unlikely to read patristic writings.

definitive study of parallelism in general, because of the care, precision, and conceptual sophistication brought to bear on this problem. Smith describes his work as follows:

> In discussion of the parallels I have attempted to classify them according to their various natures and have begun each chapter with an effort to define the nature of the parallels therein to be discussed. This classification seems to me one of the most important respects in which this work differs from its predecessors. Those who previously wrote on such parallels made no attempt to classify them by nature; therefore they either produced lists in which all sorts were strung together indiscriminately . . . or they divided the material according to the various academic interests of the previous students . . . a division of the subject matter according to external criteria, without consideration of its natural divisions . . . In the following chapters I have tried, also, to emphasize the difference between the facts actually revealed by the comparison of the texts, and the explanations of these facts current in the form of historical theories . . .

What Smith has done is different from anything we noticed in Ginzberg, Funk, and Gavin. Ginzberg and Funk simply cite parallels without an effort to classify or interpret. The latter provides a list organized according to the Pentateuchal books. Gavin's concrete instances are arranged by theological categories, yet his dubious assumption is that the structure of Jewish rabbinical theology on questions of interest to him has been adequately delineated or is satisfactorily portrayed by a few random sayings.

Smith's categories are as follows: First, verbal parallels, in that one word may resemble another; second, parallels of idiom; third, parallels of meaning in which the external form is of no essential importance; fourth, parallels of literary form, e.g. forms of rhetoric which depend not on a single idiomatic expression nor on grammatical peculiarities of the words, but on their meaning, or forms of argument and exegesis; fifth, parallels in types of association, that is, the principle of association on which material in a given book is selected and arranged; sixth, complete parallels, that is, passages which are parallel at once in words and in structure, in content and in literary form; seventh, parallels of parallelism, that is, the relationship which exists between the books of one literature with the relationship which exists between the books of a second literature; eighth, parallels with a fixed difference, that is, parallels in all of which the same difference appears, e.g. those of which the element from Tannaitic literature refers to God and His Law, the element from the Gospels to Jesus and his teachings.

Clearly, the study of parallels between Aphrahat and rabbinical literature must at the outset be organized according to these principles. Verbal parallels abound, beginning with reference to Scripture as 'uraita in Aphrahat, 'oraita in talmudic literature, to the disciples of Jesus as disciple-companions, that is, talmidé ḥaverim of rabbinical circles, and so forth. These parallels are numerous and significant. What they signify, as I have repeatedly emphasized, is that Babylonian rabbis and Aphrahat spoke closely related dialects of the same language and referred to similar institutions and ideas in that language. Parallels of idiom are of the same sort and signify the same fact.

As to parallels of meaning in which the external form is of no essential importance, here matters are more complex, as Smith recognizes: "Every word, from the name of the simplest thing to the name of God himself, can serve as the basis for a parallel of meaning, and on many of these parallels, of which the number is at least equal to the number of nouns and verbs in the Gospels, the standard commentators have already written." Scholars come to the question of parallels of meaning "from the side of ideas and not from the side of texts, from the side of concepts and not from the side of words," as is illustrated by Gavin. The problem is further complicated by the complexities of cultural relationships and the difficulties of the evidence. Parallels of meaning are produced by "accumulation of details, of a complete way of life." As to relationships between Aphrahat and Judaism, much more careful definition, together with exemplifications both of what is meant and of what is supposedly signified, must precede any specific inquiry.

Parallels of literary form are of two sorts, first, common exegetical devices, such as the qal veḥomer, second, common rhetorical characteristics, such as the division of a Scripture into its parts, with interpretation attached to each of the parts in terms of some other set of images, meanings, or concepts. The treatment of Gen. 2:24 and of Ex. 12 are instances of parallels of literary form. What they signify is still an open question, for studies of literary conventions in late antiquity, particularly in varieties of Semitic literature, are at an elementary stage. To conclude at the outset that the appearance of a qal veḥomer or of an exegetical parsing of a Scripture signifies a rabbinical education is hardly justified.

As to the fifth and seventh sorts of parallels, however, I may state definitely that there are none. I know of no parallels in types of association, that is, in the principle of association on which material in a given book is selected and arranged, or parallels of parallelism, that is, cases in which the relationship which exists between books in one literature is the same as that between books of a second. There simply is no resemblance whatever between the kind of writing done by Aphrahat and the literature of the rabbinical schools of third and fourth-century Babylonia. Aphrahat wrote essays. The rabbis, if they wrote at all, prepared commentaries to the Mishnah, case reports, stories and sayings in no way to be compared to essays. Since the two sorts of writing are quite unrelated, we cannot expect to find parallels in types of association or parallels of parallelism.

The sixth and eighth sorts of parallels have repeatedly come to our attention. We indeed observed a few complete parallels, in which passages seemed approximately similar in words, structure, content, and literary form. But as we noticed, those few parallels did not signify the existence of relationships or contacts between Aphrahat and rabbis. The eighth kind is everywhere before us. Nothing is so common as parallels in which the same difference recurs, in which one element constant in rabbinical materials is replaced by another constant in Aphrahat's writing, e.g. Christ for Torah, church for Israel, completed redemption for future hope. But what this commonplace parallel proves is first, that Aphrahat was Christian and the rabbis were Jews, and second, that they stood on a common scriptural foundation.

I do not suggest the work is done. The task of careful and detailed comparison of Aphrahat and rabbinical writings is not yet begun. My purpose has been to show prevailing impressions to be imprecise and their implications exaggerated, falsely interpreted, or, at the very least, open to question. The relationships of Aphrahat's and rabbinical exegeses to the Peshitto also require close consideration, needless to say, and here the persistence of Massoretic citations in rabbinical literature and of anything but the Massoretic tradition in Aphrahat raises still more difficult questions. A study on Aphrahat's New Testament citations is now in preparation by Professor T. Baarda. I know no systematic inquiry into the relationship between Aphrahat's citations of the Hebrew Scriptures, almost invariably *different* from the Massoretic text, and other translations and textual and exegetical traditions, the *Targumim* and Peshitto above all. These are tasks for biblical scholars, expert not only in the translations and versions in general, but in Syriac language and literature in particular. Here a mere historian stands aside to await the results of persons qualified to do the work.

CHAPTER FOURTEEN

APHRAHAT AND THE PATRISTIC CRITIQUE OF JUDAISM

I. INTRODUCTION

Aphrahat was a pupil of Christ, not of rabbis. This fact will become clear as we compare his thought on Judaism with that of the Church Fathers who preceded him, particularly of those Fathers who like him composed lengthy, systematic demonstrations on Judaism. We shall survey comments on Jews and Judaism in the ante-Nicene fathers. It is not my purpose either to place Aphrahat into the context of Patristic literature generally or to show the relationships between his theology and that of his predecessors. I merely hope to point to some similarities and differences between his work and that which went before. This will demonstrate not his dependence on earlier writers, but the opposite. We have no need to enter the question of whether he had read widely in earlier Christian literature. The earlier arguments about the nature and meaning of parallels apply here. We know Aphrahat knew the New Testament and may readily assume his thought on Judaism was shaped by what he found there. For the rest the purpose of our comparison merely is to locate, not parallels, but similarities and differences. We shall see that Aphrahat generally follows well-established lines of argument, but within them shows striking originality and inventiveness.

The question of his relationships to earlier Patristic literature is far too complex to be dealt with in this limited study, and I am not competent to deal with it.[1] But it seems to me valuable to investigate the relationships of the arguments — if not of the man — to those that went before. We shall observe that the range of Christian thought on Judaism was narrow and, by the middle of the fourth century, formal and highly conventional. The

---

[1] See Marcel Simon, *Verus Israel*, pp. 166-7, for a critique of Williams, *Adversus Judaeos*. Williams fails to show the relationships between the various materials, as Simon says, "Il considère que chaque traité se suffit à lui-même. Les ressemblances, superficielles à son avis, qui peuvent exister entre certains d'entre eux, s'expliquent par la persistance des mêmes méthods d'argumentation et un usage identique des mêmes textes scripturaires; elles n'attestent à peu près jamais de filiation directe."

dictates of logic and the demands of Scripture and Christian doctrine [2] therefore must have much to do with the particular shape of Aphrahat's thought. But it remains for others to discern just what particular influences affected Aphrahat's thought and how they did so. What I find striking is not direct connections, let alone parallels, but first, simply the limited range of Christian themes on Judaism and the manifest place of Aphrahat within that range, and second, Aphrahat's originality in treating those themes.

The dialogues with the Jews have been neatly described by Amos B. Hulen (in "The 'Dialogues with the Jews' as Sources for the Early Jewish Argument against Christianity," *JBL* 51, 1932, pp. 58-70; quotation is on p. 58) as follows:

> The student of the early literature of Christianity must be impressed by the astounding abundance of the treatises "Against the Jews," as also by the distinguished names which, with whatever justification, have become attached to them. To list the more important, there are Barnabas, Justin Martyr, Aristo of Pella, Tertullian, Hippolytus, Origen, Cyprian, Novatian, Eusebius of Caesarea, Gregory of Nyssa, Chrysostom, Augustine, Cyril of Alexandria, Evagrius, Philip Sidetes, and Anastasius Sinaita. The documents may roughly be divided into three groups, corresponding to three stages of argument, not strictly chronological: 1) expository, addressed in large measure to the seed of Abraham, aiming at their conversion, and designed to prove to them the truth of Christianity out of the Old Testament — finished examples of this type being Cyprian's "Three Books of Testimonies" and Eusebius' "Demonstration of the Gospel;" 2) argumentative, dealing largely with Jewish objections to the new religion, represented by Justin Martyr's "Dialogue with Trypho the Jew;" and 3) denunciatory, based on the assumption that the Jews were a people abandoned of God, whose conversion was hopeless, works like Chrysostom's "Eight Orations Against the Jews." As years went by, the redemption of Israel was lost sight of, the apologies having for their main object the strengthening of the faith of believers. The timeworn arguments continued to resound, however, even though the practical situation had become altogether different.

Aphrahat — curiously missing from the list — will be seen to   stand generally within the range of antecedent arguments and themes. But his original contribution will likewise become evident.

II. WORKS CONSULTED

Juster and Simon, mentioned above (p. 12) provide the best brief and long introductions, respectively, to the thought on Judaism of the

---

[2] Not to mention Rendel Harris's "Testimony-Book," of which more below.

Church Fathers. Juster, *Les juifs dans l'empire romain* (pp. 53-61) cites the various anti-Jewish monographs before the time of Aphrahat, with references to editions and important studies up to 1914. Simon's *Verus Israel* must be read time and again, in particular pp. 87-124, and 166-213. The latter section constitutes the best general introduction to the subject. Unique among modern scholars, Simon both pays close attention to Aphrahat and places him into the context of early Christian thought on Judaism. By comparison, Williams, *Adversus Judaeos*, pp. 3-92, while a helpful survey, is a mere catalogue. Simon relates various writers and their arguments to one another. Williams simply summarizes one item after another. That does not detract from the usefulness of his book, but it is not of the same order as *Verus Israel*.

S. Krauss, "The Jews in the Works of the Church Fathers," *Jewish Quarterly Review*, Old Series, 5, 1893, pp. 122-157, 6, 1894, 82-99, 225-261, does not systematically treat the subject before us. Rather, Krauss deals with a number of questions, including what various fathers say about Jews and Judaism, answered cursorily, and how various fathers relate to Jewish (rabbinical) exegeses of Scriptures, answered in great detail. Krauss's chief interest (like Ginzberg's, Goldfahn's and Funk's) is in the Church fathers and the *Aggadah*. Krauss refers to Justin, Clement of Alexandria, Origen, Eusebius, and others after Aphrahat. Hulen's "Dialogues with the Jews," *JBL* 1932, pp. 55ff, cited above, should be read in the light of Simon's criticism, *Verus Israel*, p. 173. M. Freimann, "Die Wortführer des Judentums in den ältesten Kontroversen zwischen Juden und Christen," *Monatsschrift für die Geschichte und Wissenschaft des Judenthums* 55, 1911, pp. 555-585, 56, 1912, 49-64, 164-180, discusses the Jews represented in first- and second-century Christian dialogues on Judaism. Leonhard Goppelt, *Christentum und Judentum in ersten und zweiten Jahrhundert* (Gütersloh, 1954), pp. 284-310, was of interest. His bibliography provides a good starting point for the early centuries.

A thorough, convenient survey, of considerable value, is Robert Wilde, *The Treatment of the Jews in the Greek Christian Writers of the First Three Centuries* (Washington, 1949: *Catholic University of America Patristic Studies* Vol. 81). Wilde summarizes the attitude toward the Jews in profane Greek literature (pp. 32-77), the apostolic fathers to Justin (pp. 78-97), Justin to the Epistle of Diognetus (pp. 98-140), Western writers, Clement, Origen, and so forth. His summary of each writer hardly relieves the student of the need to consult the original, but he is a valuable guide on whom to consult. He makes no effort to do more than refer to one writer after another; there is little thoughtful consideration of the problem as a whole, or of themes within it. James Parkes, *Judaism and Christianity* (Chicago, 1948) pp. 113-139, and Hans Joachim Schoeps, *The Jewish-Christian Argument. A History of Theologies in Conflict* (N.Y., 1963) pp. 18-52, may be safely ignored.

III. APHRAHAT AND THE NEW TESTAMENT

What Aphrahat learned about Judaism and the Jews from the New Testament is not exhausted by the Scriptures he cited. For a rapid summary of doctrines, we shall review Gregory Baum, *The Jews and the Gospel* (Westminster, 1961). We need to assume only that the fundamental attitudes and ideas of New Testament writers were known to Aphrahat; we do not have to undertake Baarda's work in advance and ask just how Aphrahat quoted and understood particular New Testament passages. I restrict my comments to some rather general observations on the earliest doctrines on Jews and Judaism.

The first doctrine is that Jesus came to "the Jews" and that those in the Gospel accounts called "Jews" rejected him. Aphrahat needed to go no further than the Gospels to find that the Jews rejected Jesus and consequently were themselves rejected as God's people. Second, from the Gospels, particularly Matthew, Aphrahat learned that Jesus's life and passion fulfilled the predictions of the prophets of ancient Israel, and he derived from these same materials a repertoire of Scriptural testimonies, that is, Scriptures referring to, or fulfilled by, Jesus in his life and passion. Third, Aphrahat learned from the New Testament not only to regard the Hebrew Scriptures as the Old Testament, but also to speak in terms of a new covenant between God and Israel, a covenant of love made with the new people of God. The old and the new stood in opposition, the one worldly and temporal, the other spiritual and eternal. "With the death and resurrection of Jesus, the community of salvation passed from the age of the temple and its economy into a new era, the age of the Church" (Baum, p. 36). Fourth, from Matthew he learned to read the prophets' condemnation of ancient sins in terms of the Israel of his own day. From the Fourth Gospel he discerned the distinction between "the Jews" and Israel, a distinction of importance in explaining how the "people that is of the peoples" acquired the birthright of the Jews. Fifth, from the Fourth Gospel he learned that the Sabbath may be of less than salvific consequence, and that Jesus initiated the ultimate period of rest (Baum, p. 114).

We have now found in the Gospels the main outlines of the primary argument and method of Aphrahat (above, pp. 127-144). The particular prooftexts cited by Aphrahat will be considered below. What is lacking is the second main theme of Aphrahat's Judaic critique, that Judaism's particular religious practices do not and *never* did have salvific value. For this argument, Aphrahat turned to Paul. Clearly, from Paul he learned about the abrogation of the law. The law was God's will: "Giving commandments belongs to God's way of ruling the universe" (in Baum's summary, p. 189). But the law was a means of "educating the people for an elevated and spiritual morality." It pointed to a future salvation: "The law was temporal, limited to a particular age of the people; it was provisional, destined to be replaced by a superior institution" (Baum, p. 192). Here we come very close to Aphrahat's fundamental principle, but not to his particular applications of that principle. The issue of the abrogation of the law was taken for granted by Aphrahat. The question of whether the laws had ever brought salvation or distinguished between death and life, is another matter. For the future the law obviously could have no effect. But if it *had* served to prepare the way for salvation, then Aphrahat's tenacious insistence that the law had *never* served to lead to salvation cannot be traced to Paul's thought. Baum's judgment (p. 197) is this: "I am convinced that when Paul speaks of the Law as the cause of sin and a way of death, he is *not* trying to describe the role of the Law in the history of Israel's past." There is "no effort to discredit Israel's religious past, rather a judgment made in the light of the new event, Christ's victory" (p. 203). These general observations set the stage for a comparison of Aphrahat's repertoire of proof texts with that found in the New Testament. We shall now see to what degree he based his choice of testimonies on the Christian Scriptures.

Our examination of the Scriptures cited by Aphrahat in connection with his demonstrations against Judaism is intended merely to study the extent of his dependence on the New Testament usages of these same Scriptures. For that purpose it suffices to show how the repertoire of Hebrew Scriptural citations evident in New Testament writings recurs in Aphrahat. While it will become clear that Aphrahat stands well within parts of the antecedent Christian tradition on use of Hebrew Scriptural references to the Jews and Judaism, we do not have to enter the difficult question of the alleged existence of a book of Testimonies, laying forth the appropriate Scriptures by which Christians would interpret the life and meaning of Jesus. For our purpose, whether such a book of Testimonies existed is of no consequence. I do not think that Aphrahat, had he known it (and he certainly did not), would have depended on Cyprian's catalogue in preference to the New Testament. I do not imagine a book of Testimonies survived in its original form to the times of Aphrahat, or, if it did, reached the Iranian churches. Hence I shall not enter the question raised in fullest form by J. Rendell Harris with the assistance of Vacher Burch in *Testimonies* (Cambridge, vol. I, 1916, vol. II, 1920). It suffices to say that, as in many other matters, C. H. Dodd has spoken the last word, in *According to the Scriptures. The Sub-Structure of New Testament Theology* (Digswell Place, 1952), and summarized in his *The Old Testament in the New* (Philadelphia, 1952). Dodd's conclusion (p. 59-60) is as follows: ". . . our study has surely created a certain presumption that New Testament writers were guided in their use of the Old Testament by certain agreed principles or conventions. It has also suggested that such guidance may not have taken the form of an anthology of single, isolated proof-texts, as has often been supposed. It points rather to the hypothesis that there were some parts of Scripture which were early recognized as appropriate sources from which *testimonia* might be drawn." Dodd's view is especially important, for it suggests that Aphrahat might have turned to the Hebrew Scriptures as readily as to New Testament citations of those same Scriptures. Hence his general reliance on what he found before him in the New Testament places him within the conventional Christian tradition. In this connection, I also consulted R. V. G. Tasker, *The Old Testament in the New Testament* (Grand Rapids, 1963; first published, 1946) and Barnabas Lindars, *New Testament Apologetic. The Doctrinal Significance of the Old Testament Quotations* (Philadelphia, 1961). My tables depend upon, and summarize, Crawford Howell Toy, *Quotations in the New Testament* (N.Y., 1884), and further discussion of each item is indicated by the reference to page numbers in Toy, Dodd, and Lindars.

Scripture	Aphrahat	New Testament
1. Ex. 12:33	I, 849 Jews rejected redemption.	No reference.
2. Deut. 9:24	I, 468, 852-3 Israel always rebellious.	No reference.
3. Deut. 31:29	I, 748, 852, 874 Moses predicted Israel's future sin.	No reference.

Scripture	Aphrahat	New Testament
4. Deut. 32:21	I, 469, 511, 760, 782, 854 Provoke with people which is no people.	I Cor. 10:22, Toy, p. 175 Rom. 10:19, Toy, p. 151
5. Deut. 32:32	I, 468, 511, 765, 782, 852, 860 God never accepted Israel's repentence.	No reference.
6. I Sam. 3:14	I, 748-9 Sin of Eli not expiated through sacrifice.	No reference.
7. I Sam. 15:14	I, 748-9 No use for sacrifice.	No reference.
8. Is. 1:2	I, 773, 790 Jews were heirs.	No reference.
9. Is. 1:9-10	I, 468, 469, 472, 533, 765, 963 Israel = Sodom	Rom. 9:29, Toy, p. 144
10. Is. 2:5-6	I, 765 House of Jacob = gentiles.	No reference.
11. Is. 5:1-6	I, 469, 861 Wild grapes produced by vineyard.	Matt. 21:33 Mark 12:2 } Toy, p. 55 Luke 20:9 The parable is found, but not the application given by Aphrahat.
12. Is. 11:11	I, 868 Redemption a second time, no third time.	No reference.
13. Is. 29:13	I, 768, 888 Israel rejected.	Matt. 15:8-9 } Mark 7:6-7 } Toy, p. 42
14. Is. 30:1	I, 468, 766 Rebellious Israel.	No reference.
15. Is. 33:1	I, 849 Prophetic promises can be annulled.	No reference.

	Scripture	Aphrahat	New Testament
16.	Is. 33:13	I, 514, 773 Called gentiles.	No reference.
17.	Is. 34:4	I, 949ff. Israel never gave up idolatry.	II Pet. 3:12, Toy, p. 248
18.	Is. 43:24	I, 565 Israel burdened God.	No reference.
19.	Is. 50:1	I, 564 Israel burdened God.	No reference.
20.	Is. 52:11	I, 864 Rejection of Israel.	II Tim. 2:19, Toy, p. 203 Rev. 18:4, Toy, p. 271 II Cor. 6:17, Toy, p. 185
21.	Is. 54:9	I, 949 God no longer angry because Jerusalem desolated *forever*.	No reference.
22.	Is. 55:5	I, 773ff. Called gentiles.	No reference.
23.	Is. 59:2	I, 773ff. Rejected Israel.	No reference.
24.	Is. 66:3	I, 748-9 Sacrifices no good.	No reference.
25.	Jer. 2:10-13	I, 952 Israel worshipped heavens.	No reference.
26.	Jer. 2:21	I, 469, 765, 860 Alien vine, bad wine.	No reference.
27.	Jer. 3:8	I, 860, 886, 953 Rejection.	No reference.
28.	Jer. 3:16	I, 509, 532 Rejection: illegal for Jews to make ark of covenant.	No reference.
29.	Jer. 6:30	I, 468, 753, 765, 768, 853, 939 Rejected silver.	No reference.

	Scripture	Aphrahat	New Testament
30.	Jer. 9:10	I, 533 Jews annulled covenant.	No reference.
31.	Jer. 12:1	I, 953	No reference.
32.	Jer. 12:7	I, 753 Rejected Israel and its sacrifices.	No reference.
34.	Jer. 18:7-10	I, 852 God can change mind.	No reference.
35.	Jer. 31:31-2	I, 499, 533 Jews say God will make new covenant, but they are rejected.	Heb. 8:8-12, II Cor. 3; I Cor. 11:25, Matt. 26:28, etc., Heb. 8:8-12, Toy, p. 222; Dodd, Scriptures, pp. 44-6.
36.	Jer. 31:34	I, 499, 773ff. God called gentiles.	Heb. 10:16-17, Toy, p. 222
37.	Jer. 44:16-17	I, 761-4, 888 Rejection of Israel.	No reference.
38.	Ez. 8:10	I, 768-9 Rejection of Israel.	No reference.
39.	Ez. 8:10-12	I, 768, 773ff. Rejection of Israel.	No reference.
40.	Ez. 15:4	I, 469, 766, 769, 861, 886 Fire burned bough.	No reference.
41.	Ez. 16:45	I, 768, 765 Israel descends from Amorites and Hittites.	No reference.
42.	Ez. 16:48-9, 52-55	I, 472, 936ff. Israel is like Sodom, therefore will never be rebuilt.	No reference.
43.	Ez. 23:4	I, 769 Both Israel and Judah rejected.	No reference.
44.	Hos. 2:2, 3, 15	I, 768-9 Both Judah and Israel rejected.	No reference.

	Scripture	Aphrahat	New Testament
45.	Hos. 2:11	I, 509 Rejection of sacrifices.	No reference.
46.	Hos. 3:4	I, 509 Rejection of sacrifices.	No reference.
47.	Hos. 5:7	I, 768-9 Israel rejected.	No reference.
48.	Hos. 6:4-5, 8	I, 853-6, 949-952 Israel rejected.	II Thes. 2:8, Toy, p. 202
49.	Hos. 7:13	I, 853-6 Israel rejected.	No reference.
50.	Hos. 9:10, 11, 12, 15, 17	I, 853-6 Israel rejected.	No reference.
51.	Hos. 10:1, 6	I, 853-6 Israel rejected.	No reference.
52.	Hos. 11:12	I, 768-9, 853-6 Israel rejected.	No reference.
53.	Hos. 13:9, 11	I, 853-6 Israel rejected.	No reference.
54.	Amos 4:9	I, 857-60	Jude 23, Toy, p. 252
55.	Amos 4:11	I, 857-60	No reference.
56.	Amos 5:2, 16, 21, 22-25	I, 749-9, 857-60, 948 No further hope.	Acts 7:42-3, Toy, p. 112
57.	Amos 8:11-12	I, 773ff. Israel rejected.	No reference.
58.	Amos 9:7-8	I, 857-60	No reference.
59.	Micah 2:3, 2:10, 3:17	I, 856 Rejection of Israel.	No reference.
60.	Micah 7:4, 14, 17	I, 864 Rejection of Israel.	No reference.
61.	Nahum 2:13	I, 864 Rejection of Israel.	No reference.

	Scripture	Aphrahat	New Testament
62.	Nahum 3:1	I, 864 Rejection of Israel.	No reference.
63.	Haggai 1:8, 2:5-8, 10	I, 865 Redemption in the past.	[Hag. 2:6 = Heb. 12:26, Toy, p. 234; not in same sense as Aphrahat]
63a.	Joel 2:28-32	I, 776 Applies to gentiles.	Acts 2:17-21, Dodd, *Scriptures*, pp. 46-8; Lindars, *Apologetic*, pp. 36-8
64.	Zech. 1:14-15, 17	I, 865, 868-9 Redemption in the past.	No reference.
65.	Zech. 2:4-5, 6-7, 12	I, 868-9 Redemption in the past.	No reference.
66.	Zech. 4:9	Redemption in the past.	No reference.
67.	Zech. 7:6	I, 748-9 Sacrifice no good.	No reference.
68.	Mal. 2:8	I, 863 Rejection of Israel.	No reference.
69.	Mal. 2:9	I, 863 Rejection of Israel.	No reference.
70.	Mal. 2:11	I, 863 Rejection of Israel.	No reference.
71.	Mal. 2:17	I, 863 Rejection of Israel.	No reference.
72.	Mal. 3:6-7	I, 863 Rejection of Israel.	No reference.
73.	Ps. 49:13-15	I, 748-9 Sacrifice no good.	No reference.
74.	Ps. 69:28	I, 769 God rejected Israel.	No reference.
75.	Ps. 80:8, 9, 13	I, 861 God rejected Israel.	No reference.

	Scripture	*Aphrahat*	*New Testament*
76.	Daniel's Vision Chapter 9	I, 869ff. Vision of the future, no redemption after destruction.	Matt. 24:15 Mark 13:14 } Toy, p. 64 Luke 21:20
77.	Gen. 17:5	I, 468, 498, 534, 760 Gentiles called before Israel.	Rom. 4:17, Toy, p. 135
78.	Gen. 49:10	I, 760, 805, 886 Jacob spoke of Messiah, gentiles' salvation.	[Rev. 5:5, Toy, p. 258; not proved]
79.	Ex. 32:10	I, 772-3 Vocation of peoples.	No reference.
80.	Num. 24:21	I, 598, 777-780 Jethro better than Israelite.	No reference.
81.	Deut. 32:21	I, 509, 513 Fulfilled in gentiles' church.	See No. 4.
82.	Is. 2:2	I, 513, 760-1, 861-4 Addressed to church.	No reference.
83.	Is. 33:13 (See Deut. 32:21)	I, 513, 775 Addressed to church.	No reference.
84.	Is. 42:6 (See Deut. 32:21)	I, 781-2 Israel prevented from idolatry by shame before gentiles who worship God.	No reference.
85.	Is. 49:6, 51:4	I, 772-3 Vocation of peoples.	Is. 49:6 = Acts 13:47, Toy, p. 119
86.	Jer. 6:8-9	I, 761-4 Vocation of peoples.	No reference.
87.	Jer. 6:16-18	I, 512-3, 763 When Jews would not listen, Jeremiah turned to gentiles and rejected Israel.	No reference.

Scriptures	Aphrahat	New Testament
88. Jer. 12:7-9	I, 512, 754, 764-5, 859 Painted bird = church.	No reference.
89. Jer. 16:19	I, 761 Conversion of gentiles.	No reference.
90. Mal. 1:11	I, 768 Gentiles chosen.	No reference.
91. Ps. 18:44-5	I, 772-3, 813 Christians are sons.	No reference.
92. Ps. 22:28	I, 773ff. Vocation of gentiles.	No reference.
93. Ps. 47:1	I, 773ff. Gentiles called.	No reference.
94. Ps. 69:28-9	I, 769 Rejection of Israel and vo- cation of gentiles.	No reference.
95. Ps. 74:2	I, 513, 773 Refers to church.	No reference.
96. Ps. 87:6	I, 769 God counts gentiles.	No reference.
97. Gen. 49:10	I, 804, 885 Fulfilled in Christ, proved by me, Aphrahat.	See No. 78.
98. Ex. 4:22-3	I, 774, 788-9, 846 Israel called sons of God.	No reference.
99. Ex. 7:1-2	I, 788 Moses called God.	No reference.
100. Ex. 12:5 (see also Ex. 12:4, 9, 11)	I, 505, 525 Interpreted in terms of passion.	John 19:36, Toy, p. 91
101. II Sam. 7:14	I, 788 Solomon called son of God.	Rev. 21:7, Toy, p. 276 II Cor. 6:18, Toy, p. 186 Heb. 1:5
102. Is. 7:14	I, 804 Christ foretold.	Matt. 1:23, Toy, p. 1; Lindars, Apologetic, pp. 213-219

Scripture	Aphrahat	New Testament
103. Is. 9:6-7	I, 804ff. Christ foretold.	No reference.
104. Is. 52:13-15, 53:2, 5, 10	I, 808ff., 812 Apply to Christ.	Is. 52:15 = Rom. 15:21, Toy, p. 168 Is. 53:5 = I Pet. 2:24, Toy, p. 243
105. Is. 53 & Ex. 12	I, 516 Apply to Passion.	NT references to Is. 53 cited by Toy are as follows: 53:1 = John 12:38, Rom. 10:16, Toy, p. 88; 53:4 = Matt. 8:17, John 1:29, I Pet. 2:24, Toy, p. 29; 53:4-5 = I Pet. 2:24, Toy, p. 243; 53:7 = Rev. 5:6, 12, Toy, p. 259, Acts 8:32-3, Toy, p. 115; 53:9 = I Pet. 2:22, Toy, p. 243; 53:12 = Luke 22:37, Toy, p. 80; 53:12, 6 = Rom. 4:25, Toy, p. 135. It is clear that the interpretation of Is. 53 in reference to Christ and the passion derives from NT materials. See also Dodd, *Scriptures*, pp. 39, 88-96; Lindars, *Apologetic*, pp. 77-88.
106. Zech. 9:10	I, 761 Applies to Christ.	No reference.
106a. Zech. 13:7	I, 812 Applies to Christ.	Matt. 26:13, Mark 14:24; Lindars, *Apologetic*, pp. 127-132.
107. Zech. 14:6-7	I, 812 Foretold passion.	No reference.
108. Ps. 2:6-7	I, 804 Applies to Christ.	Acts 13:33 ⎱ Toy, Heb. 1:5, 2:6-8, 5:5 ⎰ p. 118; Dodd, *Scriptures*, pp. 31-34, 104-5; Lindars, *Apologetic*, pp. 139-144.

Scripture	Aphrahat	New Testament
109. Ps. 16:10	I, 808ff. Applies to Christ.	Acts 13:35, Toy, pp. 99, 118; Lindars, *Apologetic*, pp. 45-51.
110. Ps. 22:17-18, 23	I, 808ff. Applies to Christ, Passion.	John 19:24, Toy, p. 90; Heb. 2:12, Toy, p. 212; Dodd, *Scriptures*, pp. 96-8; Lindars, *Apologetic*, pp. 89-93.
111. Ps. 69:21, 26	I, 812 Applies to Christ.	No reference.
112. Ps. 110:1-3	I, 796, 804ff. Applies to Christ.	Mark 12:36, Acts 2:34-5 Dodd, *Scriptures*, pp. 34-5; Harris, *Testimonies*, I, pp. 14-15, etc.
113. Ps. 118:22	I, 16 Jesus is stoned, rejected.	Matt. 21:42 Mark 12:10-11 Luke 20-17 } Toy, p. 56 Acts 4:11 I Pet. 2:7 Dodd, *Scriptures*, pp. 35-6, 99-100; Lindars, *Apologetic*, pp. 169-224.
114. Dan. 9:26-7	I, 805, 882, 939, 943 Daniel foresaw Jesus.	See No. 76
115. Gen. 2:24	I, 840 Means you should be celibate, love Father and Holy Spirit.	Eph. 5:31 [See Toy, p. 46. But no relationship between Aphrahat's exegesis and Matt. 19:5, Mark 10:7, 8, I Cor. 6:16. Aphrahat follows Eph. 5:31]
116. Ex. 19:15	I, 825 No revelation until people celibate.	No reference.

Scripture	Aphrahat	New Testament
117. Jer. 16:2, 17:16	I, 833 Why Jeremiah did not marry.	No reference.
118. Gen. 1:29	I, 736 Any food all right, but not blood.	No reference.
119. Gen. 7:1ff.	I, 549-51, 555 Noah did not keep Sabbath.	No reference.
120. Gen. 15:6	I, 476, 558 Faith, not circumcision.	Rom. 4:3, 9 Gal. 3:6 } Toy, p. 132 Jas. 2:23 Lindars, *Apologetic*, pp. 225-228
121. Gen. 17:10	I, 476 Circumcision valid for limited time.	No reference.
122. Gen. 39:9	I, 557 Joseph did not keep Sabbath.	No reference.
123. Gen. 43:32	I, 736 Egyptians worshipped oxen.	No reference.
124. Num. 33:4	I, 740 Egyptians worshipped cows and sheep.	No reference.
125. Deut. 10:16	I, 481, 435 Circumcise heart, flesh without heart no value.	No reference.
126. Josh. 5:2, 5, 6	I, 486 Israelites not circumcised before; 2nd time—first time was of the heart.	No reference.
127. Josh. 6:4	I, 568 Joshua violated Sabbath at Jericho.	Heb. 4:8-9

	Scripture	*Aphrahat*	*New Testament*
128.	Josh. 24:15-22	I, 740-1, 963 Israelites worshipped gods of Egyptians.	No reference.
129.	Judges 15:18	I, 744 Samson ate food from lion, unclean animal.	No reference.
130.	Is. 28:12	I, 569-72 Sabbath of God.	I Cor. 14:21, Toy, p. 175
131.	Is. 56:4	I, 569-72 Sabbath of God.	No reference.
132.	Is. 65:5	I, 569-72 Sabbath of God.	No reference.
133.	Jer. 4:4	I, 500 Circumcise hearts.	No reference.
134.	Jer. 9:25-6	I, 480 Circumcision without faith of no value.	No reference.
135.	Ez. 4:13-14	I, 508-9 Jews will eat among unclean peoples.	No reference.
136.	Ez. 20:11, 25-6	I, 753 Evil commandments are purity laws, etc.	No reference.
137.	Is. 65:8	XXIII: The Grapecluster.	No reference.

In addition to the specific Scriptural references surveyed, we should note the following New Testament doctrines and arguments alluded to by Aphrahat:

Doctrine	*NT Source*	*Aphrahat Demonstration*
True circumcision is a matter of the heart.	Rom. 2:25-29	XI
True child of Abraham is one who obeys God.	Rom. 9:6ff.	XI
Christ, our paschal lamb, has been sacrificed.	I Cor. 5:7	XII

Doctrine	NT Source	Aphrahat Demonstration
Dietary laws are of no account.	I Cor. 6:12ff I Cor. 8:1-13	XV
Dietary laws, festivals, new moons, and Sabbath are only a shadow of what is to come.	I Col. 2:16	XIII, XV
Sin of wilderness was unbelief.	Heb. 3:16-19	XI
Christ and Melchizedek.	Heb. 5:6, 6:13ff., 7:1-10	XI
End of sacrifices.	Heb. Chs. 9-10	XV
Scriptural Heroes Abel, Enoch, Noah, Abraham, Moses, Gideon, Barak, Samson, Jephthah, David, Samuel.	Heb. 11	XXI

What Hebrew Scriptures did Aphrahat cite following the New Testament testimonies? Among the first group, on the rejection of Israel and vocation of the gentiles, we found No. 4 (Deut. 32:21); No. 9 (Is. 1:9-10), the comparison of Israel and Sodom; No. 11 (Is. 5:1ff.), the wild grapes produced by the vineyard, but with the qualification that the parable is not used by Aphrahat in the same way as in the New Testament; No. 13 (Is. 29:13); No. 17 (Is. 34:4); No. 20 (Is. 52:11); No. 35 (Jer. 31:31-2); No. 36 (Jer. 31:34) on the new covenant in Jeremiah; No. 48 (Hos. 6:4-5); No. 55 (Amos 4:11); No. 56 (Amos 5:2, etc.); No. 63a (Joel 2:28-32); and a brief allusion to No. 76 (Daniel 9) and Nos. 77-8 (Gen. 17:5, 49:10). Of the seventy-eight passages under investigation, we therefore find only thirteen instances, 15%, in which Aphrahat presumably selected a Hebrew Scriptural reference from the repertoire of testimonies in the New Testament on Israel and the gentiles.

By contrast, among Nos. 79-114, on "Christ in the Old Testament," we found a considerably higher proportion, 56%, as follows: No. 81 (Deut. 32:21); No. 85 (Is. 49:6); No. 100 (Ex. 12); No. 101 (II Sam. 7:14); No. 102 (Is. 7:14); No. 104 (Is. 52-53); No. 105 (Is. 53 and Ex. 12); No. 106a (Zech. 13:7); No. 108 (Ps. 2:7); No. 109 (Ps. 16:10); No. 110 (Ps. 22); No. 112 (Ps. 110); No. 113 (Ps. 118:22) No. 114 (= No. 76), that is to say out of twenty-five Scriptures on the figure of the Christ in the Old Testament in Aphrahat, fourteen are drawn from New Testament materials. We may therefore conclude that Aphrahat certainly learned from the New

Testament testimonies how to read Hebrew Scriptural references in the
light of the life and passion of Jesus. But his repertoire of materials on the
rejection of Israel and vocation of the peoples is to a considerably smaller
degree based upon New Testament precedents.

In addition we found that Aphrahat's striking exegesis of Gen. 2:24
(No. 115) is in fact a citation of Ephesians 5:31. The basic arguments for
circumcision were buttressed with No. 120 (Gen. 15:6); the example of
Joshua at Jericho (No. 127) comes from Heb. 4:8-9; and the Sabbath of
God (Is. 28:12, No. 130) derives from I Cor. 14:21. I am unable to find a
New Testament reference to Is. 65:8 (No. 137). In addition we also noted
that the major arguments of Aphrahat concerning circumcision derive
from Romans; on Christ as the paschal lamb from Corinthians; on the
dietary laws from Corinthians; on the end of sacrifices from Hebrews 9-
10; and the repertoire of Scriptural heroes owes much to Hebrews 11.

As we review the Hebrew Scriptures cited in the New Testament and
referred to by Aphrahat, we see several facts. First of all, in general, as we
supposed at the outset, most of the important doctrines of Aphrahat on
the Jews and Judaism are present in New Testament materials,
including references to the rejection of Israel and the vocation of the
gentiles, the abrogation of the law in general, and of the Sabbath,
circumcision, and dietary laws in particular, and, we need hardly add, the
Christian axiom of the end of the Jews' messianic hope. The only
significant matter left open is the issue of whether fulfilling the specific
laws of Sinai had *ever* served a salvific purpose. Aphrahat denies it, and
the New Testament writers seem to me not to do so. We shall therefore
look for evidences of such a view in earlier patristic writers on Judaism.

It now is quite clear that many proof-texts cited by Aphrahat were not
part of the New Testament repertoire at all. Some texts cited by Aphrahat
were referred to in New Testament writings in entirely other ways. We
shall now compare Aphrahat's views of Judaism to those of the Church
fathers who preceded him, both for general points of similarity and
difference, and for specific instances in which Scriptures cited by
Aphrahat were quoted by his predecessors in much the same manner.
We eliminate those Scriptures used in the New Testament, in the
presumption that Aphrahat drew on the New Testament testimonies
where these existed.

IV. APHRAHAT AND THE APOSTOLIC FATHERS

Our interest is in three questions. First and predominating is the
inquiry into earlier appearances of Aphrahat's arguments and judgments

on Judaism. Second, we shall seek evidences that the Scriptures he cited had earlier received attention in the context of the same issues and arguments. The results are given all together, in part ix. Finally, we shall look for some obvious differences between Aphrahat and his predecessors. Since in no way can I be considered a qualified student of patristic literature, I rely on Johannes Quaesten, *Patrology* (Westminster, Utrecht-Brussels, 1950), I. *The Beginnings of Patristic Literature*, and II. *The Ante-Nicene Literature after Irenaeus.* Quaesten's judgments guide me in all questions of date, text, authenticity, and other matters. I survey Alexander Roberts and James Donaldson, eds., *The Ante-Nicene Fathers. Translations of the Writings of the Fathers down to A.D. 325* (Repr. Grand Rapids, n.d., of 1884-6 edition, rev. by A. C. Coxe). Page references are to volume and page in this edition. I realize this is not a complete collection of ante-Nicene Christian writings, but for my purposes it proves satisfactory to review a representative sample of the whole literature.

Epistle to Diognetus (Quaesten, I, pp. 248-53), possibly to be dated at the beginning of the third century, refers (Chapter IV, I, p. 26) to the Jews' scrupulousness concerning meats, their superstition in respect to the Sabbath, their boasting about circumcision, and their fancies about fasting and the new moons. Dietary laws reflect negatively on some of the things created by God; the Sabbath law forbids doing what is good on Sabbath-days; and circumcision is no proof of election. Observing months and days is not unlike astrology. We see here in brief the themes of Aphrahat's arguments in Demonstrations XI, XIII, and XV, but not the ways Aphrahat treats them. He refers only in passing to fast days and new moons.

Ignatius of Antioch (d. ca. 115) (Quaesten, I, pp. 63-76), in the Epistle to the Magnesians (Chapters VIII-IX, I, pp. 62-3) warns against circumcision and keeping the Sabbath. His argument on the latter is that one should not be lazy. In the long recension he refers to not eating things prepared the day before, nor using lukewarm drinks, nor walking within a prescribed space, nor finding delight "in dancing and plaudits." These specific references to Jewish observance are important evidence that Ignatius knew something of rabbinical Sabbath-rites. By contrast we hear nothing so specific from Aphrahat. Indeed, "walking within a prescribed space" calls to mind the Oral Tradition on 'eruvin. We do not know whether Ignatius's Jews knew the rabbinical procedures to permit a wider framework for walking on the Sabbath. We can be fairly sure that Aphrahat's Jews gave him no indication they kept such laws. Since the original prohibition is Scriptural—each person was to stay within his tent—it is of interest that the Scriptural Judaism of Aphrahat's Jews seems not to have included that rule.

Epistle of Barnabas (Quaesten, I, pp. 85-91) derives from Alexandria and cannot be dated after 138 (Chapter II, I, pp. 138-9). Barnabas argues that the Jewish sacrifices were never needed by God. The fasts of the Jews are not acceptable to God (Chapter III, I, p. 138). God rejected Israel at Sinai, when Moses broke the tables of the covenant. Circumcision was widely practiced in antiquity. The Egyptians also practice circumcision, as do Syrians, Arabs, and all the priests of idols (Chapter VIII, p. 142). As to making distinctions among foods, Moses spoke with a spiritual reference (Chapter X, I, p. 143). When people live like swine, they forget God. The Christians, not the Jews, have inherited the covenant. The younger takes precedence over the older. God has given the Christians the testament broken by Moses. As to the Sabbath, Scripture refers to the "eighth day, that is, a beginning of another world."

Barnabas strikingly differs from Aphrahat. His critique of the Sabbath and the dietary laws has nothing to do with the historical bases for these practices. The argument on circumcision, on the other hand, is similar to Aphrahat's, but it is not developed, merely stated. Barnabas does not draw the same conclusions from the argument. Barnabas' Epistle shows us a completely different way of phrasing the critique of Judaism. For Barnabas the Jews err chiefly because they interpret the Torah literally. The true, spiritual meaning consists of an allegorical explanation of biblical doctrines and commandments. God wants not material gifts but the heart, not circumcision of the flesh but of the heart and ear, not abstinence of flesh but renunciation of sins symbolized by various animals (Quaesten, I, p. 86).

In the *Apocryphal New Testament*, trans. Montague Rhodes James (Oxford, 1924, repr. 1955), I could find nothing pertinent to the Judaic Demonstrations of Aphrahat, no common themes, no Scriptures used for much the same proposition, no shared arguments concerning specific aspects of Judaism. To be sure, in several of the documents (e.g. in the Apostolic History of Abdias, James, p. 462ff.) Jews appear, and arguments about the messiahship of Jesus, buttressed by Scriptural references, are presented. But these are generally well within the New Testament formulation, and in any event the place of the Jewish disputes is inconsiderable. The acts of the various apostles are mostly stories of events and miracles and contain nothing equivalent to the discourses of Paul or the exegeses of the letter of Barnabas.

v. Aphrahat and Justin Martyr and Irenaeus

Justin's *Apologies* and *Dialogue with Trypho* are the first important, systematic Christian critiques of Judaism after Romans 9-11 and Paul's letters. As we saw, the intervening century produced nothing of much interest. Justin, who wrote between 148 and 161 (Quaesten, I, pp. 197-219), was born in Samaria, son of gentile parents, about 114, and was martyred about 165. Justin's knowledge of the Jews and Judaism derives mainly from Scripture (Wilde, p. 105).

In the *First Apology*, directed toward pagans, Justin argues that Jesus was predicted by the prophets (Chapters XXXI-XXXV, I, pp. 173-4). The *Second Apology* contains nothing pertinent. The *Dialogue with Trypho* cannot be briefly summarized; it contains one-hundred forty-two chapters. Trypho's critique is practical. He cannot understand how Christians, professing to be pious, do not separate themselves from the nations, observe festivals and the Sabbath, and keep the rite of circumcision. Justin replies that the true Israel is spiritual, marked not by circumcision but by faith. The Jews therefore require a second circumcision (Chapter XII, I, p. 200). The Jews understand everything in a carnal sense, e.g. by refraining from eating unleavened bread. But the unleavened bread symbolizes the old wicked deeds. The purpose of circumcision was to separate the Jews from the nations, "and so that you alone may suffer that which you now justly suffer" (Chapter XVI, I, p. 202). While this superficially resembles Aphrahat's view, the thrust of Justin's argument is national, not personal: "Your land is desolate, your cities, burned, strangers eat your crops — you are set apart for these by the mark of circumcision." Aphrahat's argument pertains to an individual who might deny he was an Israelite, therefore subject to the punishment of the law. But Justin then remarks that Christians know why circumcision, Sabbath, and other feasts were commanded, "namely, on account of transgressions and the hardness of your hearts" (Chapter XVIII, I, p. 203, XCII, I, p. 245).

As to circumcision, if it were of value, God would have created Adam already circumcised, would have paid no respect to Abel, would not have been pleased with Enoch, would not have saved Noah. Melchizedek's blessing would have been valueless, for he too was uncircumcised. The same righteous men kept no Sabbaths, but still pleased God. The priests did not sin when they carried out the sacrificial rites on the Sabbath, and circumcision may take place on the Sabbath without sin. God enjoined sacrifices on account of the idolatry of the generation of the wilderness, "in order that you might not serve idols." The Sabbaths are merely a memorial of God. The abstinence from certain kinds of food was to counteract the Jews' tendency to "wax fat and forsake God." In fact, Noah was allowed to eat anything that was dead, "and he was ready to say, 'as the green herbs' ". Sacrifices were likewise caused by Israel's sinfulness.

The same God who in olden times favored Enoch and the rest who did not circumcise, keep the Sabbath and other rites, is the one who saved mankind. There was no need of circumcision and Sabbath before Moses, and none now. For the interim, it was the Jews' sinfulness that necessitated the commandments. The Christian circumcision is with knives of stone. Here we come very close to Aphrahat's general view of the practical commandments. Justin seems to deny that the commandments had ever saved anyone (Chapter XLIII, I, p. 216). They were of this-worldly significance, meant to keep the Jews from sinning against God, but in no way led to salvation.

The reference to the generations before Sinai, indeed before Abraham, appears. Aphrahat's reference to Melchizedek, who was uncircumcised, yet blessed the circumcised Abraham is found in pretty much the same form. Three central points in Aphrahat's argument, however, are lacking. First, the Sabbath is a day of rest for man and beast, a sign of God's compassion for his creatures. Second, the dietary laws counteracted the Israelites' worship of the gods of the Egyptians. Third, circumcision was meant to separate the Israelites from the Canaanites. While in a general way Aphrahat's interpretation is similar to Justin's, in particulars we find important differences. What is striking is that the classical critique of Judaism by Justin's time included reference to circumcision, Passover, the Sabbath, dietary laws, and the messianic hope (Chapters XLIV, I, p. 216-7, LXXX, I, p. 239). The repertoire of themes is by now constant. The way in which they are worked out is not.

Trypho argues that the prophetic Scriptures referring to the Messiah will be fulfilled in the future. To this Justin answers (Chapter XXXII, I, pp. 210f) that the Scriptures pertain to Jesus, and those which have not been fulfilled will be carried out in the second coming (Chapter LXXX, 1, p. 239). Like Aphrahat Justin shows that Ps. 110 applies to Jesus, not to Hezekiah, as the Jews maintain (Chapter XXXIII, I, p. 211).

While arguing in much the same framework, Aphrahat and Justin therefore differ markedly. Aphrahat's chief concern is to demonstrate the rejection of Israel and the formation of the people which is of the peoples in place of ancient Israel. While Justin does likewise (Chapters

CXIX-CXX, I, pp. 258-260), he wants moreover to prove from Scriptures that various details of Christian theology, e.g. the Trinity and the virgin birth, were foretold of old. The two fathers by and large do not emphasize the same matters at all. Further, the exegetical argument dominates in Justin, while, though Aphrahat also copiously cites Scripture, he in the end concentrates on things which have happened, historical reasons for laws, and the like. For Aphrahat the Hebrew Scriptures are a historical source, not primarily a collection of proof-texts to be read allegorically. Aphrahat to be sure follows the earlier tendencies to spiritualize various laws and commandments or to treat them as allegories. But Justin carries this to far greater extreme (e.g. the bells on the priest's robe were a figure of the apostles, Chapter XLII, I, p. 215-6), so even here, the two are not really comparable. The fundamental difference is that while Justin's chief interest was to expound the Christian faith in great detail and to show the Scriptural foundations of that faith, Aphrahat concentrated on the task of refuting and criticizing Judaism. It was one thing to compare Jesus to former biblical heroes, such as Joshua (Chapter CXIII, I, p. 255). This Aphrahat did many times. It was quite another to read vast segments of the Hebrew Scriptures into the Jewish-Christian debate. Aphrahat did not do so. Justin did little else.

In the setting of his arguments in *Against Heresies*, Irenaeus (b. ca. 140-160, Quaesten, I, pp. 287-313) also turns to Judaism and briefly covers the by-now standard themes. In Book IV, Chapters VIIIff. (I, pp. 470ff.), he asserts that the Jews departed from God in not accepting Christ. The bondage of the law was loosed by Christ. It was permitted to circumcise and to heal on the Sabbath, and so Jesus both fulfilled the law and loosed its requirements by his actions (Chapter VIII, 2-4, I, p. 471). In this context Irenaeus stresses that there is but one author and one end to both covenants, a point made in passing by Aphrahat as well. From the fact that the Old Testament foretells the advent and passion of Christ it follows that they were inspired by one and the same God (Chapter X, I, p. 473), apparently important against the Marcionites. Circumcision was a sign so that the race of Abraham might continue to be recognized (Book IV, Chapter XVI, I, p. 480); likewise the Sabbath was a sign. Abraham without circumcision and Sabbath-observance was righteous because of his faith. God did not require sacrifices for his own need, but rather (Chapter XVI, 3), "that, forgetting the idolatry of the Egyptians, they should be able to hear the voice of the Lord." Irenaeus comes near Aphrahat's position, but he does not in the end contend the Jews worshipped the animals they now were told to eat and to sacrifice. These points are not central to Irenaeus' discussion, and there is no detailed comparison to be made with Aphrahat's Demonstrations.

VI. Aphrahat and Tertullian

Born in Carthage in 155, Tertullian produced his immense corpus of writings from 195 to 220 (Quaesten, II, pp. 246-340). His *Answer to the Jews* [3] represents only a tiny part of the whole (in quantity, roughly 3 %), by contrast to the substantial place (40.9 %) of Aphrahat's Judaic demonstrations in his writings.

Tertullian first shows that gentiles participate in divine grace. Both Israel and the gentiles are called "people" and "nation." The Jewish people came first, "while ours is less." But the prior people must serve the greater, for Israel forsook God and worshipped idols even in the wilderness, while the lesser people abandoned idolatry and attained grace (Chapter I, III, pp. 151-2). God first gave to Adam the law not to eat the fruit of the tree, and that law would have continued had it been kept. But Adam disobeyed, so God gave the law through Moses. This argument comes close to Aphrahat's, that when God saw covenants broken, he changed them. But Tertullian draws other conclusions from the law given to Adam. He says that the law given to Adam contained within it the *whole* of the commandments. Noah was righteous because he kept natural law. Abraham was a friend of God. Melchizedek was the priest of God before the priesthood. Thus God's law "was anterior even to Moses and was not first given in Sinai but in paradise" (Chapter II, III, p. 152-3). God has the power to reform the law's precepts "in response to the circumstances of the times, with a view to man's salvation." Aphrahat, in a general way, holds the same view.

The Sabbath, circumcision and the like in past time were kept by righteous men. But circumcision does not purge a man, since God made Adam uncircumcised, and Adam, Abel, and Noah, Enoch, and Melchizedek were not circumcised and did not keep the Sabbath. Abraham was circumcised only after he had pleased God through believing (Chapter III, III, pp. 153-4). Like Justin, Tertullian then argues that circumcision was given as a sign so that Jews thereby would be distinguished and hence prevented from entering Jerusalem. Carnal circumcision was merely a sign, but spiritual circumcision, as described by Jeremiah, was for the salvation of the peoples. As in the exegesis of

---

[3] For the fullest recent discussion, see Hermann Tränkle, *Q.S.F. Tertulliani, Adversus Iudaeos, mit Einleitung und kritischem Kommentar* (Wiesbaden, 1964).

Aphrahat, Is. 2:2-5 refers to Jacob, "the second, that is, our people, whose mount is Christ." "We who are fully taught by the new law observe these practices." The old law no longer applies. "We are the people referred to in Ps. 18:43," which was ignorant of God and now give heed to him, having forsaken idols.

Just as circumcision was valid for a time, so the Sabbath "is demonstrated to have been temporary" (Chapter IV, III, p. 155). "We keep all days free of servile work." The temporal Sabbath is human, the eternal one divine. The temporal Sabbath foreshadowed the eternal one, just as the temporal circumcision foreshadowed the eternal one. Adam, Abel, Enoch, Noah, and Melchizedek all pleased God without keeping the Sabbath. Joshua made war against Jericho on the Sabbath. The Maccabees fought on the Sabbath. Therefore the commandments were temporary in value. Aphrahat cites the same facts, but draws a more radical conclusion from them.

Sacrifices prefigured the spiritual sacrifice of Christ. The sacrifices of the peoples were foreshadowed in that of Abel. Thus temporal and eternal are symbolized in the same commandments, circumcision, Sabbath, and sacrifices. The temporal ceremonies were annulled in the New Testament. "The giver of the new law, observer of the spiritual Sabbath, priest of the eternal sacrifices, eternal ruler of the eternal kingdom" (Chapter VI, III, p. 157) must be shown to have come in Christ. This is proved in the prophetic writings which foretell Christ.

Daniel 9 is then cited at length, just as in Aphrahat, and spelled out in much the same way. Daniel predicted "seventy hebdomads within which, if they receive him, the times will be renewed." God foresaw they would not receive, but would kill him. Tertullian then shows that the Christ came within the seventy-second and a half hebdomad from the first year of Darius. His calculation is to be compared to Aphrahat's:

Tertullian		*Aphrahat*
Darius	18 years	*490 years from Daniel to 70 A.D.*
		49 years = Zerubbabel
Artaxerxes	41	*434 years = Zerubbabel to 70 A.D.*
Ochus/Cyrus	24	Darius
Argus	1	Belteshazzar
Darius/Melas	21	Cyrus
Alexander	12	
Soter	35	
Philadelphus	38	
Euergetes	25	

Tertullian		*Aphrahat*
Philopator	17 years	
Epiphanes	24	
Euergetes	29	
Soter	38	
Ptolemy	37	
Cleopatra	20 5/12	
Cleopatra/Augustus	13	
Augustus	43	
Christ is born eight years after the death of Cleopatra. From then to Vespasian:		
From birth of Christ to death of Augustus	15	
Tiberius	20 7/12'	
Caligula	3	
Nero	11	
Galba	7	
Otho		
Vitellius	492 years (approximately)	

Vespasian completed the seventy hebdomads predicted in Daniel. The contrast is striking. While Tertullian spells out the history of Palestine under Ptolemies and Caesars, Aphrahat simply refers to the overall calculation, as if the rest of the detailed facts were known, taken for granted, or unimportant. Why he omits reference to all the intervening events I cannot say. If he actually had read Tertullian, then one would understand his omission of the details on how the vision of Daniel was fulfilled for Palestine. He would have concentrated his brief comments on events in the Persian reign, in which, presumably, his readers, living in Iran, would be especially interested.

But this does not prove Aphrahat knew Tertullian's interpretation of Daniel 9, nor can we say that Aphrahat must have drawn on Tertullian even for the selection of Daniel 9 as a useful text for the Christian interpretation of Jewish history, for the text was briefly alluded to in New Testament testimonies. In our review of Scriptures commented on by both Aphrahat and earlier Christian writers, we shall see no significant pattern in the selection of Scriptures for the anti-Judaic arguments constructed by the respective fathers. The few texts in common are not quoted in the same order or connection. If Aphrahat knew Tertullian, he did not slavishly copy his Scriptural proof-texts, for he introduced Zechariah's vision as well. At best Aphrahat merely assumed the general conclusions of Tertullian's testimony and made use of them for the purposes of his argument. But I do not think Aphrahat knew Tertullian's *Answer to the Jews* at all.

Tertullian's selection of the prophecies of the birth and achievements of Christ (Chapter IX, III, pp. 160-4) need not detain us. He cites the usual Scriptures to prove Isaiah foretold the birth of Jesus, expounding the proof-texts against possible Jewish opposition. What is of somewhat greater interest is the reference to Israel of the time of Isaiah as "rulers of Sodom and people of Gomorrah" (Is. 1:10), and "your father was an Amorite and mother a Hittite" (Ezek. 16:3, 45). But these passages do not serve the same purpose as they do for Aphrahat. Here they are intended to show that Scriptures "figuratively use a transference of name grounded on parallelism of crimes" (III, p. 162). For Aphrahat, a more concrete, specific case is served by Is. 1:10 and Ez. 16:45.

Much argument is devoted to the fact that Jesus was not a warrior-messiah. Tertullian takes pains to prove that Christ need not have been a warrior "because he was not predicted as such by Isaiah." "Because Jesus Christ was to introduce the second people (which is composed of us nations, lingering deserted in the world) into the land of promise flowing with milk and honey (that is, into the possession of eternal life . . .), and this had to come about not through Moses (that is, not through the law's discipline) but through Joshua (that is, through the new law's grace) after our circumcision with a knife of rock (that is, with Christ's precepts, for Christ is in many ways and figures predicted as a rock) therefore the man who was being prepared to act as images of this sacrament was in-augurated under the figure of the Lord's name, even so as to be named Jesus." This explanation of the name of Jesus is of interest, not only because Aphrahat makes use of the same Joshua/Jesus parallel. It also highlights how different is the style of Aphrahat's discussion from Tertullian's. The ideas are much the same: new people, brought into the promise, through Joshua, with circumcision with a knife of rock, and so on. But Aphrahat's use of these images is always phrased in terms of things which have actually happened, not of the interpretation of religious symbolism in allegorical terms. While Aphrahat used allegory, he was not an allegorist. While Tertullian referred to facts of history, he always remained the lawyer-allegorist.

The prefiguring of the passion in various Scriptures is carefully worked out (Chapter X-XIV, III, pp. 164-172). Other references to Jews and Judaism pertinent to the Jewish-Christian argument are in "On Prescription against the Heretics" (Chapter IX, III, p. 247): "all Christ's words to the Jews are for us, not as specific commands but as principles

to be applied"; "Against Marcion" (Book II, Chapter XXI, III, p. 312),
that the minute prescriptions of the law were meant to keep the
people dependent on God, and "Against Marcion" (Book IV, Chapter
XII, III, p. 362), that Christ had restored the original purpose of the
Sabbath.

While we observe a few important similarities in selection and
treatment of Hebrew Scriptural materials, I see no general pattern
showing that Aphrahat followed the same Scriptural references as
Tertullian. On the contrary, the few items noted earlier, though striking,
actually are the only points in common. Hence if Aphrahat read
Tertullian, he took only a little of what he found. But, as I said, I doubt
that he knew Tertullian at all. Aphrahat to be sure discusses the people
which is of the peoples and the rejection of Israel, but the details of his
discussion owe nothing to Tertullian, and the themes are not new in
Tertullian. Aphrahat likewise argues that those who came before Sinai
were justified without the law, but this argument he takes from Hebrews.
At decisive points Aphrahat shows no relationship whatever to
Tertullian. First, Tertullian nowhere discusses the dietary laws, to which
Aphrahat devoted an entire demonstration. Second, for Tertullian the
primary issue of the Jewish-Christian debate is the Jewish critique of the
Christian's theological understanding of the Hebrew Scriptures. For
Aphrahat the primary issue is the Jewish critique of the Christians'
worldly situation, their stress on celibacy, their suffering and
persecution. The point to be debated is hardly theological, rather
historical and concrete. Third and most important, Aphrahat repeatedly
denies that keeping the law was intended to lead to salvation, while
Tertullian takes for granted that for a time the commandments
concerning the Sabbath, circumcision, and the like were of some value.
In this matter Aphrahat stands quite apart.

VII. APHRAHAT AND ORIGEN

Origen of Alexandria (Quaesten, II, pp. 37-101) (b. ca. 185, d. 263)
spent much of his life in Caesarea, in Palestine. In replying to the
critique of Christianity offered by the pagan Celsus (ca. 177-180,
following Henry Chadwick, *Origen: Contra Celsum* [Cambridge, 1953],
p. xxviii), he composed a critique of Judaism in ca. 246-8 (Chadwick,
p. xiv).

His earlier writings contain numerous references to the Hebrew
Scriptures, Jews, and Judaism. For instance, in *De Principiis* (Book IV,

Chapter I, Paragraph 22, IV, p. 371, Latin version) he distinguishes between Israel according to the flesh and Israel according to the spirit. Our interest, however, is in the systematic account of Judaism provided in *Contra Celsum*. Origen copiously answers the critique presented by Celsus in the name of Judaism concerning the person and life of Jesus. He cites the Hebrew Scriptures to prove that the Holy Spirit may take the form of a dove (Book I, Chapter XLIII, IV, p. 414), defends the New Testament miracle stories by pointing out that the law and prophets are full of marvels similar to those recorded of Jesus at his baptism (Book I, Chapter XLVI, IV, p. 415), and cites various prophetic Scriptures in the usual way. Jewish worship consisted in the pattern and shadow of certain heavenly things (Book II, Chapter II, IV, p. 430). In general the Jewish critique for Origen is based mainly on the Gospel stories. Jesus invented the tale of his birth from a virgin, though he was the illegitimate son of a Roman soldier, Panthera. Because of his poverty he went to Egypt and studied magic. The interpretation of various Scriptures is debated, e.g. Ps. 45. And so on through the life of Jesus.

Further, the Christians have abandoned the law. Jesus taught nothing new about resurrection and judgment. Jesus is arrogant and a liar, an impostor. Jesus cannot be God, for he fled, tried to escape, and was betrayed. The story of the resurrection is a fabrication. He was not really wounded so severely. Williams comments (p. 90), ". . . these arguments used by Origen are not made with the view of winning the Jews to Christ, but with that of rebutting objections made by them . . . through the medium of a Gentile."

I have not at length summarized the apology of Origen, because it shows little, if any, grounds for comparison with the Demonstrations of Aphrahat. Only once does Aphrahat refer to a Jewish critic's citing the New Testament, and never does he mention extensive interfaith discussions about the life and teachings of Jesus. On the contrary the substance of the Jewish critique was directed not toward the person of Jesus but rather against the Christians' worshipping him as God and calling him Christ. Here Aphrahat's defense is so unlike Origen's that no basis for contrast exists. The Jew of Celsus learned much from the Gospels (e.g. Book II, Chapter XI, IV, p. 435), while the Jew of Aphrahat knew practically nothing. Origen says, "We blame the Jews who have been brought up under the training of the law and the prophets (which foretell the coming of Christ) because they neither refute the argument which we lay before them to prove that He is the Messiah, . . . nor yet, while not offering any refutation, do they believe in him . . ." (Book II,

Chapter XXXVIII, IV, p. 446). This sort of criticism was open to Aphrahat, but he did not make it.

Celsus accuses the Jews of thinking they are holier than others because they are circumcised, but the Egyptians and others did it before they did. They abstain from pigs, but so do the Egyptians and others (Book V, Chapter XLI, p. 561). But, Origen argues, the Jewish laws are most admirable (Book V, Chapter XLII, IV, p. 562, Book VIII, Chapter XXIX, IV, p. 650). Circumcision is practiced among the Jews not for the same reason as among the Egyptians. Their sacrifices are not to the same god. They abstain from pork not because "it is some great thing," but because pigs are unclean (Book V, Chapter XLIX, IV, p. 565). We are very far indeed from the world of Aphrahat. To be sure, the "meaning of the law of Moses has been concealed from those who have not welcomed the way which is by Jesus Christ" (Book V, Chapter LX, IV, p. 569). But Aphrahat would not agree that those laws ever really had led to salvation. He never defended Judaism and its mysteries.

It is striking that Origen and Aphrahat scarcely comment on the same Scriptures. In only three instances, Gen. 49:10 (No. 78), Jer. 16:19 (No. 89), and Is. 9:6 (No. 103) do they say much the same thing about the same verse — and in all three instances, the exegesis conforms to the plain sense usually drawn by Christian interpreters.

Origen strongly hints he thinks Celsus has invented the whole Jewish case: "Celsus, in adopting the character of the Jew, could not discover any objections to be urged against the Gospel which might not be retorted on him as liable to be brought also against the law and the prophets" (Book II, Chapter LXXVI, IV, p. 462). That seems to me to explain the substantial difference between the Judaic Demonstrations of Aphrahat and *Against Celsus*. In the end Origen's argument is not with Jews but with pagans, and the thrust of Aphrahat's arguments was invariably directed against Judaism. By contrast, Origen not infrequently defends Judaism's Scriptures and beliefs.

Origen thus is really primarily arguing not with Jews but with pagans. Celsus's holds that there is a "true doctrine, of the greatest antiquity, held by the most ancient and pious races and the wisest of men. It has been perverted or misunderstood first by the Jews, then by the Christians, who are only an offshoot from an already corrupt stem, Judaism" (Chadwick, p. xxi). Therefore, Chadwick observes, Celsus appeals to Christians "to return to take their stand upon the old paths and abandon this newly invented absurdity of worshipping a Jew recently crucified in disgraceful circumstances. Let them return to the old polytheism, to the customs of their fathers" (Chadwick, p. xxi). To counter such principles, Origen must either defend Judaism outright, or mute Christian criticism directed against it. He does both.

Studies by G. Bardy, "Les traditions juives dans l'œuvre d'Origène," *Revue biblique* 34, 1925, pp. 217-52, M. Lods, "Étude sur les sources juives de la polemique de Celse contre les chrétiens," *Revue d'histoire et de philosophie religieuses* 21, 1941, pp. 1-31, which are listed by Chadwick, as well as W. Bacher, *Aggadot Amora'é 'Erez Yisra'el* (Tel Aviv, 1925) V, pp. 91-109, and Crawford Howell Toy, "Origen," *JE* 9, pp. 433b-434b have examined the question of rabbinic parallels in Origen. Toy notes, "Origen speaks of consulting learned Jews on the meaning of Old Testament words and passages . . . In the *Contra Celsum* he throughout defends the Jewish faith against the philosopher's attacks." Origen was the first Christian scholar to study Hebrew, but, Toy says, "There is no indication that he was acquainted with the Midrash." This judgment required modification in the light of later studies. Origen also refers to a Jewish patriarch, generally identified as Judah II, and with R. Hoshaiah. By contrast, Aphrahat does not seem to have known anyone in authority in the Babylonian Jewish community and almost certainly knew no one who was part of the rabbinical movement. The implications of these facts for the comparison of the two fathers are not entirely clear to me. On the one hand, Origen's Scriptural citations are not to the Hebrew text, Toy says, and Origen's knowledge of rabbinical exegesis, in Toy's view, is slight. But if after careful, thorough study it should prove otherwise, we should have little difficulty in explaining the appearance of attested, contemporary rabbinical comments in Origen's writings, by reference to his documented contacts with the Caesarean Jewish community and rabbinate. But if it should prove otherwise, as Toy judges, that fact would be even more striking. Second, I do not think Origen moderates his treatment of Judaism on account of personal relationships, rather because of the exigencies of the debate with the pagans. Hence I am unclear as to what relationships with rabbis actually meant to the first church father known to have been acquainted with rabbis. I am unsure as to what contrary inferences are to be drawn from the probable absence of such relationships in Aphrahat's social and religious life.

VIII. APHRAHAT AND LACTANTIUS AND THE
DIALOGUE OF TIMOTHY AND AQUILA; EUSEBIUS

Lactantius (ca. 260-330) (Quaesten, II, pp. 392-410), a North African, wrote in Book IV of his *Divine Institutes* (Chapters Xff, VII, pp. 108-123) about the classical set of themes pertinent to the Jews and Judaism. He first reviews the biblical account of Israelite history, the Exodus from Egypt, and so forth. Because God was disappointed in the Jews for resisting "wholesome precepts" and departing divine law, he sent prophets to rebuke the people. They failed to listen, so he determined "to change his covenant and bestow the inheritance of eternal life upon foreign nations" and "collected to Himself a more faithful people out of those who were aliens by birth." Then Lactantius reviews the birth, life, death, and resurrection of Jesus, and cites the prophetic testimonies pertaining to these matters.

As to Jewish practices, he notes that Jesus "destroyed the obligation of the law given by Moses, that is, that he did not rest on the Sabbath but labored for the good of men; that he abolished circumcision; and that he took away the necessity of abstaining from the flesh of swine." In these things "the mysteries of the Jewish religion consist" (Chapter XVII, VII, pp. 118-9). The people therefore were incited against Jesus. Moses however had predicted that the law would be abrogated. Isaiah prophesied concerning the abolition of circumcision (the reference is to Jer. 4:3-4). Joshua the son of Nun likewise referred to a second circumcision, not of the flesh, but of the heart and spirit. Circumcision is irrational. If God wanted it, he would have created man circumcised. As to the prohibition of pork, God wanted the Israelites to understand that they should abstain from sins and impurities symbolized by the pig. The passion was foretold (Chapter XVIII, VII, pp. 119-20).

These arguments in general are already familiar to us. The "mysteries" of Judaism are by now assumed to be the three practical commandments repeatedly referred to and criticized by most church fathers writing on Judaism. The claim of the fulfilment of prophecies in the life and death of Jesus had already recurred for nearly three hundred years before Lactantius. Lactantius is neither closer to, nor more distant from, Aphrahat than any of his predecessors. Scriptures serving both writers as proof-texts occur in a random pattern.

Dialogue of Timothy and Aquila, dated by Williams (p. 66) at ca. 200, was published by F. C. Conybeare, *Anecdota Oxoniensia, The Dialogues of Athanasius and Zacchaeus and of Timothy and Aquila* (Oxford, 1898). Williams summarizes the treatise as follows: I. The Trinity and the Incarnation; II. The Rejection of Israel in favor of the Gentiles; III. The Passion and Resurrection of Christ and the future judgment by him. In the epilogue, the Jew is converted and baptized. The issues in part I are, first, Does God have a son? Is the cross prefigured in the Hebrew

Scriptures? Is the Trinity mentioned? Many texts concerning the life of Jesus are cited from Hebrew Scriptures, generally in an allegorical framework. The Christian, for instance, says the cross was foretold by Moses' stretching out his hands when fighting against Amalek (Ex. 17:12), the anti-Christ. The Trinity derives from Is. 6:1-3.

As to the rejection of the Jews, the Christian holds that the covenant of Sinai has been abolished, citing Jer. 31:31-3 and Hos. chapters 1 and 2. Moses in Deut. 31:16 and 32:37, 43, refers to the punishment of Israel and the turning of the gentiles to God. Various events in the life of Jesus are debated, e.g. how can you reconcile Jesus' willingness to die with his being judge of all? The Christian shows that the death was foretold, in even minor details. Like other such debates we have briefly considered, this one bear little resemblance to the Demonstrations of Aphrahat.

Conybeare says (p. xxxiv) that *Athanasius and Zacchaeus* "did not assume its present for much before 300 A.D." While the work was known before that time, we have no reason to suppose Aphrahat was familiar with it, any more than with any of the earlier works *Adversus Judaeos*. The sorts of definitive proofs Conybeare provides to show relationships between Justin, Tertullian and others and the Dialogue cannot be provided for Aphrahat here or anywhere else. Indeed, the success of Conybeare in this regard shows that the absence of similar parallels of language (e.g. pp. xlvii-1), conceptions and arguments is consequential, indeed probative of Aphrahat's virtual independence in particulars and details from the whole earlier Christian polemical literature.

Eusebius *Demonstratio Evangelica* (translated by W. J. Ferrar, *The Proof of the Gospel* [N.Y., 1920], Vols. I-II), addressed chiefly to the faithful, was written between 314 and 318. The thesis is that Christianity is "a republication of the primitive religion of the patriarchs, from which the Mosaic religion was a declension" (Ferrar, I, p. xiii). Ferrar shows that Eusebius knew Justin's and Origen's writings, "After two centuries of defensive warfare against Jews and Greeks, the lines of controversy were clearly defined" (p. xv). The Jews are mentioned repeatedly, but the primary critique is directed against their unbelief in Jesus, rather than against their actual beliefs and practices, as in Aphrahat. The argument is summarized as follows (Book I, ch. 1, Ferrar, I, p. 3):

> The most ancient Hebrew oracles present all these things definitely about One Who would come in the last times, and Who would undergo such sufferings among men, and they clearly tell the source of their foreknowledge. They bear witness to the Resurrection from the dead of the Being Whom they revealed, His appearance to His disciples, His gift of the Holy Spirit to them, His return to heaven, His establishment as King on His

Father's throne and His glorious second Advent yet to be at the consummation of the age. In addition to all this you can hear the wailings and lamentations of each of the prophets, wailing and lamenting characteristically over the calamities which will overtake the Jewish people because of their impiety to Him Who had been foretold.

He further states, (Book I, ch. 1, Ferrar, I, p. 5):

And this is why in attacking this subject myself I must of course endeavour, with God's help, to supply a complete treatment of the Proof of the Gospel from these Hebrew theologians. And the importance of my writing does not lie in the fact that it is, as might be suggested, a polemic against the Jews. Perish the thought, far from that! For if they would fairly consider it, it is really on their side. For as it establishes Christianity on the basis of the antecedent prophecies, so it establishes Judaism from the complete fulfilment of its prophecies.

And finally (Book IX, ch. 1, Ferrar II, p. 185):

Even so of old, when they saw Him Incarnate and working miracles among them, they did not behold Him with the eyes of their soul and with understanding vision, nor had they any vision of spiritual inspiration, so as to understand what power it was that worked so wondrously and so prodigally among them. Yes, they who were counted worthy to receive with their eyes the words of eternal life, and listen to the voice of divine wisdom, did not hear with the ears of their understanding, and so made themselves an evident fulfilment of the prophecy. And even until now, through the power of Christ, by which every race of mankind, divorced from its ancestral superstition, is being led to the Christian religion, is so obvious to them, yet they do not regard it with their understanding, nor consider that what neither Moses nor his successors among the prophets achieved has been brought to pass by these alone, namely, to give up idolatry and pay no heed to polytheistic error, which has been accomplished among all nations by the power of our Saviour. And so when they read the witness of the prophets concerning Him, they hear with their ears and do not understand, and the prophecy before us is literally even now fulfilled against them.

Eusebius stresses that Enoch, Noah, Seth, and others including Job pleased God before the laws of Moses. Moses' laws were applicable only to the Jews. "We reject the Jews' way of life, but accept their writings" (I, ch. 4, Ferrar, I, p. 23):

You see here that he distinguishes two covenants, the old and the new, and says that the new would not be like the old which was given to the fathers. For the old covenant was given as a law to the Jews, when they had fallen from the religion of their forefathers, and had embraced the manners and life of the Egyptians, and had declined to the errors of polytheism, and the idolatrous superstitions of the Gentiles.

Joseph and Moses did not keep the Sabbath and dietary laws in Pharaoh's palace (I, ch. 6, Ferrar I, p. 30), nor was circumcision a means of salvation. Moses' laws were "to heal Jews from Egyptian idolatry" (I, ch. 6, Ferrar I, pp. 33-4):

> And it was in this intermediate period, while the ideal of the new covenant was hidden from men, and as it were asleep, that the law of Moses was interposed in the interval. It was like a nurse and governess of childish and imperfect souls. It was like a doctor to heal the whole Jewish race, worn away by the terrible disease of Egypt. As such it offered a lower and less perfect way of life to the children of Abraham, who were too weak to follow in the steps of their forefathers. For through their long sojourn in Egypt, after the death of their godly forefathers, they adopted Egyptian customs, and, as I said, fell into idolatrous superstition. They aimed no higher than the Egyptians, they became in all respects like them, both in worshipping idols, and in other matters. Moses tore them from their godless polytheism, he led them back to God, the Creator of all things; he drew them up as it were from an abyss of evil, but it was natural for him to build first this step of holiness at the threshold and entrance of the Temple of the more Perfect . . . He rescued them from their wild and savage life, and gave them a polity based on better reason and good law as the times went, and was the first lawgiver to codify his enactments in writing, a practice which was not yet known to all men. He dealt with them as imperfect, and when he forbade idolatry, he commanded them to worship the One Omnipotent God by sacrifices and bodily ceremonies. He enacted that they should conduct by certain mystic symbols the ritual that he ordained, which the Holy Spirit taught him in a wonderful way was only to be temporary; he drew a circle round one place and forbade them to celebrate his ordinances anywhere, except in one place alone, namely at the Temple in Jerusalem, and never outside it. And to this day it is forbidden for the children of the Hebrews outside the boundaries of their ruined mother-city to sacrifice according to the law, to build a temple or an altar, to anoint kings or priests, to celebrate the Mosaic gatherings and feasts, to be cleansed from pollution, to be loosed from offenses, to bear gifts to God, or to propitiate Him according to the legal requirements.

For the rest, the interest of Eusebius is in prophetic predictions of Jesus as Christ, Christological issues and doctrines, references in the Hebrew Scriptures to the pre-existence of Christ, to his sojourn among men, his passion, death, and resurrection.

Eusebius devotes some attention to Daniel 9:20-27, then (Book VIII, ch. 2, Ferrar II, pp. 118):

> It is quite clear that seven times seventy weeks reckoned in years amounts to 490. That was therefore the period determined for Daniel's people, which limited the total length of the Jewish nation's existence. And he no longer calls them here "God's people," but Daniel's, saying, "thy people." Just as

when they sinned and worshipped idols in the wilderness, God called them no more, His people, but Moses', saying, "Go, descend, for thy people has sinned." In the same way here too he explains why the definite limit of time is determined for them. It was that they might know they were no longer worthy to be called the people of God.

Although the ideas are much the same, the treatment of the passage by Aphrahat bears no great resemblance. As in the instances of the other Western writers, so with Eusebius we encounter a very different style of thought. Aphrahat sometimes makes use of much the same ideas, e.g. the assimilation of the Israelites in Egypt. But his development and application of these themes is entirely different from that of Eusebius. He speaks a different language, uses different idioms, and his fundamental mode of argumentation has in common only the resort to proof-texts, but Aphrahat chooses different proof-texts as well.

IX. SCRIPTURAL TESTIMONIES IN APHRAHAT AND OTHER CHURCH FATHERS

Aphrahat occasionally cited Scriptures which earlier served as testimonies for other Church Fathers, specifically, Nos. 8, 10, 14, 15, 18, 22, 24, 25, 34, 41, 50, 51, 60, 65, 67, 70, 72, 78, 82, 83, 84, 87, 89, 90, 91, 92, 99, 103, 111, 114, 116, 118, 121, 122, 125, 126, 133, 134, 136, and 137 (excluding Eusebius). But many of these citations were not for the same purpose or in the same sense, e.g. No. 136, Ez. 20:11 is referred to in Justin's Dialogue, but the reference is not spelled out as in Aphrahat; Origen's use of the same Scripture is in no way comparable to Aphrahat's. Some of the Scriptures important to Aphrahat were mentioned but not in a similar framework, e.g. No. 137, Is. 65:8, the grapecluster, is briefly referred to by Justin, while Aphrahat devoted a whole Demonstration to spelling out the "history" of the grapecluster. Aphrahat's treatment of No. 10, Is. 2:5-6, is well attested; apparently several fathers had earlier interpreted the "House of Jacob" to mean the gentiles.

Many of the Scriptures read in pretty much the same way by Aphrahat and earlier Church Fathers were interpreted in the plain and obvious sense to begin with. Scriptures proving that Israel was rebellious in the past, that sacrifice was not so important as obedience, and the like, occur in several of the essays against Judaism. The tendency to read references to the nations as meaning the Church is present in Justin, Tertullian, Novatian, and Cyprian, for example (No. 22). But we can hardly imagine Aphrahat depended for his repertoire of Scriptural testimonies on earlier

Church Fathers. Clearly, he followed the New Testament testimonies, and proceeded along the lines of exegesis set forth there. I do not think he was similarly influenced by any Church Father. No pattern of citations suggests he conscientiously followed the Scriptural testimonies of Cyprian, all the more so of others. On the contrary, the Scriptures cited in common exhibit no scheme at all. No one predecessor predominated, nor does the whole range of selections of an earlier Father recur in Aphrahat.

In the actual interpretation of Scriptural testimonies, moreover, Aphrahat does not allegorize in the manner of most of his predecessors. He does, to be sure, tend to spiritualize commandments, but not like Lactantius on the pig, or Novatian, Barnabas, or Hippolytus, on the three Jewish mysteries. Hence even though Scriptures are used to prove much the same point, that does not mean Aphrahat had much in common with others who earlier made similar use of those Scriptures. In a great number of cases, not only are Aphrahat's arguments entirely original, but also the Scriptures (eighty-one of one hundred and twenty-one) cited to prove his point are entirely of his own choice, never having been earlier cited in the Christian polemic against Judaism.

Key to Abbreviations in the following table

Volume and page references are to *The Ante-Nicene Fathers. Translations of the Writings of the Fathers down to A.D. 325*, edited by Alexander Roberts and James Donaldson (Repr. Grand Rapids, n.d.). *The Proof of the Gospel* by Eusebius in *Werke*, VI. *Die Demonstratio Evangelica*, ed. Ivar A. Heikel (Leipzig, 1913) and *Preparation of the Gospel*, in *Werke* VIII, 1-2, *Die Praeparatio Evangelica* ed. Karl Mras (Berlin, 1954) cannot be easily summarized, but should not be ignored. I have therefore included in the following table citations to the above works, according to the Heikel and Mras (I-II) editions, respectively. I see nothing but a few coincidences in which Aphrahat and Eusebius cited the same Scripture at random; but there is no correlation of testimonies to suggest Aphrahat followed either Eusebius's choices, or the arguments based upon the Scriptures in Eusebius's repertoire of proof-texts.

Page references for *Athanasius and Zacchaeus* are to Conybeare.

Ath.	=	*Athanasius and Zacchaeus etc.*
Ba.	=	Barnabas, *Epistle*
Cyp.	=	Cyprian, *Three Books of Testimonies against the Jews*
EusD.	=	Eusebius, *Demonstratio Evangelica* (Heikel)
EusP.	=	Eusebius, *Praeparatio Evangelica* (Mras)
Hip.	=	Hippolytus, *Against the Jews*
Ir.	=	Irenaeus, *Against Heresies*
JuA1	=	Justin, *First Apology*

JuA2 = Justin, *Second Apology*
JuD   = Justin, *Dialogue with Trypho*
Lac. = Lactantius, *Divine Institutes* (Book IV, Chapters X-XXI only)
Nov. = Novatian, *On the Jewish Foods*
Or.   = Origen, *Contra Celsum*
Ter. = Tertullian, *Answer to the Jews*

	Scripture	*Aphrahat*	*Earlier Writers against Judaism*
1.	Ex. 12:33	I, 849 Jews rejected redemption.	No reference.
2.	Deut. 9:24	I, 468, 852-3 Israel always rebellious.	No reference.
3.	Deut. 31:29	I, 748, 852, 874 Moses predicted Israel's future sin.	No reference.
5.	Deut. 32:32	I, 468, 511, 765, 782, 852, 860 God never accepted Israel's repentence.	No reference.
6.	I Sam. 3:14	I, 748-9 Sin of Eli not expiated through sacrifice.	No reference.
7.	I Sam. 15:14	I, 748-9 No use for sacrifice.	No reference.
8.	Is. 1:2	I, 773, 790 Jews were heirs.	Ir. I, 525; Ter. III, 154, 155, 162; [Cyp. V, 495]; Lac. VII, 110.
10.	Is. 2:5-6	I, 765 House of Jacob = gentiles.	JuA1, I, 175: refers to apostles who taught peace to gentiles; JuD I, 267; Ter. III, 154; Cyp. V, 510; EusD 73.5, 63.7, 74.21 etc.
12.	Is. 11:11	I, 868 Redemption a second time, no third time.	EusD 81.23, 82.5, etc.
14.	Is. 30:1	I, 468, 766 Rebellious Israel.	JuD I, 238; Ir. I, 485; [Nov. V, 657][Cyp. V, 341, 592].

Scripture	Aphrahat	Earlier Writers against Judaism
15. Is. 33:1	I, 849 Prophetic promises can be annulled.	JuD I, 234.
16. Is. 33:13	I, 514, 733 Called gentiles.	No reference.
18. Is. 43:24	I, 565 Israel burdened God.	Ir. I, 483, sacrifice not important; EusD 64.9.
19. Is. 50:1	I, 564 Israel burdened God.	EusD 273.30, 291.24.
21. Is. 54:9	I, 949 God no longer angry because Jerusalem desolated *forever*.	No reference.
22. Is. 55:5	I, 773ff. Called gentiles.	JuD I, 200, 202, call to gentiles; Nov. V, 618; Cyp. V, 513.
23. Is. 59:2	I, 773ff. Rejected Israel.	No reference.
24. Is. 66:3	I, 748-9 Sacrifices no good.	Ir. I, 485, sacrifices no good.
25. Jer. 2:10-13	I, 952 Israel worshipped heavens.	Ba. I, 144 re baptism; JuD I, 203 re Jewish baptism; Ir. I, 458; Ter. III, 170; [Cyp. V, 376, 549]; Cyp. V, 509; Lac. VII, 133.
26. Jer. 2:21	I, 469, 765, 860 Alien vine, bad wine.	EusP II, 175.4.
27. Jer. 3:8	I, 860, 886, 953 Rejection.	No reference.
28. Jer. 3:16	I, 509, 532 Rejection; illegal for Jews to make ark of covenant.	EusD 89.13.
29. Jer. 6:30	I, 468, 753, 765, 768, 853, 939 Rejected silver.	No reference.

	Scripture	Aphrahat	Earlier Writers against Judaism
30.	Jer. 9:10	I, 533 Jews annulled covenant.	No reference.
31.	Jer. 12:1	I, 953	No reference.
32.	Jer. 12:7	I, 766, 860	EusD 465.31.
33.	Jer. 15:1-2	I, 753 Rejected Israel and its sacrifices.	No reference.
34.	Jer. 18:7-10	I, 852 God can change mind.	[Cyp. V, 593].
37.	Jer. 44:16-17	I, 761-4, 888 Rejection of Israel.	No reference.
38.	Ez. 8:10	I, 768-9 Rejection of Israel.	No reference.
39.	Ez. 8:10-12	I, 768, 773ff. Rejection of Israel.	No reference.
40.	Ez. 15:4	I, 469, 766, 769, 861, 886 Fire burned bough.	No reference.
41.	Ez. 16:45	I, 468, 765 Israel descends from Amorites and Hittites.	Ter. III, 162.
42.	Ez. 16:48-9 52-55	I, 472, 936ff. Israel is like Sodom, therefore will never be rebuilt.	No reference.
43.	Ez. 23:4	I, 769 Both Israel and Judah rejected.	No reference.
44.	Hos. 2:2, 3, 15	I, 768-9 Both Judah and Israel rejected.	EusD 274.1.
45.	Hos. 2:11	I, 509 Rejection of sacrifices.	No reference.
46.	Hos. 3:4	I, 509 Rejection of sacrifices.	No reference.

	Scripture	*Aphrahat*	*Earlier Writers against Judaism*
47.	Hos. 5:7	I, 768-9 Israel rejected.	No reference.
49.	Hos. 7:13	I, 853-6 Israel rejected.	No reference.
50.	Hos. 9:10, 11, 12, 15, 17	I, 853-6 Israel rejected.	Ir. I, 578.
51.	Hos. 10:1, 6	I, 853-6 Israel rejected.	JuD I, 251.
52.	Hos. 11:12	I, 768-9, 853-6 Israel rejected.	No reference.
53.	Hos. 13:9, 11	I, 853-6 Israel rejected.	No reference.
54.	Amos 4:9	I, 857-60	No reference.
57.	Amos 8:11-12	I, 773ff. Israel rejected.	EusD 469.4.
58.	Amos 9:7-6	I, 857-60	No reference.
59.	Micah 2:3, 2:10, 3:17	I, 856 Rejection of Israel.	No reference.
60.	Micah 7:4, 14, 17	I, 864 Rejection of Israel.	[Cyp. V, 541].
61.	Nahum 2:13	I, 864 Rejection of Israel.	No reference.
62.	Nahum 3:1	I, 864 Rejection of Israel.	No reference.
64.	Zech. 1:14-15, 17	I, 865, 868-9 Redemption in the past.	No reference.
65.	Zech. 2:4-5, 6-7, 12	I, 868-9 Redemption in the past.	JuD I, 256, applies to Christians.
66.	Zech. 4:9	I, 868-9 Redemption in the past.	No reference.
67.	Zech. 7:6	I, 748-9 Sacrifice no good.	Nov. V, 649, God does not eat or drink.

	Scripture	Aphrahat	Earlier Writers against Judaism
68.	Mal. 2:8	I, 863 Rejection of Israel.	No reference.
69.	Mal. 2:9	I, 863 Rejection of Israel.	No reference.
70.	Mal. 2:11	I, 863 Rejection of Israel.	Cyp. V, 508
71.	Mal. 2:17	I, 863 Rejection of Israel.	No reference.
72.	Mal. 3:6-7	I, 863 Rejection of Israel.	[Or. IV, 405, God changes not; Nov. V, 614, God changes not; Cyp. V, 485]; EusP II 28.15, 175.21. EusD 254.22; Ath. 129.
73.	Ps. 49:13-15	I, 748-9 Sacrifice no good.	No reference.
74.	Ps. 69:28	I, 769 God rejected Israel.	No reference.
75.	Ps. 80:8, 9, 13	I, 861 God rejected Israel.	Ath. 1.
78.	Gen. 49:10	I, 760, 805, 886 Jacob spoke of Messiah, gentiles' salvation.	JuA1, I, 173: refers to Jesus —"until he comes for whom the sceptre is reserved"; JuD I, 259; Ir. I, 474, refers to Jesus; Or. IV, 419; Nov. V, 618; Cyp. V, 513; EusD 18.11, 58.6, 68.9, etc. (many more); Ath. 47.
79.	Ex. 32:10	I, 772-3 Vocation of peoples.	No reference.
82.	Is. 2:2	I, 513, 760-1, 861-4 Adressed to church.	Ter. III, 154; [Cyp. V, 390]; Cyp. V, 510, 523; EusD 74.19, 270.34.
83.	Is. 33:13 (See Deut. 32:21)	I, 513, 775 Addressed to church.	JuD I, 234, refers to bread which Christ gave us to eat.
84.	Is. 42:6 (See Deut. 32:21)	I, 781-2 Israel prevented from idolatry by shame before gentiles who worship God.	[Cyp. V, 518, not in same sense] Lac. VII, 123, refers to gentiles; EusD 59.9; EusP I, 384.10-12.

	Scripture	*Aphrahat*	*Earlier Writers against Judaism*
86.	Jer. 6:8-9	I, 761-4 Vocation of peoples.	No reference.
87.	Jer. 6:16-18	I, 512-3, 763 When Jews would not listen, Jeremiah turned to gentiles and rejected Israel.	Ir. I, 515; Cyp. V, 513; EusD. 60.27.
88.	Jer. 12:7-9	I, 512, 754, 764-5, 859 Painted bird = church.	EusD. 465.31.
89.	Jer. 16:19	I, 761 Conversion of gentiles. 14.2-5	Or. IV, 558, refers to conversion of gentiles; EusD. 248.29; EusP. I, 14.2-5.
90.	Mal. 1:11	I, 768 Gentiles chosen.	JuD I, 208, 215, 257 applies to gentiles; Ir. I, 574, refers to Christians; Ter. III, 156, fulfilled by gentiles; Cyp. V, 512 [290, 409]; Lac. VII, 109; EusD 29.27.
91.	Ps. 18:44-5	I, 772-3, 813 Christians are sons.	Ir. I, 525; Ter. III, 154; Cyp. V, 513; Lac. VII, 109.
92.	Ps. 22:28	I, 773ff. Vocation of gentiles.	[Cyp. V, 527].
93.	Ps. 47:1	I, 773ff. Gentiles called.	No reference.
94.	Ps. 69:28-9	I, 769 Rejection of Israel and vocation of gentiles.	No reference.
95.	Ps. 74:2	I, 513, 773 Refers to church.	No reference.
96.	Ps. 87:6	I, 769 God counts gentiles.	No reference.
98.	Ex. 4:22-3	I, 774, 788-9, 846 Israel called sons of God.	EusD 358.14.

	Scripture	Aphrahat	Earlier Writers against Judaism
99.	Ex. 7:1-2	I, 788 Moses was called God.	Ir. I, 420, Moses was not God or Lord; [Hip. V, 187, Moses was worshipped as God by the Egyptians]; Nov. V, 631, if Moses was called God, how much the more so Jesus.
103.	Is. 9:6-7	I, 804ff. Christ foretold.	JuA1, I, p. 174: Applies to cross; JuD I, 236; Ir. I, 441, 449, 509; Ter. III, 166; Or. IV, 566, 649; Nov. V, 628-9, 632, 639; [Cyp. V, 524]; Lac. VII, III; EusD 3.13, 168.6, etc. (many references); Ath. 28.
106.	Zech. 9:10	I, 761 Applies to Christ.	EusD 396.21f., 397.1f., 440.33, 441.20, 442.4.
107.	Zech. 14:6-7	I, 812 Foretold passion.	EusD 282.21, 469.27, 470.6.
111.	Ps. 69:21, 26	I, 812 Applies to Christ.	Ir. I, 510; Nov. V, 639; Lac. VII, Lac. VII, 120.
114.	Dan. 9	I, 869ff. Daniel's prayer was already answered.	Ter. III, 158-160; Or. IV, 595, re anti-Christ; Hip. V, 190, 179, 213, 247-8; EusD 367-388, pass.; Ath. 121.
116.	Ex. 19:15	I, 825 No revelation until people celibate.	[Cyp. V, 544, same sense]; Lac. VII, 118.
117.	Jer. 16:2, 17:16	I, 833 Why Jeremiah did not marry.	No reference.
118.	Gen. 1:29	I, 736 Any food all right, but not blood.	JuD I, 203-4, addressed to Noah re eating all food. (Aphrahat has Adam and Noah; the point is the same.)
121.	Gen. 17:10	I, 476 Circumcision valid for limited time.	Ir. I, 480.

	Scripture	Aphrahat	Earlier Writers against Judaism
122.	Gen. 39:9	I, 557 Joseph did not keep Sabbath.	[Cyp. V, 513, not in same sense.]
123.	Gen. 43:32	I, 736 Egyptians worshipped oxen.	No reference.
124.	Num. 33:4	I, 740 Egyptians worshipped cows and sheep.	No reference.
125.	Deut. 10:16	I, 481, 485 Circumcise heart, flesh without heart no value.	JuD I, 202.
126.	Josh. 5:2, 5, 6	I, 486 Israelites not circumcised before; 2nd time — first time was of the heart.	JuD I, 206, allusion to Joshua; Ter. III, 163; Cyp. V, 510; Lac. VII, 118.
128.	Josh. 24:15-22	I, 740-1, 963 Israelites worshipped gods of Egyptians.	No reference.
129.	Judges 15:18	I, 744 Samson ate food from lion, unclean animal.	No reference.
131.	Is. 56:4	I, 569-72 Sabbath of God.	[Hip. V, 205].
132.	Is. 65:5	I, 569-72 Sabbath of God.	No reference.
133.	Jer. 4:4	I, 500 Circumcise heart.	Ter. III, 154; Cyp. V, 510; Lac. VII, 118.
134.	Jer. 9:25-6	I, 480 Circumcision without faith of no value.	Ba. I, 142; JuA1, I, 181.
135.	Ez. 4:13-14	I, 508-9 Jews will eat among unclean peoples.	No reference.

Scripture	Aphrahat	Earlier Writers against Judaism
136. Ez. 20:11, 25-6	I, 753 Evil commandments are purity law, etc.	[JuD I, 205, reference not spelled out; Or. IV, 619, not pertinent].
137. Is. 65:8	II, 1ff. Grapecluster.	JuD I, 267-8, Jews in rejecting Christ rejected God's blessing.

x. Conclusion

If, living in Seleucia, Edessa, Antioch, Alexandria, Carthage, or Rome in the year 340, we were asked to predict what a Christian would write concerning Judaism, we should readily have outlined the major themes of the argument: Sabbath, circumcision, dietary laws, the futility of the Jews' messianic hope, and the election of the peoples in place of the people. If we in addition were instructed that the master addressed himself to an oppressed Christian minority living among, and subjected to the active criticism of, Jews, we might have included apologies on two further themes: celibacy and the persecution of the Christians. The former themes would have demanded attention because everything said about Judaism up to that time included reference to them. The latter themes would have been less obvious, but no less a matter of common sense. Clearly, therefore, in selecting his topics, Aphrahat remains well within the antecedent conventions of Christianity east and west. But in developing his ideas, choosing Hebrew Scriptures to illustrate or demonstrate them, presenting reasons for the Christians' convictions, Aphrahat stands generally alone, original, inventive. His most strikingly novel contributions, moreover, are not merely the unique historical analyses of the origins of the practical commandments, though these are remarkable, but his historical interpretation of Daniel 9 and the Grapecluster (Is. 65:8), to which he devoted considerable effort. These are the summa and climax of his argument. It seems to me he was first fully to exploit the polemical usefulness of these (excepting Dan. 9 in Tertullian) and many other materials in the defense of the faith.

In support of the judgment that Aphrahat is fundamentally original, we shall rapidly review our observations on the comparison of Aphrahat to earlier Church Fathers on Judaism. The Epistle to Diognetus, like Aphrahat, refers to dietary laws, Sabbath, circumcision, also to fasting and new moon. The critique is different from Aphrahat's, for the Epistle contains no reference to historical reasons for the institution of the practical commandments. Rather the argument is that the commandments simply are not reasonable. Similarly, Ignatius of Antioch argues that various Jewish practices in observance of the Sabbath signified that the Jews were lazy. The arguments of Barnabas are, in the Alexandrian mode, highly allegorical. The reference of dietary laws was spiritual: One should not live like a pig. Barnabas treats circumcision in some ways as does Aphrahat, emphasizing that the practice was a widespread custom. But the argument is undeveloped. The spiritual meaning of Scriptures and of the practical commandments lies at the base of Barnabas's argument. For Aphrahat the spiritual sense is referred to, but the primary argument is based on historical, not allegorical, considerations.

Justin repeats the argument that the Jews understand everything in a carnal sense, rather than in the allegorical mode preferred by the Church. The arguments about circumcision are very similar, but both Justin and Aphrahat in this regard rely on New Testament motifs.

The primary difference is in Justin's concern (like Eusebius's) to demonstrate from Scriptures various elements in Christian theology, an effort on the whole subordinate in Aphrahat's anti-Judaic writings. No meaningful comparisons are to be drawn between Aphrahat and Irenaeus and Origen. Tertullian is probably closest, in a general way, to Aphrahat's mode of argument. Yet even here, when we approach matters of detail, such as the spelling out of Daniel 9, we can hardly find much correspondence or locate many agreements, verbal or merely substantive, in concrete matters. We discern no significant common pattern of citations of the same Scriptures for much the same points. In fact, the comparison between the two underlines how much they differed. The likenesses are general, the differences are specific.

The basic difference between Aphrahat and Lactantius consists in the latter's allegorization of the laws, the dismissal of circumcision on grounds that God did not really want it, for if he had, he would have created man already circumcised. The issue of salvation is never raised by Lactantius. I imagine he might well have denied salvific value to pre-Christian circumcision and regarded observance of the taboo against pork as of value only for a moral purpose. But his reasons for such opinions would have differed from Aphrahat's.

The *Dialogues* published by Conybeare bear many affinities, even close linguistic parallels (as Conybeare proved) to Justin and Tertullian, none at all to Aphrahat. The chief concern is to prove Christian theological convictions about the Trinity and Incarnation, which never occur in Aphrahat, the Passion and Resurrection, and the rejection of Israel. The third is commonplace. The use of Hosea is important, but the specific Scriptures cited in the Dialogues are not so numerous as those used by Aphrahat, and the pattern of citations as before reveals nothing more than some random coincidences.

Unlike the rabbis, who are, to be sure, not the only Jewish parties to the argument known to us, Aphrahat does not hide from the realities of the argument, but faces them honestly and squarely. The rabbis' mode of dealing with the Christian critique, in contrast, was to answer, if at all, by indirection, mainly through reshaping Scriptural figures to meet the needs of the dispute. In all rabbinic literature of late antiquity, we have not got the remotest equivalent to the *Demonstrations* of Aphrahat. We can hardly reconstruct out of the remnants of rabbinical exegeses a single coherent argument against Christianity, just nasty stories about Jesus. The fact that the Christians' beliefs were "unthinkable" hardly changes matters, for the Jews' convictions were no less incredible to Aphrahat. But he made the effort to come to grips with them, and rabbis did not seem to have responded, even by indirection, to his viewpoint and to opinions similar to his which they must have known. Others, such as the Jews of Celsus, Justin, and Tertullian, argued more to the point than did rabbis known to us. But the framework of argument was established by the Christian apologists who portrayed these Jews, and there is no reason to doubt such Jews were fabricated to begin with.

Of all parties to the argument between Judaism and Christianity in late antiquity, Aphrahat therefore is most impressive for his reasonable arguments, his careful attention to materials actually held in common by both sides, and the articulated and wholly lucid, worldly character of his argumentation. On the Christian side, he stands practically alone for his interest in the opinions of actual, not imaginary Jewish opponents. Unlike many of the earlier Christian apologists he has taken the trouble to learn what his opponents really say against Christianity. He has not merely constructed out of Scriptures an imaginary argument for refuting the other side and defending theological propositions of no real interest to the Jewish opposition. Unlike the rabbinical parties to the argument he admitted an important issue was at hand, and he met the opposition mostly on the neutral grounds provided by Hebrew Scriptures and Israelite history. Considering the elevated matters under discussion and their importance to both parties, I judge Aphrahat the worthiest participant in the Jewish-Christian dialogue put forward in antiquity by either side.

INDEX
OF BIBLICAL AND TALMUDIC PASSAGES [1]

I. Books of the Bible

Genesis

1:28	76-77
1:29	30, 53, 181, 211, 240
1:31	81
2:1-3	47
2:24	82, 178-79, 194, 210, 214
4:15	156
6:3	156
6:7	44, 77
7:1	43-44, 181, 211
9:3	53
9:7	76
9:27	113
15:5	76
15:6	22, 46, 181, 184, 211, 214
16:12	26, 28
17:5	19, 28, 39, 60, 172, 207, 213
17:10	21, 181, 211, 240
18:14	99
21:20	26
22:18	39
26:5	186
36:33	27
39:9	46, 182, 211, 241
43:32	54, 182, 241
49:10	60, 73, 95, 130, 172, 174-75, 177, 207-08, 213, 226, 238

Exodus

1:22	26
3:6	1, 4, 15, 70
4:19	104
4:22	64
4:22-23	69, 84, 175, 177, 208, 239
4:23	64
7:1	69

Exodus

7:1-2	175, 208, 240
7:2	69
8:18	65
8:20	25, 26, 54
12	153, 176, 194, 209, 213
12:3	5-6, 31
12:4	9, 11, 176, 208
12:5	176, 208
12:9	37
12:11	37-38
12:33	85, 160, 201, 234
12:44	45, 32, 38
12:45	37
12:46	32, 37
14:12	85
16:48-49, 52-55	204
17:12	229
19:10	78
19:15	78, 178-80, 210
20:9-11	41
20:10	42
20:13	42
20:14	42
20:19	79
23:10-11	46
23:12	42
23:36	76
32:10	64, 172, 207, 238
32:31-33	63
34:14	68, 159

Leviticus

13:45-46	87
15:5	59
17:13	53
20:17	42
20:12	70, 79, 119
26:11-12	72, 153
26:44	98, 159-60

[1] Indices were prepared by Mr. Arthur Woodman, Canaan, New Hampshire, on a grant from Brown University.

II. Palestinian Talmud

III. Babylonian Talmud

B.B.	
75b	166

Ber.	
5a	176
19a	162
24b	183
32a	172
35b	165
56b	165
59a	165

Bekh.	
12a	176
26b	167

'Eruv.	
101a	166

Giṭ.	
57b	159

Ḥag.	
6b	166

Hor.	
11b	172

Ḥul.	
92a	167

Ket.	
8b	162

M.Q.	
16b	166

Meg.	
11a	159
32a	183

Men.	
110a	173

Ned.	
31b	183

Pes.	
68a	159, 166
88a	164
119a	177

Qid.	
70a	165

R.H.	
17b	174
18a	161

Sanh.	
5a	172
59b	181
65b	163
82a	167
91b	159
92b	164
94a	176
97b	166-67
98b	172
99a	163
104b	164
105a	162
106a	172

Shab.	
31a	175
32b-33a	165
55a	176
118b	183
138b	166

Soṭ.	
11a	163

Suk.	
49a	162

Ta.	
6b	165
20a	167
28b	177

Yev.	
17a	165
62b	178
63b	161
105a	161

Yoma	
28b	186

Zev.	
25b	176
119a	173

IV. Midrashic Compilations

GENERAL INDEX

A

Aaron, 69, 75, 79, 115

Abba, R., 165

Abbahu, R., 172

Abel, 9, 111, 133, 213; circumcision, 200-21; covenant, 22

Abijah, 116

Abiud, 118

Abraham, 6, 9, 39, 75, 177; circumcision, 19-26, 28, 30, 142-43, 156-57, 181, 184-86, 218-20; dietary laws, 53, 55; grapecluster, 114-15; Israel rejected 60, 66-67; marriage and celibacy, 76, 78; persecutions, 99, 101; Sabbath observance, 46; vocation of Gentiles, 134, 139, 172, 174

Absalom, 82

Achan, 30, 80, 105, 132

Achim, 118

Adam, 152; celibacy, 76-77, 81, 131-32; circumcision, 141, 143, 217, 220-21; covenant, 21, 28; dietary laws, 53, 141, 181, 184-85; grapecluster, 113, 117, 119; Sabbath observance, 41, 43-45, 140

Adiabene, xi, 2, 3, 148

Ahab, 102, 106, 110, 116

Ahasuerus, 91, 95

Ahaz, 116

Ahaziah, 116

Alexander, 100, 221

Alexandria, 6, 216, 242

Allegory, Aphrahat avoiding, 4-7

Altaner, B., 7

Amalek, 6, 104, 229

Amaziah, 116

Aminadab, 115

Ammon, 101-02, 117, 178; celibacy, 82, 132, 178; circumcision, 19, 23, 25-28

Amorites, 20

Amos, 138, 170

Anastasius Sinaita, 197

Antioch, 242

Anti-Semitism and Aphrahat, 5

Aphrahat, allegory, 4-7; anti-Semitism, 5; Apostolic Fathers, 214-16; celibacy, 76-83; circumcision, 19-30; Christian Passover, 34-36; debate, mode of, 4-7; dietary laws, 51-59; Eusebius, 227-32; Gentiles, 60-67; grapecluster, 113-19; Irenaeus and Justin Martyr, 217-20; Jewish Passover, 31-33; Judaism, 123-49; Justin Martyr and Irenaeus, 217-20; Lactantius and the Dialogue of Timothy and Aquila, 227-32; Messiah, 68-75; New Testament, 199-214; and Origen, 224-27; Paschal sacrifice, 31-40; Passover, 31-40; Patristic critique of Judaism, 196-244; persecution, 97-112; Rabbis, 150-95; Sabbath, 41-50; scriptural testimonies, 232-42; and Tertullian, 220-24

Apostolic Fathers, 7, 214-16

'Aqiva, R., 145, 148, 151, 166, 171

Aram, 88, 118, 172

Araunah the Jebusite, 101

E

F

G

U

Ur, 22, 114
Urbina, *see* Ortiz de Urbina, Ignatius
Uriah the Hittite, 60, 66
Uzziah, 87, 116

V

Valentius, 8
Vashti, 109
Vespasian, 222
Virginity, *see* Celibacy
Vitellius, 222
Vööbus, Arthur, 3-4, 8, 12

W

Wace, Henry, 68n
Wallace, Henry, 7
Wellhausen, 150, 188
Wiessner, Gernot, 10
Wilde, Robert, 198, 217
Williams, A. Lukyn, 11, 196n, 198, 225, 228
Wright, William, xii, 7-8; celibacy and marriage, 76-83; circumcision, 19-30; dietary laws, 51-59; grapecluster, 113-19; Jesus, son of God, 68-75; Messiah and Jews gathered together, 94-96; Paschal sacrifice, 31-40; persecution, 97-112; Sabbath observance, 41-50

Y

Yoḥanan, R., 164, 183
Yoḥanan ben Zakkai, 184
Yonah, *see* Avi-Yonah, Michael
Yosi, R., 162
Yudan, R., 176
Yufna, 25

Z

Zadok, 118
Zechariah, 87, 90, 137, 222
Zedekiah, 111, 118
Zerah, 27
Zerubbabel, 90, 94, 118, 221
Zimri, 80, 132
Zorastrianism, xi, 125, 152-53

South Florida Studies in the History of Judaism

South Florida Academic Commentary Series

	and the Talmud of Babylonia, Volume F, Tractates Besah, Taanit and Megillah	Neusner
243066	The Two Talmuds Compared, I. Tractate Berakhot and the Division of Appointed Times in the Talmud of the Land of Israel and the Talmud of Babylonia, Volume G, Tractates Rosh Hashanah and Moed Qatan	Neusner
243067	The Talmud of Babylonia, An Academic Commentary, Volume XXII, Bavli Tractate Baba Batra, B. Chapters VII through XI	Neusner
243068	The Talmud of Babylonia, An Academic Commentary, Volume XXIII, Bavli Tractate Sanhedrin, B. Chapters VIII through XII	Neusner
243069	The Talmud of Babylonia, An Academic Commentary, Volume XIV, Bavli Tractate Ketubot, B. ChaptersVII through XIV	Neusner
243070	The Talmud of Babylonia, An Academic Commentary, Volume IV, Bavli Tractate Pesahim, B. Chapters VIII through XI	Neusner
243071	The Talmud of Babylonia, An Academic Commentary, Volume XXIX, Bavli Tractate Menahot, B. Chapters VII through XIV	Neusner
243072	The Talmud of Babylonia, An Academic Commentary, Volume XXVIII, Bavli Tractate Zebahim B. Chapters VIII through XV	Neusner
243073	The Talmud of Babylonia, An Academic Commentary, Volume XXI, Bavli Tractate Baba Mesia, B. Chapters VIII through XI	Neusner
243074	The Talmud of Babylonia, An Academic Commentary, Volume III, Bavli Tractate Erubin, A. ChaptersVI through XI	Neusner
243075	The Components of the Rabbinic Documents: From the Whole to the Parts, I. Sifra, Part One	Neusner
243076	The Components of the Rabbinic Documents: From the Whole to the Parts, I. Sifra, Part Two	Neusner
243077	The Components of the Rabbinic Documents: From the Whole to the Parts, I. Sifra, Part Three	Neusner
243078	The Components of the Rabbinic Documents: From the Whole to the Parts, I. Sifra, Part Four	Neusner
243079	The Components of the Rabbinic Documents: From the Whole to the Parts, II. Esther Rabbah I	Neusner
243080	The Components of the Rabbinic Documents: From the Whole to the Parts, III. Ruth Rabbah	Neusner
243081	The Components of the Rabbinic Documents: From the Whole to the Parts, IV. Lamemtations Rabbah	Neusner
243082	The Components of the Rabbinic Documents: From the Whole to the Parts, V. Song of Songs Rabbah, Part One	Neusner
243083	The Components of the Rabbinic Documents: From the Whole to the Parts, V. Song of Songs Rabbah, Part Two	Neusner
243084	The Components of the Rabbinic Documents: From the Whole to the Parts, VI. The Fathers According to Rabbi Nathan	Neusner
243085	The Components of the Rabbinic Documents: From the Whole to the Parts, VII. Sifré to Deuteronomy, Part One	Neusner

South Florida-Rochester-Saint Louis
Studies on Religion and the Social Order

South Florida International Studies in
Formative Christianity and Judaism